JOSSEY-BASS TEACHER

Jossey-Bass Teacher provides educators with practical knowledge and tools to create a positive and lifelong impact on student learning. We offer classroom-tested and research-based teaching resources for a variety of grade levels and subject areas. Whether you are an aspiring, new, or veteran teacher, we want to help you make every teaching day your best.

From ready-to-use classroom activities to the latest teaching framework, our value-packed books provide insightful, practical, and comprehensive materials on the topics that matter most to K–12 teachers. We hope to become your trusted source for the best ideas from the most experienced and respected experts in the field.

More Praise for *Teaching Content Outrageously*

"Pogrow is one of the nation's most inventive educators. He demonstrates his creativity, and that of the teachers he works with, in this powerful reminder that lively lessons produce engaged learners. A wonderful book demonstrating that creative teaching is within the grasp of all who are privileged enough to be called teacher."

> — ***David C. Berliner***, *Former President, American Educational Research Association, Former Dean and Regents' Professor, Mary Lou Fulton College of Education, Arizona State University*

"Dr. Pogrow tells not only what outrageous content teaching is, but how to do it effectively, and how to train others to do it. The book is vital for teachers and professional developers interested in accelerating student learning as well as in improving teacher practices. The book is informative, practical, and fun. It's a must read for every serious educator."

> — ***Dr. Ahmes Askia***, *Director, Professional Development, National Urban Alliance, Atlanta GA*

Teaching Content Outrageously

HOW TO CAPTIVATE *ALL* STUDENTS AND ACCELERATE LEARNING, GRADES 4–12

Stanley Pogrow

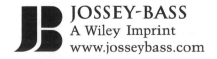

JOSSEY-BASS
A Wiley Imprint
www.josseybass.com

Published by Jossey-Bass
A Wiley Imprint
989 Market Street, San Francisco, CA 94103-1741—www.josseybass.com

Jossey-Bass books and products are available through most bookstores. To contact Jossey-Bass directly call our Customer Care Department within the U.S. at 800-956-7739, outside the U.S. at 317-572-3986, or fax 317-572-4002.

Jossey-Bass also publishes its books in a variety of electronic formats. Some content that appears in print may not be available in electronic books.

Library of Congress Cataloging-in-Publication Data

Pogrow, Stanley.
    Teaching content outrageously : how to captivate all students and accelerate
learning, grades 4-12 / Stanley Pogrow. —1st ed.
        p. cm.
    Includes bibliographical references and index.
    ISBN 978-0-470-18026-6 (pbk.)
    1. Education—Experimental methods. 2. Teaching—Aids and devices. 3.
    Creative teaching. 4. Drama in education. I. Title.
    LB1027.3.P64 2008
    371.1—dc22
                                                                2008041908

Printed in the United States of America
FIRST EDITION

PB Printing   10 9 8 7 6 5 4 3

CONTENTS

About This Book   vii

About the Author   xv

Acknowledgments   xix

ONE Why Teach Outrageously in All the Content Areas?   1

TWO Perspectives on Dramatizing Content Instruction   17

THREE From Discipline to Outrageous Teaching: Classroom Use
of Dramatic Techniques   39

FOUR How to Design Outrageous Lessons: Essential Steps   69

FIVE Outrageous Lessons: Examples from the Classroom   89

SIX Suspense and Surprise: Why Outrageous Lessons Work   143

SEVEN Getting Started   165

EIGHT So...Let's Do It!   185

Appendix A: The Origins of Drama   193

Appendix B: Games and Quizzes—Selected Resources   197

Appendix C: Simulation Units—Selected Resources   201

Appendix D: Lesson Plans for the Sample Lessons   207

Appendix E: Teaching Outrageously in the Early Grades   221

References   225

Index   229

ABOUT THIS BOOK

All teachers face a set of problems that at times seem unsolvable. For example:

- What do you do on those days when students are bored, uncooperative, uninterested—or even actively resistant to learning?

- What do you do when the required content objectives seem too abstract or too difficult for most students to understand or appreciate no matter how you try to explain them?

- How do you handle a class in which the moment you start to teach, half the students decide they need to sharpen a pencil or go to the bathroom?

- What do you do when the best instructional practices fail to work?

There are also ongoing challenges, such as the following:

- How do you get students who are two or more years behind in reading and math to write essays and solve math word problems?

- How do you get students to reflect on key ideas rather than just learn facts, and how do you get those who are preoccupied with doing well on test questions to truly engage fundamental ideas?

- How do you teach the YouTube generation, which expects on-demand, individualized entertainment and learning experiences?

These are everyday problems for most teachers and principals. In addition, as public schools in the United States become increasingly segregated by race, and as accountability pressures grow, all of these problems are exacerbated.

In such an environment, teachers rely on the old standbys of (a) telling students "you need to learn it because it is on the test and if you do not do well you will not get promoted," (b) sending the unruly to the office and complaining to their parents, (c) ignoring passive learners after initial attempts to get them to respond, or (d) making the lesson "authentic" and telling students, "You will understand why this is important when you become adults."

None of these techniques are ideal. The problems with the first three are obvious. The problem with the fourth is that adolescents go through stages in which they think adults are dorks, and most efforts to provide "authentic" curricula focus on applications from the adult world—which can serve to reinforce students' belief that the content is uncool.

What is a teacher to do?

The best solution is to convert those content lessons into learning experiences that are so fascinating and entertaining that students cannot help but be drawn into what you are trying to get them to learn, and hang onto your every word and gesture!

Impossible? A pipe dream? A fantasy?

Not really. It actually is possible to draw *all* students deeply into what you are trying to teach, pretty much whenever you want to. This book describes a methodology for creating lessons and units for teaching any content, be it traditional or standards based, in ways that engage and inspire even the most reluctant, resistant, and superficial learner. The techniques provide a way for teachers to have fun teaching those lessons and units that have formerly been trouble, while increasing student learning.

In this book you will meet teachers across the content areas who are teaching in such an unusual and daring fashion that the only adjectives that apply to describe these lessons and units are *outrageous* and *highly effective*. These types of lessons and units are hereafter referred to in this book as *Outrageous Teaching*, or *teaching content Outrageously*. The Outrageous Teaching approach is designed to teach conventional content objectives more effectively and quickly than traditional approaches. It is the fusion of art, creativity, imagination, and emotion—and pragmatics.

The techniques of Outrageous Teaching are designed to be employed by any teacher with a bit of daring in any content area in grades 4 through 12. The focus is on these grades because they are the ones in which content objectives become increasingly specialized and complex, and because once students in these grades fall behind or lose interest in a content area, they tend to go downhill thereafter.

PURPOSE

This book presents a validated methodology for designing highly dramatic and unconventional lessons for meeting standards-based content objectives (or any other content objectives) that any teacher can use in any curricular area. Most teachers already use some of these techniques in their everyday instruction to maintain discipline and for other instructional management purposes. Outrageous Teaching incorporates many of these everyday techniques, such as the use of signals to get students' attention, along with others such as role-playing. It then modifies and intensifies the dramatic intensity of these techniques in systematic ways that (a) immediately capture students' attention, (b) captivate them throughout the lesson, (c) make them want to learn the content, and (d) make the teaching, learning, and application of the content a seamless process.

If you would like to experience this amazing transformation in your classroom, read and use this book, which provides a specific planning methodology called the *Dramatized Content Planning Method*. This method makes it possible for all teachers in all content areas to design such lessons. In addition, the book provides extensive examples of teachers using these techniques in different content areas. You will find here lessons that are masterful. Can you design such lessons? Yes! Although you may at first feel intimidated by how good these lessons are, please keep in mind that *most of the highlighted lessons were designed by inexperienced student teachers*. If they could tap their imagination to create these types of show-stopping lessons, you too can develop highly original and creative Outrageous lessons that convert even the most prosaic topics into captivating and effective learning experiences. All the sample lessons and units in this book are highlighted.

The techniques presented in this book are highly practical—albeit a bit weird. They are derived from my research and successful experience using drama as a curricular technique in the large-scale reform programs I have developed over the past twenty-six years, and from my work with student teachers at the University of Arizona.

The reform for which I am most known is the Higher Order Thinking Skills (HOTS) program for low-income and learning-disabled students in grades

4 through 8. This program integrated theories of learning, technology, and drama to create a powerful Socratic learning environment for developing the types of thinking and literacy skills that underlie all learning, and it substituted these activities for remedial instruction. I also designed Supermath, which is an alternative approach to teaching the pre-algebra topics that are most difficult for all students to learn, such as word problems. Supermath used technology to create fantasy contexts in which math content was critical for resolving dilemmas that were of interest to students, as a way to teach both mathematical reasoning and content objectives. Both of these programs incorporated heavy doses of dramatic technique, humor, and fantasy, and led to key discoveries about the conditions under which a dramatic approach could increase and deepen learning to a greater degree than relying on conventional approaches.

Could such knowledge be used by all teachers in their everyday teaching? To find out, I asked each of my student teachers to prepare a highly dramatic lesson for me to observe. Over time I refined how I prepared them to create such lessons. The result was some of the most amazing teaching I have ever seen. (Examples of these lessons and units are found in Chapters Five and Seven.) Indeed, it is the lessons taught by my student teachers that were the inspiration for this book, and the methods I used to prepare these students are the book's backbone.

Thus, the techniques presented in this book have been developed, used, and validated over an extended period. All of the sample lessons and units described here are ones I witnessed teachers using successfully with students—often in the toughest classrooms and schools. In addition, to give a better sense of what it is like to develop and teach these types of lessons and units, each example not only describes the lesson but also describes the background of its development, the reaction of the teacher and students, and the aftermath and effects of the lesson.

So, every time you find yourself thinking, "This could not possibly work," please keep in mind that *it has worked*. This means that if you open the creative part of your mind, you can make "it"—or something similarly different, strange, and wonderful—work with your students.

This book is designed to enable all teachers who have a sense of humor, a dash of daring, and a desire to reach their students more deeply to use the techniques of Outrageous Teaching to develop highly original, creative, and engaging ways of converting even the most prosaic content objectives and topics into captivating and effective learning experiences for their students. The book is also designed to be used by administrators and instructional leaders seeking a way to incorporate more creative instruction into their schools and districts, by teacher educators as a text for preservice training methods courses, and by teacher trainers for postservice workshops.

Outrageous Teaching has the following main advantages over conventional instruction:

- It can be used to teach concepts that otherwise might not be interesting or accessible to students, in ways that captivate them and increase their learning.
- It can make lessons meaningful and memorable to students.
- Although it helps all students, it can succeed particularly well with underperformers.

Clearly, Outrageous Teaching is not the first effort to enhance instruction through dramatic technique and the use of humor and fantasy. This practice goes back to ancient times. Many teachers already employ drama and other progressive techniques such as simulation, role-play, games, readers theater, and so on.

What makes Outrageous Teaching unique compared to traditional classroom use of dramatic technique is that, rather than relegating such techniques to review and enrichment, it is specifically designed to be the *primary* instructional technique for teaching targeted content objectives. Outrageous Teaching is designed to be used *in lieu of rather than as an addition to* conventional instruction to teach the most troublesome content objectives in your school or district's curriculum. Why not teach the content "richly" in the first place? This is the goal of Outrageous Teaching, regardless of whether the targeted curriculum objectives are mandated by state or federal standards or by the independent decision of a school or district, or selected by you, the teacher, on the basis of your own instincts about what is important for your students to learn.

Outrageous Teaching is thus both effective *and* efficient. As readers will see in the sample lessons presented in the book, Outrageous Teaching not only increases content learning and transforms the student-teacher relationship, but also does so in *less* time than traditional teaching. Also, the techniques are optimized for content learning in grades 4 through 12. This means that the techniques can be used to teach rigorous and complex concepts. Indeed, the more rigorous and complex the concepts are, the more valuable the techniques are for making them interesting and accessible to students. In addition, Outrageous Teaching is so powerful that even a few such lessons are transformative for both teachers and students, both individually and in how they interact with each other. Students who formerly were passive come alive and reveal their true capabilities.

Because Outrageous Teaching is effective, efficient, and focused on complex content objectives, its use is consistent with, though not limited to, the current emphasis on standards and accountability. Standards and accountability dictate merely what content should be taught, not *how* the content should be taught. In addition, teaching Outrageously does not require additional funds or equipment—it requires only imagination and daring.

Enough about pragmatics and standards. *The bottom line for teachers and students is that it is lots more fun to teach and to learn through Outrageous Teaching than through traditional instructional approaches.* It is hoped that reading this book will put lots of smiles on your face, with an occasional belly laugh, and above all, inspire you to venture forth.

SUMMARY OF CONTENTS

Chapter One defines what dramatic technique is in general, and what Outrageous Teaching is specifically, and why Outrageous Teaching is a powerful tool for teaching content to *all* students, and particularly to the disadvantaged. The chapter also provides a glimpse of an Outrageous lesson.

Chapter Two discusses the history of incorporating dramatic technique into education. It presents the different schools of thought and describes how the use of dramatic technique evolved differently in the United States than it did in England. This chapter also discusses the theoretical and research bases that support the use of dramatic technique as an instructional tool, and provides a follow-up glimpse of the Outrageous lesson previewed in Chapter One.

Chapter Three describes the typical uses of dramatic techniques in the classroom—from maintaining discipline and providing instructional management to using student role-play strategies, including games and simulations, to review and reinforce content learning. The chapter then discusses how many of these widely used, valuable techniques form the building blocks of Outrageous Teaching. It then compares how Outrageous Teaching differs in its application of those techniques and why it tends to be more efficient and effective for teaching standards-based content, or any teacher-initiated content. The example of the Outrageous lesson glimpsed in earlier chapters is then presented in its entirety to show how the approach extends conventional use of dramatic classroom technique, and why the lesson is so effective.

Chapters Four through Seven focus on the how-to and practical aspects of implementing Outrageous lessons and units, along with lots of examples, and advice on how to get started. The sample lessons are highlighted with a gray screen.

Chapter Four describes the daily-lesson planning method used to create Outrageous lessons and links the techniques discussed in the preceding chapters to the sample lesson presented in Chapter Three. Lots of additional examples are presented to illustrate how to plan each part of an Outrageous lesson. A lesson-planning template is also provided.

Chapter Five presents additional examples of teachers conducting Outrageous lessons in a variety of content areas with students in grades 4 through 12. It discusses how the lessons were developed, and the reactions of the students and teachers to these very different types of lessons. The techniques used to develop the lessons are compared, and the lesson plan template for each lesson is provided.

Chapter Six describes what can be learned from the experiences of the teachers and students in the sample lessons presented earlier, in terms of the benefits for students and teachers and for the process of lesson development.

Chapter Seven discusses how everyone, from individual teachers to schools and the profession as a whole, can get started using Outrageous lessons. It also discusses how the planning techniques can be extended to create Outrageous units, and to develop lessons for the earliest grades.

Chapter Eight reviews the rationales for and benefits from teaching content Outrageously.

Together these chapters provide both a theoretical rationale and a specific, validated methodology that all teachers can use to apply dramatic technique, humor, and imagination to their teaching in order to enrich their professional practice and inspire transformative student learning. They also offer many inspirational examples of successful experiences.

D r. Stanley Pogrow started his career as a math teacher in the New York City public schools. He currently serves as professor of educational leadership at San Francisco State University. Dr. Pogrow is also one of the nation's leading scholars in the formulation of policies and practices for reducing the learning gap, and is especially noted for his national reform efforts, including use of advanced instructional approaches for accelerating and enriching the learning of children born into poverty and for helping all students learn complex content. He developed the Higher Order Thinking Skills (HOTS) Project, a thinking skills approach to Title I and learning disabled (LD) students in grades 4 through 8. HOTS has been used in approximately 2,600 schools in forty-eight states and has served close to a half-million Title I and LD students. HOTS has won numerous state and federal awards. Dr. Pogrow also developed Supermath, a form of pre-algebra mathematics curriculum that develops math problem-solving skills in all students. Funded by the National Science Foundation, Supermath uses technology to create dramatic contexts for applying and inferring mathematical concepts constructivistically. His latest reform effort is the Hi-Perform School, a redesign of high-poverty elementary schools to reduce the learning gap.

Dr. Pogrow's research and development work has been funded by grants from the National Science Foundation, the U.S. Department of Education, the Arizona Department of Education, the Edna McConnell Clark Foundation, the Ford Foundation, IBM, and Apple Corporation. Dr. Pogrow has served as professor at the University of Arizona, Seattle University (endowed chair), the University of Illinois at Champagne-Urbana, the University of New Mexico, and the University of Southern California (endowed chair), and has been a visiting scholar at the University of California, Los Angeles. In addition, he has worked at the National Science Foundation and the California State Department of Education. He is the author of four books, including *Education in the Computer Age: Issues of Policy, Practice, and Reform* (1983), and more than one hundred journal articles. He did a series of monographs on exemplary middle school curricula for each of the major content areas for the National Middle School Association. He has made more than 240 presentations around the United States and abroad.

Dr. Pogrow is a noted teacher educator. More than three thousand teachers have gone through his small-group, weeklong workshop on how to develop thinking skills in children born into poverty, and he has mentored more than one hundred student teachers. He continues to offer workshops on thinking development and schoolwide questioning strategies, and now plans to offer workshops on creating Outrageous lessons.

Photos of the author at work, taken by Hall Williams, Tucson, AZ.

This book is dedicated to

the memory of my parents, Morris and Rhoda,

for putting up with me, and to Deborah,

for supporting my explorations.

ACKNOWLEDGMENTS

I would like to acknowledge the wonderful teachers and student teachers I have been fortunate to work with, observe, and learn from over the course of my career. Without them, their ideas, and their dedication to students and to the craft of teaching, this book would not have been possible, nor would any of my other professional accomplishments have been possible. I would also especially like to thank the first teacher I ever observed, who was also the best—my mom, Rhoda (may she rest in peace).

A very special thanks goes to Christie Hakim, associate editor at Jossey-Bass, for maintaining her interest and support over the four-year period from when I first broached the idea for this book to when I had the time to start writing it. Her enthusiasm for new ideas is inspiring. In addition, her critical insights were always on target and an invaluable guide.

Finally, I would like to thank my research assistant, Penney Radillo, for her research on the history of theater, and Barbara (Bobbi) McKean, associate professor of theater arts education at the University of Arizona, for her suggestions on sources.

chapter ONE

Why Teach Outrageously in All the Content Areas?

Most teachers enter the teaching profession with an idealistic vision of impacting the lives of their students. They see themselves in a classroom in which their students hang onto their every word. It is of course a rude awakening when they actually first enter a classroom to teach, and find that they must fight for their students' attention and interest. It is a battle that is often lost.

As many teachers realize, conventional approaches to content instruction, even approaches employing state-of-the-art, best-practice strategies, are often inadequate for serving the large percentage of students in public schools who are reluctant, superficial, or resistant learners. They are often inadequate for meeting standards-based content objectives, even in high-performing schools. If anything, the problem of student disengagement is becoming more prevalent due to a combination of social problems, such as poverty and the increasing availability of on-demand entertainment options for filling one's time outside of school. Indeed, veteran teachers often report that it is increasingly difficult to hold students' attention.

A major challenge for teachers is how best to motivate and engage students who are discouraged or underachieving their true potential. Underperforming learners, be they students born into poverty or from advantaged backgrounds, often do not see purpose in what they are taught and respond with boredom, apathy, and misbehavior. Conventional approaches to instruction have been inadequate in reversing the low achievement and high dropout rates now prevalent in all too many schools. Dropouts report that boredom is a major contributor to their decision to leave school. There are also large numbers of reluctant learners who do well generally but have lost motivation to learn in a particular content area. Examples include students who have decided that they are "mathphobic" or that science is not "cool." Alternatively, they may find it impossible to understand selected key topics within content areas that are crucial to future success.

Student boredom and the resultant misbehavior are also major factors behind the high turnover rate among new teachers, who are simply unable to hold students' interest and consequently have to spend inordinate amounts of time trying to maintain order. This inability is typically viewed as not having the skills to maintain discipline. However, the discipline problems themselves are symptomatic of teachers not having the stagecraft and presence to hold their students' attention.

Indeed, little has changed since Charles Silberman documented the absolute boredom of students in the typical classroom in high-poverty schools in his classic book *Crisis in the Classroom: The Remaking of American Education* (1971). The experience of walking through a high-poverty school is much the same today as it was thirty or a hundred years ago. The dominant expression on the faces of disadvantaged students is generally boredom or resignation. The same is true when teachers in all schools and in any content area teach particular lessons and units. *But this need not be so!* And that is why this book was written.

It is time to recognize that this era of on-demand, individualized, and YouTubed entertainment is producing as fundamental a shift in communication and learning patterns today as the printing press did 550 years ago. The key to teaching reluctant and resistant learners who have grown up with unsurpassed access to on-demand entertainment is to transform the classroom into a highly intriguing learning environment, to make it entertaining, dramatic, visually captivating, and a multisensory experience.

It is time to accept that we cannot always teach content conventionally! This approach does not work anymore for most students. Unfortunately, even if you agree with this sentiment, chances are that you teachers were not trained in how to produce highly creative unconventional instructional environments that can increase learning. Nor were you administrators trained to encourage the use of unconventional instructional approaches as part of a systematic approach to school improvement.

But even if you did want to create very dramatic learning environments, most of the published work on using drama and humor focuses primarily on using them to develop the literacy or self-expression skills of young children, to review and reinforce what has been learned conventionally, or to develop students' artistic sense. All of these are important uses of dramatic techniques. However, they only scratch the surface of the potential of using dramatic instructional approaches.

MOVING FROM CONVENTIONAL TO OUTRAGEOUS TEACHING

The ideal is possible. We can transfix students even while teaching seemingly prosaic content. Later in this book you will read about lessons in which hard-core problem students and classes in the toughest schools were transfixed and hanging on every word and gesture of their teacher. When that happens, it is an inspirational and fun moment for the teacher as well. After even one such experience, student and teacher come to view each other differently—with mutual heightened respect and admiration.

The big need is for a practical way to use dramatic approaches as a primary technique for teaching new content across the curriculum in grades 4 through 12—that is, to teach the content Outrageously. Outrageous Teaching is a powerful tool for all teachers to use to stimulate learning in those lessons and students for which conventional instruction is not likely to be effective. This book goes beyond conventional notions of using dramatic technique in education. The goal is to use dramatic technique, humor, and imagination in combination to create lessons that are so different from conventional instruction, and so far out, that the only words to characterize them are *Outrageous* and *amazingly effective.*

What is Outrageous Teaching and why is it so effective? Why is it able to captivate reluctant and resistant learners and squirrelly classes? Why is it able to stimulate high levels of learning in otherwise passive or confused students? Can drama and humor really be the basis of a large-scale tool for improving content instruction and increasing academic achievement? To understand what Outrageous Teaching is and why it is so effective, it is important first to understand dramatic technique, the base on which the method is built.

DEFINITION OF DRAMATIC TECHNIQUE

Some key components of drama are as follows:

> "A composition . . . intended to portray life or character or to tell a story
> usually involving conflict and emotions through action and dialogue. . . ."
> (Merriam-Webster Online Dictionary)

"Exciting, tense, and gripping . . . either in a work of art or in a real-life situation." (Encarta World English Dictionary)

"'A deed' or 'an action.' So anytime you've acted something out, you've done drama!" ("The Play's The Thing: Drama Definition," retrieved from http://jfg.girlscouts.org/how/girlslife/dramadef.htm. *Note:* This site no longer exists. The quote currently appears at http://suzynarita.blogspot.com/2004_12_01_archive.html.)

"A collective experiencing, celebrating, or commenting, not on how we are different from each other, but on what we share. . ." (Bolton, 2001, p. 154).

On the basis of these definitions, this book views classroom use of dramatic technique as

> Teacher actions that turn lessons into a collective experience by creating a story or context that produces excitement and other emotions central to acquiring and consciously processing the key content ideas and knowledge.

Although this definition includes what most educators think of as drama—that is, theatrical productions—it is a much broader definition that includes all aspects of artistic expression that performers—in this case, teachers—can use to create a dramatic tension that enthralls and draws in an audience—in this case, their students.

THE POWER OF DRAMA AS AN INSTRUCTIONAL TOOL

Dramatizing content instruction has tremendous potential for teaching students who have not been successful learners or are intimidated by a particular subject or type of content, because it taps into their deeply held emotions and beliefs, their imagination, their sense of life's possibilities, and their role in the cosmos. As such, it is the most underused and powerful teaching technique in American education.

Philosophers as far back as Confucius and Aristotle have been fascinated with the power of drama as a teaching tool, as evidenced by the following quotes:

"I hear, I know. I see, I remember. I do, I understand." (Confucius, 551 B.C.–479 B.C. http://www.brainyquote.com/quotes/authors/c/confucius.html)

"Tell me and I will forget. Show me and I will remember. Involve me and I will understand." (Attributed to Aristotle by some and said to be a Chinese Proverb by others; originally retrieved from http://www.geocities.com/broadway/alley/3765/why.html—*Note:* This site no longer exists. In addition, another version of this quote has as the middle phrase, "Show me and I may remember.")

Indeed, drama has been used as a teaching technique since ancient times. (See the history of drama use in Appendix A.)

Dramatic practices are also widely used in the modern classroom. Many teachers are already familiar with conventional techniques that engage students in role-playing, improvisations, games, and simulated experiences. These practices are most often used to "supplement" lessons previously taught—to develop particular skills, such as reading fluency; to deepen understanding of a particular content topic; or to review and reinforce learning. Although these practices are important, they barely scratch the surface of the potential of using dramatic technique as a teaching and learning tool.

The method featured in this book places great importance on the role of the teacher in incorporating dramatic practices into the design and staging of the original content instruction, rather than first teaching the content conventionally. The goal of these practices is to capture the attention of students at the onset of the content instruction, and to gain their willingness and commitment to fulfill specified content learning objectives.

DEFINING OUTRAGEOUS TEACHING

Most conceptions of using drama to teach content involve first teaching a lesson using conventional approaches and then using dramatic techniques such as student role-plays, reader's theater, games, and simulations to review, reinforce, and deepen the learning. Although the conventional reinforcement approach to using dramatic technique is valuable, it tends to be inefficient. In other words, you are basically teaching the content objectives twice—first conventionally and then using dramatic technique to reinforce it. Why not just teach the content from the beginning using the more creative, enriched approach? That is the goal of Outrageous Teaching.

Outrageous Teaching it is not designed to replace all instruction. However, for those lessons and content objectives that a teacher has decided will be of greatest value, Outrageous Teaching is used as *the* primary teaching approach. It is how the content objectives are taught from the very beginning—as opposed to being merely a supplemental approach. In Outrageous Teaching, the teacher teaches the same lessons he or she would teach using conventional methods, covering the same content, but in a very different, far more compelling fashion. No lessons are added to a unit to incorporate Outrageous Teaching. Outrageous Teaching is thus the first classroom use of dramatic technique that does not require incorporating additional lessons to teach content in an enriched fashion.

Outrageous Teaching integrates humor, imagination, and dramatic technique to develop inventive storylines that provide a context that seems important to students in terms of how they think. For most of the lesson, students have no idea what the content objective is—even as they are learning the content. In the early parts of the lesson, a sense of suspense is created and students do not recognize what the teacher is trying to accomplish or the reasons for the teacher's behavior. All they know is that whatever is happening seems interesting and strange.

The storyline also contains a dilemma that students are called on to resolve and, in doing so, to unknowingly, at first, learn and apply the formal content. The more Outrageous the storyline is, the better it is. (The specific techniques for creating such storylines and for planning Outrageous lessons are presented in Chapter 4, and examples of real lessons and storylines are presented in Chapter 5.)

This form of teaching is called Outrageous Teaching because although the same content objectives are being taught as in conventional teaching, the resulting lessons are different from and more imaginative than those taught by conventional teaching methods. Outrageous Teaching provides a whole new motivation and a new context for the student learning to occur in.

Outrageous Teaching is equally applicable across all content areas in grades 4 through 12, and equally applicable to all students and to all content objectives. The techniques are especially valuable for lessons in which all the other techniques a teacher has tried have failed to create student interest or understanding, or to engage resistant and reluctant learners.

Outrageous Teaching is a powerful tool that all teachers can employ to

- Increase simultaneously, in powerful ways, how much students learn and their interest in learning.
- Deepen understanding.
- Enrich the quality of school life for both teacher and student while creating new bonds between them.

- Involve students who previously have not responded to conventional instruction, whether across the board, in specific content areas, or in meeting specific content objectives.

Indeed, although Outrageous Teaching derives from the traditions of dramatic technique and humor, the methodology provides a practical way to operationalize other progressive conceptions such as constructivism and discovery learning.

Of course the best way to understand Outrageous Teaching is to observe an example of it. (All of the sample lessons and units in this book are highlighted.)

DWIGHT'S OUTRAGEOUS LESSON: INTRODUCTION

What does Outrageous Teaching look like?

Let me introduce a lesson taught by one of my student teachers, whom I will call Dwight, to a class of high school sophomores.

The Lesson Begins

The students file in, and once they are settled, the teacher announces that Dwight is home sick today but a special guest is coming to make them an exciting offer.

The visitor then arrives. He has a huge, bushy white beard; wears a tall, Amish-style black hat; is dressed in overalls; and carries a tree stump. He emphatically puts the tree stump on the floor and announces in a booming voice:

> I am a master salesman and have heard that all of you in this
> room have wonderful social skills and would make great salespeople.
> I am here as part of a national search to find the next generation
> of salespeople to sell a new, exciting line of products, the next great
> product, a complete line of stumps!

By now the students have recognized Dwight and are starting to titter a bit, although they are also curious. Dwight continues:

> I see that you are skeptical about the importance and sales potential
> of stumps. Well, let me tell you all the things you can do with stumps
> and I am sure that in five minutes you are all going to want to know
> where you can buy one.

What Is Going On?

Dwight is teaching a traditional content objective that is very hard to communicate and get students interested in. Most of them struggle with learning the content. What objective do you think he is addressing? And in what content area do you think he is teaching?

Hint: He is not teaching a woodworking shop course, and he is not preparing students to learn how to use a chainsaw.

If Dwight is correctly using the techniques described in this book, at this point you should be as much in the dark as the students are about what is going on. Dwight's opening is not just a spur-of-the-moment idiosyncratic creative outburst, nor is he being Outrageous for the sake of being Outrageous. Dwight is using, in a very conscious manner, specific techniques described later in this book, and the lesson is designed to teach a critical content objective.

You will be exposed to more of Dwight's lesson in subsequent chapters.

WHY TEACH OUTRAGEOUSLY?

As you might assume, daring to conduct a lesson such as the one taught by Dwight might take more preparation time, not to mention a bit of courage. Why go to this trouble? Why does Dwight feel it is worth the effort and daring to make a critical content objective come alive for his students?

Teaching the Reluctant or Resistant Learner

Some students have become reluctant to learn from conventional instruction and others actively resist such learning. They have stopped responding across the board and are unmotivated, or unable, to make more than minimal effort. They find conventional instruction boring or unenlightening. Other students do not understand what is being taught even when and if they try to learn it. Such students are disproportionately composed of students born into poverty, minority students, those whose native language is not English, and those with special needs. As these students experience difficulty and even failure, their reluctance to learn turns to active resistance. This results in social concerns about inequity in educational outcomes—the unfortunate learning gap.

One of the revelations that teachers often experience when they teach an Outrageous lesson is that reluctant and resistant students suddenly emerge and shine and their innate intelligence comes to the fore. Many students who have not responded to conventional approaches or other suggested best practices suddenly seem to come alive. The emergence of such students is not only a revelation to the teacher but also an affirmation to the student that he or she really can excel and that the classwork is relevant and interesting.

Other reluctant learners are highly motivated and do well generally but have a dread and a seeming inability to learn the concepts of particular types of content. Math phobia, whether real or imagined, is an example. Most students dread certain academic areas or content topics, and all teachers do not look forward to teaching particular lessons and units because they know that students will have trouble or purposely resist. We all, whether students or teachers, are weak in certain academic areas. For example, as a student I was able to understand the intimidating subject of calculus but could not grasp the details of chemistry, and almost all of the middle and high school students I taught had trouble with math word problems.

What were your weak content areas and topics as a student? I suspect you would have benefited if your teachers had used some Outrageous Teaching, and your students will benefit if you use it now to teach selected learning objectives.

Finally, some students generally do well but learn superficially. They learn by relying on their memory, or they want to learn only what they need to know to answer test questions correctly. Such students are reluctant to understand the deeper meaning or inferences of what they are learning. These reluctant learners generally do well in the early years of schooling but are at a disadvantage at some point later on.

Reducing the Learning Gap

The learning gap in our public schools is one of the most vexing social problems facing our society. As education becomes more important in achieving economic success, a persistently large gap remains between the performance of white students and that of African Americans and Latinos. The gap exists when students start school, and grows ever larger after the fourth grade. Progress was made in reducing the gap between 1965 and 1988, but it widened again thereafter. (You can examine the national trend of the learning gap by downloading the National Center for Educational Statistics' report card *Trends in Academic Progress* from http://nces.ed.gov/nationsreportcard/pdf/main2005/2005464.pdf. The graphs on page 33 show that the black-white reading gap for thirteen- and seventeen-year-olds was smaller in 1988 than in 2004.) The consequences for individuals of color are higher dropout rates and fewer opportunities after school. The consequences for society are the continued marginalization of a substantial portion of our population and a major social inequity.

Recent reform efforts to reduce the learning gap have relied on conceptions of learning from behavioral psychology, which view poor test performance as simply lack of knowledge, and students as vessels that have simply to be filled up with knowledge. If they have not learned it, teach it again, and again, and again—the same way. *Pound it in!* Some schools are now teaching basic reading skills three hours a day in an effort to get test scores up.

This approach simply has not worked. As recently as 2005, after a decade of such reform, results of the National Assessment of Educational Progress (NAEP) showed that approximately half of urban black and Hispanic students are not meeting basic standards in fourth grade reading. Another effect of sole reliance on simplistic instructional approaches is the high dropout rate. A recent study funded by the Gates Foundation found that almost half of high school dropouts report being bored with what was being taught (Bridgeland, Dilulio, and Morison, 2006).

Clearly, relying on force-feeding content to students is not reducing the learning gap. Something more, or something else, is needed. Judicious use of Outrageous Teaching provides potential to produce substantially higher and deeper learning outcomes and test scores for reluctant and resistant learners than relying only on traditional, or teach-to-the-test, approaches. *Indeed, Outrageous lessons and units are viewed as key tools for reducing the learning gap between advantaged and disadvantaged students.*

It is therefore important that Outrageous Teaching not follow the traditional pattern, in which progressive techniques are adopted only in high socioeconomic status schools. Although the techniques are appropriate for such schools, I hope they will also be widely adopted for teaching those reluctant and resistant learners who were born into poor families, they can make an even bigger difference, and help solve one of our most vexing social problems: the learning gap.

Yellow Feathers, Pus, and Warfare: Tapping into Students' Sense of Culture and Reality

The biggest cultural shock that many students face when they first arrive in school is that *the teacher is not wearing yellow feathers*. Research has shown that students raised in caring, low-income homes generally have substantially less verbal interaction with adults at home compared to their peers from moderate and high-income households (Hart and Risley, 1995). As a result, most of their preschool learning comes from passive TV watching. Even children from higher-income households are raised on a heavy diet of TV. Children who grow up watching Sesame Street and other cartoons and video games come to view learning as watching animated characters engaged in dramatic situations and getting new information from dramatic contexts. When they walk into the first grade classroom, the culture shock is that the teacher is not a big bird—there is no costume, no graphics, no animation, and no compelling dramatic contexts. There is just an adult talking . . . and talking . . . and talking!

My point is not to argue that such massive passive learning from entertainment is good. Rather, schools need to recognize the dissonance experienced by students when they enter dramaless learning environments such as those typically found in American classrooms—particularly now that we are so sensitive to other forms of cultural disconnect. We have made great strides in making instruction more sensitive to students' cultural heritage relative to race and ethnicity. We continue, however, to ignore the need to gear instruction to the cultural sense of youth—in other words, to the shared experiences of youth worldwide in learning from dramatic contexts.

Educators also need to recognize that the dramatic contexts of TV shows and YouTube promote powerful forms of learning. Of course our students are often learning things we would prefer they did not. Indeed, there is an old joke that TV is called a medium because it is seldom well done. At the same time, it makes sense for schools to capitalize on the power of dramatic contexts to teach that which we in fact do want students to learn.

Whenever educators address the issue of cultural differences, they always gravitate immediately to thinking in terms of racial and ethnic differences. Although these differences are important, there is a cultural divide that is generally ignored and that is limiting the usefulness of instructional approaches. This ignored cultural divide is between "kidness" and adulthood.

Kids all over the world share bonds of knowledge and perspective that are outside the realm of what most adults know and experience. Youngsters in Harlem, New York, and youth in Bush, Alaska, who have access to satellite TV and the Internet can have more knowledge and perspectives in common than they have with the adults in their own community. I could design a test of cultural knowledge that these seemingly disparate students would all pass but that the adults in both communities would fail.

The use of drama and humor to design highly creative and unusual lessons is a way to engage students' natural experiences and instincts in a productive learning process, regardless of whether the students are at the "yellow feathers" stage (that is, the elementary level), the "pus" stage (that is, the middle school level, where students are increasingly fascinated with their bodies and the changes occurring there), or the "warfare" stage (that is, the high school level, where senses of turf, place, and interest are increasingly set in place).

Transitioning from "Authentic" to "Creatively Authentic" Learning

Conventional instruction often strives to stimulate learning by providing "authentic" learning experiences. The teacher tries to convince students that something is important to them now because it will be important to them when they become adults. *But the students are not adults.* Indeed, many of them may even be rebelling against or intimidated by adults and adulthood—which can cause them to further rebel against learning the content. Such a seemingly progressive notion of instruction is in effect a capitulation to the notion that it is impossible to make the ideas important to students in their current state, and is in effect a demeaning view of what students are capable of appreciating and responding to. The concept of authentic instruction is in reality a diminished view of the craft of teaching and of students' capabilities.

Creatively Authentic instruction, on the other hand, seeks to make the same ideas and content important and intelligible to students on the basis of the "culture of kidness." It seeks to tap into students' views of what life is about and what is important to them. Although the young are immature in many ways, they do have heightened insight into important human concepts such as fairness and friendship that are often eroded in the adult world. Outrageous instruction is built around Creative Authenticity, i.e., teaching what adults want students to learn, but teaching it in a context that is consistent with students' cultural view of life.

Connecting with High School Adolescents

High school teachers at general education conferences often lament that almost all of the innovative ideas seem to be geared to younger students. In addition, the general reaction to dramatic technique is usually, "It will work fine at the elementary level, but it will never work at the high school level, or with complex instructional and learning objectives, or with jaded students." The fact that Outrageous lessons are as effective at the high school level as they are with fourth graders means that middle and high school teachers have an important additional tool for reaching their students in powerful ways. Examples of Outrageous Teaching being used effectively to teach complex content and difficult classes at the high school level—including with low-performing seniors—are provided throughout the book.

Outrageous Teaching is more than just an additional tool, however. Even a single lesson is a transformative experience for teachers. It reaffirms their craft skills, and it feels like a pioneering achievement, because it is probably the first time the content objective has ever been taught that way. It hones, recalibrates, and affirms one's instincts about what is possible.

In addition, Outrageous Teaching builds a new relationship between the students and the teacher. Barriers fall and are replaced by mutual respect. Students react to such lessons as evidence that their teacher really cares about their learning and is willing to go the extra mile and take chances to make sure they succeed. After such a lesson, students respond more positively even to conventional instruction and feel heightened respect for their teacher. Teachers also gain a new perspective on the creative and thinking capabilities of their students, particularly of those who have been reluctant and resistant learners.

IS THERE A METHOD TO DWIGHT'S OUTRAGEOUSNESS?

Although the notion of using drama or any art form to increase the pragmatic outcomes of content learning and improve test scores may seem counterintuitive or a sellout of the artistic ideal, the goal of theater has always been to increase the audience's awareness of something. Using highly dramatic techniques to increase content learning is a natural extension of the theatrical tradition, and it produces powerful results. Indeed, the root of progressive advocacy in favor of incorporating drama into education was the desire to teach content in more effective and meaningful ways.

Nevertheless, it is not obvious how drama and humor and imagination can be used to teach content in ways that provide a consistent advantage over conventional instruction. To accomplish this purpose, formal methodologies are needed, along with a knowledge base of accumulated experience. Methodology is used in all the creative arts. Dancers have choreography, musicians have instruments and music notation. Similarly, a methodology is needed for organizing the kind of highly creative instruction that is described and advocated in this book.

Chapter 4 describes the methodology of being constructively Outrageous, which I have called the Dramatized Content Planning Method.

WHY IS DWIGHT TEACHING AN OUTRAGEOUS LESSON?

The short answer to the question of why Dwight was teaching an Outrageous lesson is that I required it of my student teachers. Yet once he started planning the lesson, his work became a genuine exploration of technique and of his own ability to be highly creative with a "difficult" class. He wanted to discover if he could teach unconventionally without losing control of his class or looking foolish. Would students buy into his ideas? Would they pay attention? Would they learn?

These are questions that all teachers could reasonably ask, regardless of how experienced they are when they explore a new, very different technique. These questions were of particular concern to Dwight given his inexperience, and that this class was one with which he had gotten frustrated. I had observed this class several times. It was a difficult one to teach because the majority of the students did not like to participate, and some even delighted in being unruly. Most simply enjoyed looking bored and spacing out. I came to think of them as "loungers." They had little passion for learning. On most days, the first fifteen minutes of the period were lost to student groans and excuses, requests for pencils, requests to go to the bathroom, and so on. It was worse on days when Dwight introduced a new topic. Teaching this content using conventional instructional methods was like passing a kidney stone, so he was apprehensive about how the class would respond to an Outrageous lesson.

Perhaps a better question to ask is, Why did Dwight pick that particular lesson to teach Outrageously?

The lesson Dwight picked was the first one in a unit that the district had defined as a major learning objective. It was a critical lesson. It was also one that teachers throughout the district had trouble teaching to most students. He also knew that the lesson and unit would bore his students to the point of resisting and stalling them using the wide array of techniques that sophomores have available for such purposes.

As Dwight's lesson unfolds in subsequent chapters, keep in mind that he had not already taught the lesson conventionally. This was the first time the students were taught this critical content. This was *the* learning experience. And even though for the most part Dwight would teach the follow-up lessons conventionally, this first lesson provided a context that he used to bind together his subsequent teaching for the remainder of the unit.

What was the content objective? Was the lesson successful? Did Dwight or the students get splinters? Did he get reprimanded by his principal? Was he ostracized by other teachers? Stay tuned.

Can You Teach Like Dwight?

Yes! Keep in mind that Dwight was not an extrovert or a jokester by nature. Nor was he very experienced. His lesson was a calculated professional process. Therefore, if someone as inexperienced as Dwight could change his persona for a lesson and make it effective, anyone can. He was merely tapping into the wellspring of imagination that all teachers have, and attempting to tap into his students' senses of imagination, wonder, and hope. When that happens, all things are possible, and I think you will be amazed at the results of Dwight's lesson.

The lessons we can learn from Dwight's instruction and from the other examples of Outrageous Teaching presented in this book are as follows:

- Any teacher can create terrific Outrageous lessons and units, and although such lessons require a bit more planning than traditional lessons, the results are worth it, and a little bit goes a long way.

- Any content lesson, no matter how boring and pedantic, can be converted into a riveting Outrageous lesson that increases student learning, interest, and retention.

- Creating Outrageous instruction is only a matter of thinking in divergent, creative, and weird ways.

- Although this form of teaching is beneficial for all students, it is of particular value for reluctant and resistant learners, and it is a critical tool for reducing the learning gap.

Yes! You can be like Dwight and all the other teachers whose Creatively Authentic Outrageous lessons and units are described in the upcoming chapters.

Although teachers often instinctively respond to the notion of drama and being dramatic as "that is not me," the reality is that all good teachers use drama to some degree. Indeed, it may be impossible to teach a really good conventional lesson without the use of dramatic technique. Even maintaining discipline requires the use of dramatic elements. Discipline is not just laying down the rules. It is also adopting a convincing persona. The persona may be one of kindness or of marshal order ("Grave things will happen if you transgress"). In any case, something you do has to convince students that they should obey you.

So, chances are you already use dramatic technique. Outrageous Teaching merely requires you to embellish these techniques in a more imaginative fashion to reach a different goal—enhancing content learning.

SUMMARY

Advances made in knowledge about curriculum and learning have not been matched by progress in making learning fascinating to the vast majority of underachieving learners. Teachers have tremendous untapped creative potential that is critical to improving education in a wide variety of dimensions, from increasing student interest in a given content area to general school improvement and to reducing the learning gap. It is time to tap this creativity to create more dynamic learning environments for reluctant and underperforming and resistant learners.

Organizing Outrageous lessons in grades 4 through 12 requires only a vivid imagination and courage. It does not require special training beyond reading this book. Because such lessons require extra planning, the methods offered here should be used strategically, where they can do the most good. If Dwight and the other student teachers could develop tremendously creative and effective Outrageous lessons, experienced teachers certainly can. In addition, because Outrageous Teaching techniques focus on teaching the content objectives that are already in the curriculum, the methods suggested here are consistent with the push for accountability and standards. More important, however, the use of Outrageous lessons and units represents good practice under any conditions, and provides high levels and unique types of satisfaction for both teachers and students. *They are also lots of fun for everyone!*

Perspectives on Dramatizing Content Instruction

Should dramatic technique be incorporated into instruction—and if so, how and why? The answers to these questions are examined in this chapter from a historical perspective, then from a research perspective, and finally from a theoretical perspective.

Consideration of the instructional role and uses of drama has always evoked heated debate. Many ideals, rationales, and methods for its use have come and gone, or coexisted, or more commonly, competed for attention. To capture this rich dialogue, this chapter first discusses the history of incorporating dramatic technique into instruction. It shows how the proposal for Outrageous Teaching is a rekindling of an enduring—although bumpy—constant going back to the ancient roots of drama: the use of dramatic technique as a pragmatic teaching tool. The chapter shows how this historical phenomenon is the basis of the ideas and techniques proposed in this book, and why it had fallen out of favor.

The relatively low level of creative teaching that incorporates drama in the typical American classroom is surprising given that from ancient times the impulse behind drama was to teach. The ancient Greeks created drama to teach civic values and responsibilities. They used it as a tool to convey the content deemed critical by the rulers of the time. (See Appendix A for a brief summary of these origins.) The use of drama in American education, however, evolved somewhat differently.

The chapter also discusses the available research on the use of dramatic technique to support content learning. It then looks at the latest theoretical perspectives from a wide variety of disciplines that (a) support the use of dramatic technique as an instructional tool, (b) suggest the conditions under which it is likely to be effective, and (c) draw implications for how such use should be designed.

INSTRUCTIONAL USE OF DRAMATIC TECHNIQUE: RECENT EVOLUTION

A number of movements in education have made the use of drama a centerpiece of curriculum and instruction.

Progressive Origins

In 1870 the concept of child-centered education was developed. This view combined a Rousseauesque view of the child as an unsullied little being with the growing interest of evolutionists in the phenomenon of child's play as a common developmental behavior across species. Some early progressive educators, in looking for good examples of an enlightened approach to teaching, saw drama as the centerpiece of such an approach. Acting behavior seemed close to child's play; it was child rather than subject centered, process rather than product oriented, active rather than passive, and above all, self-expressive. Drama was introduced into schools under the rationales of supporting child-centeredness, promoting an activity method of instruction, and developing self-expression (Bolton, 2001).

The most notable practitioner of this progressive approach was Harriet Finlay-Johnson (1897–1910). In her role as headmistress of Sompting School, West Sussex, England, her ideas attracted national and international interest. Finlay-Johnson translated these ideal into practice and introduced dramatic methods of teaching (Bolton, 2001). She introduced such techniques as nature rambles, educational visits to museums and libraries, lessons out-of-doors, and incorporating cookery, handicrafts, art, and drama into the curriculum. She allowed her pupils a degree of freedom and autonomy that was unheard of in other Victorian schools. Progressives argued that children "would enjoy learning facts if they were illustrated in this attractively active way" (Bolton, 2001, p. 152).

Although Ms. Finlay-Johnson's teaching approach required pupils to be active and playful in their learning, the purpose of this pioneering freedom was the learning of facts connected with nature study, history, scripture, and other subjects. The focus was not primarily on the child's opportunity for self-expression but on the body of knowledge dictated by the school's curriculum. Dramatic activity was seen as a dynamic way of illuminating and promoting the acquisition of knowledge rather than as drama for the sake of art (Bolton, 2001).

The most interesting aspects of Finlay-Johnson's work were that her techniques were the first designed specifically to incorporate drama into teaching, and that from the beginning of her use of these techniques she (and other progressives) viewed drama as a better and more effective way to teach content rather than as a separate experience valued primarily for its development of artistic expression.

This original conception of drama linked with child's play and enhancing content was supplanted, however, in 1920 by the speech movement and disappeared for fifty to sixty years (Bolton, 2001). The new speech movement used drama as a form of training to help students master elocution and thereby provide them with self-confidence. The movement was led by the work of Winifred Ward, who established speech training courses as part of the teacher training program at Northwestern University. She also pioneered making creative dramatics a part of the curriculum in Northwestern's School of Speech. This was the first time that dramatics were taught in a college of education in the United States. Ward trained many of the leaders in the educational drama movement in the United States and had a profound impact on American education (Shuman, 1978).

The next step in the evolution of the use of drama in education occurred in England in the 1930s, when Peter Slade attempted to bring natural and spontaneous play into the classroom (Bolton, 2001). The focus of his work was to encourage spontaneous expression for its own sake. "He was opposed to public performances, the use of scripts, training children to act, and above all, teacher intervention in children's playing. Rather, Slade encouraged spontaneity of expression. In his view, content did not matter" (Bolton, 2001, p. 153). What was expressed was seen to be of less importance than the freedom to express it. In time the philosophy of drama as self-expression fell out of favor because teachers felt uneasy with its lack of specific purpose, direction, and progression.

Brian Way developed more formal systems of acting techniques to enable teacher's to develop their students' sensory experiences, imagination, and concentration. The focus of Way's techniques was on the "individuality of the individual" (Bolton, 2001, p. 154), and the goal was to help children "find themselves."

By 1960, Way's work was surpassed in England by the influence of Dorothy Heathcote, who moved the use of drama in the classroom in a very different direction. She rebuilt the tradition started by Finlay-Johnson to link the use of drama to classroom content. She became the biggest influence of her time in redefining the relationship between drama and education and in recasting the role of the teacher.

In rejecting the notion of drama in education as self-expressive play for its own individualistic ends or for teaching students dramatic techniques, Heathcote refocused the use of drama to enhance content learning. In doing so, she went beyond the learning of facts, which was Finley-Johnson's primary concern, to using drama to enable students to look at the "issues, principles, implications, consequences, and responsibilities behind the facts" (Bolton, 2001, p. 154). Her primary focus in using educational drama was to involve students in active role-taking situations in which they could "get inside the consciousness of other human beings and . . . experience a critical segment of life as those beings experienced it" (Shuman, 1978, p. xi). She was less concerned with what the students knew about the historical event than with deepening their understanding of it.

In Heathcote's approach, students were projected into a situation by a real dilemma that they would try to resolve for themselves and for the other participants through dialogue. She noted that "a student has essentially the same task as the poet: to make clear to himself, and thereby to others, the temporal and eternal questions which are astir in the age and in the community to which he belongs" (Wagner and Heathcote, 1976, p. 158). Heathcote established a pedagogy for teachers to design the role-playing experience and mediate the group process. The goal of such mediation was to increase the likelihood that both individual understanding and a productive group dialogue about resolving the dilemma would occur. Her work built on the concerns of progressives with creating individual understanding, but it cast that creation into a formal group process within specific content and with a specific role for the teacher.

Cognitive Transfer: A New Rationale

In the 1980s, the impetus to use drama for content skill development got a new push. In the United States, research began to appear on a new rationale for incorporating drama in schools: the concept of *cognitive transfer*.

What Is Transfer?   *Transfer* means that one type of activity or program can produce gains in many different areas. Producing transfer in education is a holy grail, similar to producing fusion energy or developing a unified theory in physics. Transfer is the most powerful potential force in education. The new transfer rationale was that involvement in the arts in general and in drama in particular could enhance overall cognitive functioning in ways that could increase learning in all areas.

The idea that participation in the arts enhances overall cognition goes back to John Dewey (1931) and Sir Herbert Read (1945). Both men promoted the idea that in important ways the arts stimulate cognition as a way of knowing, in constructing knowledge and meaning, and in the use of symbol systems. This idea was lost, however, as the field of psychology came to focus on the measurement of discrete and observable behaviors rather than on how the mind itself functioned. This approach found its most notable expression in behaviorism.

By the early 1950s, however, pioneers in cognitive psychology such as George Miller, Herbert Simon, and Lev Vygotsky challenged behaviorism and began to focus on how human beings acquire and process knowledge. This increased emphasis on cognitive processes—mental processes that cannot be seen or easily objectified—needed a basic philosophical and analytic structure. The first step was provided by Nelson Goodman, who developed a philosophy of cognition that he called "a philosophy of understanding" (Bruner, 1986, p. 95). In his seminal work *Languages of Art: An Approach to a Theory of Symbols*, Goodman (1968) advanced the theory that human beings use different kinds of symbols and symbol systems to express and achieve meaning. The arts therefore have their own symbol systems, as does writing. By presenting science and art as two different symbol systems, Goodman provided cognitive legitimacy for the arts and erased the traditional philosophical dichotomy between art and science by building a bridge between them. As a result of this cognitive revolution, both philosophers and psychologists began to look at a wide range of human thought processes, including artistic ones.

Viewing learning in terms of different symbol systems opened up the possibility that the types of understanding that resulted from learning one symbol system would increase the learning of other symbol systems. The idea that such transfer is possible was led by the large-scale work of James Catterall at the University of California, Los Angeles (UCLA) (Catterall, Chapleau, and Iwanaga, 1999; Catterall, 2007) and by my work at the University of Arizona (Pogrow, 2005). These two strands of research focused on very different uses of drama. The main emphasis of Catterall's work was on participation in the arts, while my work focused on integrating the use of drama into an intensive environment devoted to the development of Socratic thinking. Despite their different emphases, both approaches essentially reached the same conclusion—that drama use can produce transfer that improves other learning outcomes.

There are two kinds of transfer: *near* and *far*. *Near transfer* occurs when using an Outrageous lesson to introduce a unit results in greater learning not only on that day but throughout the unit. *Far transfer* occurs when learning skills in one area increases students' academic performance in other areas.

Significance of the Transfer Perspective   In a sense, the transfer rationale updates the initial progressive instinct to use drama to increase learning. There is now support from the field of cognitive psychology for the belief that the strategic use of dramatic technique can increase content learning.

Controversy in Using Drama for Instructional Purposes

The historic tension among the different philosophical perspectives on how dramatic technique should be integrated into American education continues. A wide variety of rationales, including the following, are used to argue against using dramatic technique to teach content.

It Inhibits Self-Expression   Although dramatic technique is clearly viewed as a progressive tool, modern progressives tend to gravitate toward the Slade perspective, mentioned earlier, which says that drama provides unfettered freedom of self-expression for students and teachers, and can be used as a tool for artistic discovery. Such progressives see having a specific goal—that is, the teaching of specific content objectives—as inherently antagonistic to the ideal of promoting freedom of self-expression. In addition, modern progressives tend to rail against any systemization of content delivery or requirements. This feeling has become particularly acute at the present time because content objectives are increasingly being mandated by external forces. So the worst idea from this perspective is to come up with a way to use dramatic technique in a systematic fashion to teach formal content objectives.

Although the external mandate of curriculum objectives is a problem, it is not clear from historical experience that self-expression for the sake of self-expression is a sustainable goal in and of itself, or that it is even the real goal of drama. For example, consider Bolton's (2001, p. 154) criticism of the artistry and self-expression perspective of drama use:

> To encourage individual children to search for a drama within themselves is to distort the meaning of dramatic form. Drama is not self-expression; it is a form of group symbolism seeking universal,

not individual, truths. Progressive educators throughout the century have been mistaken in their view of drama as child-centered and self-expressive, and drama teachers have been foolish to believe them.

At the same time, it is clear that self-expression is an important goal of all aspects of education and a key value of a democratic society, and that any use of dramatic technique should encourage and improve self-expression. Does Outrageous Teaching inhibit or develop self-expression? You can answer this question yourself by examining the sample lessons provided in Chapter Five.

It Inhibits Interest in Theater   Drama educators, whose primary interest is teaching about drama, tend to view the use of drama in everyday instruction as demeaning to the real meaning of drama. Heathcote's perspective on using drama has been severely criticized by theater arts advocates, even in England. In his chapter on the historical perspective on drama in education, Taylor (2000, p. 206) notes the following criticism by a prominent actor and director:

> "The emphasis on drama as a learning or pedagogical medium has 'denied students access to the culture and skills of the theater.' . . . England, which has 'one of the richest theatrical traditions in the world,' has managed to produce a generation of students who are, in effect, 'dramatically illiterate.'"

Yikes!

I certainly hope that this book's focus on using drama to improve content learning and reduce the learning gap and reduce dropouts—that is, reduce illiteracy—will not increase "dramatic illiteracy."

It Inhibits Thinking Development   It is generally assumed that teaching to specific objectives is necessarily a straightforward, literal process that suppresses thinking development. I would agree that more often than not this is the case, but it is not the fault of the content objective, which is merely a goal. The objective does not dictate how the goal should be achieved. The problem is that traditionalists generally assume that the best way to achieve content learning goals is by using the most simplistic technique—hence the "pound it in" approach described in Chapter One. That is simply not true. My work in using a higher-order approach to thinking development has consistently shown that dramatized instructional practices produce higher levels of basic skills learning.

Conversely, it is also my experience that a higher-order thinking goal, such as discovery science, can be taught prosaically with no thinking development. So it is not the goal that determines whether instruction produces higher-order thinking. Indeed, the content of a basic traditional narrow goal can be taught in a way that promotes high levels of creative thought on the part of both teachers and students. As a curriculum developer, I relish the challenge of creating thoughtful learning around specific content objectives. For example, can something as straightforward as the rules for multiplying decimals be turned into a creative, thoughtful process? To see how this was turned into an Outrageous lesson, see Stan's Lesson 1 in Chapter Five.

Do We Still Need to Teach Content?   In this era of on-demand access to information, some people question the need to learn any specific content. They argue that it is more important to learn how to access content. However, while access to and sources of content are indeed expanding, acquiring a large base of formal content remains essential for (a) success in a wide variety of fields, (b) gaining access to postsecondary education, and (c) defining our culture and society. At the same time, there is no law that says that all content must be presented in a boring, uninteresting fashion.

The Catch-22   The dueling paradigms about drama use have clearly limited its instructional use in the United States. The catch-22 in this country is that those educators who are most likely to be interested in using dramatic technique tend not to view it as a tool for enhancing content instruction. That may be one reason why the use of drama in regular instruction is more prevalent in England than in the United States. In England, drama is formally recognized as a curricular tool in the national curriculum (Catterall, Chapleau, and Iwanaga, 1999). (England also has a substantial Theater in Education movement in which theatrical companies take up residence in schools.) In the United States, the use of drama in education, and preparation in how to use it for teaching, is found largely outside of colleges of education. Instruction in how to develop and utilize drama in the classroom is rarely tied to the preparation of teachers or developed as a critical component of general pedagogy or curriculum.

Toward an Integrative Perspective

I think that all uses of dramatic technique are important and should be incorporated into education, and that all the perspectives can contribute to each other.

The self-expression school could train teachers to be more expressive and free in how they interact with students when presenting ideas. I spent a sabbatical in the theater school at UCLA studying how teaching and learning occur in the theater world. It is very different than what happens in education. I took many of the ideas and incorporated them into how we trained teachers in the Higher Order Thinking Skills (HOTS) program and into my own teaching. These ideas are key to why the training methods are so memorable to the participants, and so effective. I would love to see all teachers take a course in a theater department and be formally trained in some acting and drama creation techniques. (Actually, that would not be a bad idea for education professors as well.) In addition, as you will see later in this chapter, evidence for transfer from the use of dramatic technique comes both from my work with the HOTS program and from students participating in formal theatrical productions. So, both of these uses of dramatic technique have learning gap reduction potential, and both approaches should be incorporated into schools.

Criticism of and concerns about the use of dramatic technique to increase content learning leveled by people from the other schools of thought who are pushing their own single perspective are essentially red herrings. Although I share the current progressive impulse to rebel against externally mandated curriculum and against high-stakes accountability, the reality is that teachers have always had to teach content that students struggle with, and there have always been content objectives that are a struggle for teachers to make understandable and meaningful to their students—and there always will be. In addition, the widespread notion that if something is systematic it loses creativity and spontaneity is clearly wrong. Although drama and all of the performing arts have elements of self-expression, good drama, whether in the classroom or in the theater, also requires some specification. Actors, dancers, and singers all work from scripts. The bottom line is that the most powerful, enduring, and creative performing dramas result from a combination of systemization and improvisation, and from a blending of artistic expression and the pragmatics of doing. Playwrights of popular drama are usually pragmatic in their goals, that is, they try to teach, or generate understanding about, something specific. Dramas endure because the playwright delivers an important and timeless message in a creative form. Enduring drama is not just an exercise of self-expression or self-realization. It is a creative personal adaptation of a vision of how some important content should be delivered.

In addition, I think the argument that using dramatic technique to increase content learning will increase dramatic illiteracy is another red herring. Increasing the literacy and learning of all students can only serve to increase interest in the theater and in all the arts.

The best way to determine whether the pragmatic end of teaching content inhibits creative expression and thinking development is to read the examples of Outrageous Teaching presented later in the book. I hope that anyone who reads these examples will come away with a sense that even though the students are learning content, the experience is a process of creative self-expression and thinking development for both students and teachers.

One can only hope that the historic tensions between the various schools of advocacy around the use of dramatic technique will be reconciled, and that the strategic use of dramatic technique will be made a formal part of teacher training in the United States on a large scale. At the same time, this book focuses on the use of dramatic technique to teach content, not for the purpose of denigrating the other perspectives, but because this approach is the most underused and misunderstood. In addition, this focus is also based on the belief that the use of dramatic technique is so powerful that it needs to be brought into the core of what schools do. It is only when the use of dramatic technique comes to be viewed as essential to maximizing student achievement that other uses of dramatic technique will receive increased support. This is the spirit in which Outrageous Teaching was developed, to apply dramatic technique to teaching selected content objectives. Although it seeks to reestablish the original progressive conception of the application of dramatic technique, Outrageous Teaching is a more effective method because it also incorporates some of the ideals of the other perspectives on the use of drama in classroom education.

CAN DRAMATIC TECHNIQUES INCREASE LEARNING?

With three notable exceptions, there has been little or no research on the effects of drama use on learning outcomes. There are many claims that using dramatic techniques can increase and deepen learning, but there is very little evidence. I conducted a literature review and could find no evidence or any real research examining the benefits to content learning from classroom use of dramatic strategies.

The absence of direct evidence is a function of advocates assuming that the value of drama is self-evident, and de-emphasizing the use of drama to teach content. In other words, if schools do not adopt the use of drama to improve learning directly, it is hard to show academic benefits. It is more common to find emotional and artistic benefits. For example, Bresler (2005) cites a series of studies that found that participation in the arts increased creativity, originality, expression of imagination, taking of risks, resilience, self-regulation, and sense of identity. It is speculated, probably correctly, that these increased abilities lead to academic improvement, but only one study (discussed later) has demonstrated such growth.

There are reasons, however, to believe that "appropriate" forms of drama use do produce academic gains. There is evidence from my research and that of Catterall, both cited earlier, that suggests that such gains can be expected. There is also clear anecdotal evidence in the examples provided in Chapters Five and Seven that Outrageous lessons and units indeed consistently produce academic gains. Finally, brain research has provided new, compelling theoretical insights on how learning occurs—insights that are consistent with appropriate forms of dramatic technique.

(I keep on emphasizing the notion of "appropriate" use of dramatic technique because if dramatic interventions are not used to increase content learning, or not used with sufficient intensity, research cannot be conducted. So we have a chicken-and-egg dilemma: without research evidence it is hard to convince schools to use drama as an instructional technique, but we cannot produce research evidence without schools using drama as an instructional technique.)

Evidence of Transfer and Resultant Learning Improvement

Three major research efforts show that major transfer results from the *intensive* use of dramatic techniques, and that such techniques increase learning.

Catterall, Chapleau, and Iwanaga (1999) conducted research on the extent to which intensive involvement in the arts, particularly drama and theater and instrumental music, was associated with increases in reading and math achievement in grades 8 through 12. Their analysis of the U.S. Department of Education's National Educational Longitudinal Survey database of twenty-five thousand students found that students with high levels of arts participation outperformed "arts-poor" students. Although high socioeconomic status (SES) students were more likely than low SES students to participate in the arts, the size and diversity of this database permitted Catterall to compare high- and low-arts participants in each of the SES segments, including the lowest.

Catterall found a variety of benefits from intensive participation in drama, including acting in plays, participating in drama clubs, and taking acting lessons. Benefits included increased levels of self-concept and higher levels of tolerance of others. In particular, participation in theater and other drama activities was associated with higher reading scores for both high- and low-SES scores. *The reading gains for high-arts participation was more dramatic for the low-SES students.* Although 41.4 percent of the low-income students in grade ten who participated in theater read at the 50th percentile or higher, only 24.9 percent of those who did not participate were reading at grade level. Participation in instrumental music was associated with higher levels of mathematical achievement for both high- and low-SES students.

The result of higher gains and improved performance in reading for low-SES students who participated in theater was confirmed by the research of Heath and Roach (1999). They studied the effects of participation of at-risk students in arts-based after-school community organizations. Their research not only confirmed the benefits of arts participation for linguistic development, but it also explained how and why. They found that intensive participation in the arts encourages students to engage in planning, monitoring, reasoning, and critiquing activities in the preparation of the artistic product. These activities in turn produce dramatic increases in the sophistication of verbalization and writing activities. The study found that these at-risk students quickly experienced the following:

- A fivefold increase in the use of if-then statements
- More than a twofold increase in the use of verbs such as *consider, understand, could*, and *might*
- Nine times as many opportunities as in the classroom to write original text materials
- Six times as many opportunities as in the classroom to speak more than one sentence

It is easy to understand how such theatrical experience translates into improved reading and verbal skills.

The HOTS program used a different approach to produce transfer of skills in disadvantaged students. Instead of providing students with experience in theater productions, HOTS brought drama to the teaching and learning process in a self-contained program. The goal of the HOTS intervention was to develop the thinking skills of disadvantaged students, specifically Title I and learning disabled students, in the hope that that development would transfer to improved basic skills. HOTS provided a daily intensive-learning environment to disadvantaged students in grades 4 through 8, thirty-five to forty minutes per day for one to two years. This supplemental program was used in lieu of special remedial interventions.

In HOTS the use of dramatic techniques by the teacher was integrated into the use of technology and Socratic teaching techniques. Ultimately, HOTS was adopted in approximately 2,600 schools and served approximately a half-million disadvantaged students.

The goal of the HOTS project was to determine whether the skills learned in a thinking-development program based in dramatic teaching technique would transfer to produce greater gains in reading and content performance than additional direct help in the specific content skills. The answer is a resounding yes! The research found that HOTS students generally grew three times as much in reading comprehension compared to remediated groups of disadvantaged students. This type of relative advantage was consistent across a wide range of racial groups and settings. The results were consistent both for national standardized tests and for the new state tests.

The evidence for transfer resulting from the use of dramatic contexts in the HOTS program is even more compelling in the dissertation research of Mary Ann Darmer. Darmer (1995) compared HOTS students in grades 4 and 5 in the school where she taught to disadvantaged students from the same classrooms who experienced an alternate intervention that provided additional in-class practice in the classroom content. Darmer studied the effects of HOTS training on the following outcomes: (a) metacognition, (b) reading comprehension, (c) grade point average (GPA), (d) general intelligence, (e) writing, and (f) novel problem-solving tasks.

This study was the first to use a wide variety of measures of cognitive development to assess more accurately and comprehensively how widespread the benefits of the HOTS program were. In addition, although this study was quasi-experimental in that the students were not assigned randomly to the treatment, the study used an unusually rigorous education research methodology in that both groups had the same classroom teacher. (In most education research, the treatment and comparison groups have different teachers, so the researcher does not know for sure whether differences between the groups are a result of the treatment or from having different teachers.) As a result, whatever differences were observed were a result of the supplemental help the students received—whether drama-based thinking development provided by Darmer or extra content help provided by the classroom teacher.

Counterintuitively, the students who had less direct content instruction and who instead experienced the drama-based thinking-development activity did substantially better across the board. Fourth grade HOTS students improved substantially and significantly in all twenty-two pre-post comparisons. HOTS students significantly and substantially outperformed the other Title I students in all twelve post-test comparisons between the groups. The gains in GPA for HOTS students were substantial—almost a whole letter grade. Indeed, by the end of the year, 35 percent of the HOTS students made the honor roll. In addition, twenty-three of the students entered the school's science contest. These gains are in stark contrast to the poor performance of the comparison students who made no gains in the fourth grade. By the fifth grade, the scores of the comparison students were declining—even with additional content help. In other words, HOTS students not only substantially outperformed the comparison students in all measures of academic and cognitive development, but the HOTS students also made significant gains while the comparison students declined. This is powerful evidence of transfer.

Finally, the experience of the HOTS program over dozens of independent evaluations by school districts consistently demonstrated that when dramatic techniques were combined with Socratic dialogue, not only did content test outcomes improve to a greater degree than with traditional approaches, but students' verbalization and self-confidence also increased. In other words, students' creative expression increased. So not only did the experience improve students' content learning, but it also increased their desire for and ability in self-expression—a form of far transfer.

Although the HOTS experience was a self-contained environment, it is practical to incorporate the same dramatic techniques into regular instruction. If teachers in a department or school work cooperatively to integrate the use of dramatic technique into their content teaching, disadvantaged students will cumulatively obtain intensive drama-based learning experiences as did the students in the HOTS program, and presumably the same benefits.

The Supermath program—drama-based supplemental math units that I developed for classroom use in grades 4 through 9—confirmed that integrating the use of dramatic contexts into regular classroom instruction provided the types of benefits already described. Unpublished research from pilot projects shows that Supermath increased both math performance and interest in math for low-performing students.

As a result, there is clear evidence that employing dramatic technique—whether through participation in theatrical productions or by incorporating drama into instruction—transfers into higher levels of academic achievement for disadvantaged students in grades 4 through 10. The transfer benefits appear to result from the increasingly sophisticated uses of thinking and language that are inherent in an environment that engages students and places increased responsibility for the success of learning activities in their hands. It is not just a more active learning environment, but also a more compelling one.

THEORETICAL BASES FOR TEACHING CONTENT OUTRAGEOUSLY

A body of contemporary theory, including perspectives from psychology, learning theory, and neuroscience, has informed the thinking behind the Outrageous Teaching approach. Although it is beyond the scope of this book to explore these fields in detail, I touch on a few of the more important ideas to help guide an understanding of how and why appropriate uses of drama can stimulate content learning.

Long before the emergence of neuroscience, social psychologist Lev Vygotsky was conducting path-breaking experiments into the nature of children's learning and their development of language. His conclusions have passed the test of time and are prominently taught in colleges of education. Vygotsky (1978) documented the critical importance of play and social interaction to cognitive development and learning.

Cognitive Psychology

In designing the HOTS program, I used as the basis a branch of cognitive psychology known as information processing theory. This theory describes how the brain processes information and how it organizes itself to remember and transfer what has been learned. It has proved to be remarkably useful.

Cognitive scientists talk about *mental models*. In education, that the term refers to giving students a way of seeing ideas in their minds. It is done by linking facts and ideas to situations, games, stories, and so on that help students envision the working of these ideas. The notion of mental models was a major basis for the development of Supermath units. For example, by thinking of decimals as inhabitants of a "'hood," students were able to picture the relative size of decimals in their minds without relying on the typical math rules, and were able to make inferences about the properties of decimals that math teachers fail to achieve with the vast majority of students. Most math students could now think about these concepts the way only mathematically gifted students previously could.

Perspectives from Neuroscience

The field of neuroscience, especially brain research, also offers interesting perspectives. The theory that would probably be most useful in understanding whether, how, and why Outrageous Teaching enhances content learning, is knowledge about how the left and right sides of the brain interact with each other. Science is just beginning to understand that the brain's hemispheres interact in a more complex fashion than previously thought, and it is just beginning to look for and study the nature of these interactions. So, it may be premature to base practice on such knowledge. Still, the findings are intriguing and merit attention.

Neuroscience has established links between emotion and mood on one hand and cognition and memory on the other. Although the exact nature and mechanism of this relationship is not fully known, it is clear that it exists. There is a high correlation between the vividness of memories and the emotional level of the original event (Reisberg and Heuer, 2004). (This is a positive relationship unless the emotional level is unusually high, such as that triggered by a traumatic event.) This outcome suggests that learning in an emotional context increases retention. Bower and Forgas (2000) discuss how mood affects learning. They note that "positive moods generally lead to . . . more open, flexible, creative and inclusive processing solutions," while "negative moods . . . sometimes lead to less flexible and more routine and predictable solutions" (p. 141).

A key goal of Outrageous Teaching is to create vivid memories and a positive mood around the content being taught. You will note that in the snippet of Dwight's lesson provided in Chapter One, he is creating a surprising and vivid circumstance, and the mood of the class has quickly shifted from passive obedience to active curiosity. Although you are still not sure what he is teaching, he is demonstrating great emotion about what seems at first glance to be a silly idea.

Neuroscience is also making great strides in linking the rational with emotion and artistic expression. Jensen (2008) discusses how neurology informs brain-based teaching, and that some of the work explores the relationship between artistic development and overall brain functioning. He notes that neuroscience departments in five prestigious universities (the University of Oregon, Harvard University, the University of Michigan, Dartmouth College, and

Stanford University) currently have projects studying the impact of the arts on the brain.

Imagination and Learning

There is an array of other compelling contemporary theories on which to base Outrageous Teaching. The most intriguing of these are conceptions of the use and functioning of imagination and its role in learning.

Probably the best work on the relationship between the use of imagination and learning is that of psychologist Paul Harris. In his most recent book (Harris, 2000), he shows how pretend play and fantasy contribute to cognitive development, and how the importance of these learning components does not diminish with age as previously assumed. They retain their central importance beyond the early years. Indeed, one needs only to notice the growing prevalence of video game use among adults.

The individual who is currently doing the most to link research and theory on imagination directly to teaching is Kieran Egan (1992, 2007), who traces the evolution of philosophers' and scientists' views on the role of imagination in thinking and learning. Egan traces the evolution of philosophical thought about what rational thinking is, starting with Plato's focus on rational scientific thought, geared to discovering the truth about tangible phenomena, and which derided intangible forms of learning such as creative imagination and artistic expression. Aristotle made room for perceiving imagination as part of rational thought. Does invoking the imagination inhibit or extend rational thought and learning? This is a tug of war that has gone on for thousands of years.

The concept of rationalism in the seventeenth-century's Age of Enlightenment viewed imagination as detracting from reason, and as an amusing frill. During such periods, the evoking of imagination and its related emotions is seen as inhibiting learning. Education comes to be viewed as transmitting facts and principles bound strictly by rational thought. This view is prevalent today in the neoconservative approach to education and accountability. The Romantic period of the nineteenth century developed the contrary view that imagination is at the root of conscious thought and learning. Today's progressive educators recognize that invoking one's imagination is a critical component of making sense of the facts and principles, and rather than being in conflict with rational thought, imagination aids it.

The Aristotelean view of scientific thought has prevailed. Today, imagination plays a key role in even the most hard-core sciences. "Thought experiments" are widely used in physics. Einstein derived many of the fundamental principles for which he is most famous from thought experiments. He could not measure the effects of relativity in a lab, so he created the principles by imagining "what if. . ." For example, what if the bus he was riding on was a light beam? How would it behave in the infiniteness of space, and what would he see while riding on the beam? Watching a train go by sparked the following thought experiment: What would happen if you kept on putting energy into a train's engine to try and get it to go faster than light? Einstein came to the conclusion that the energy would be converted into mass and the train would get heavier. He then used mathematics to formally represent what he had envisioned in his imagination. Howard Gardner's (1993) revolutionary work has shown that the formal logical model of thought extolled by Plato is but one of many types of formal intelligence that humans possess.

All of this modern experience supports the central roles of imagination, mental image making, and artistic sense as central to learning. Even the ancients knew this. Long before Einstein's famous thought experiments, ancient cultures invented myths to create mind pictures as a way of learning. Egan (1992) speculates that myths originated in ancient culture as a way to remember things considered to be important. Tying the information to compelling stories that stimulated the imagination was a strategy for transmitting knowledge deemed important. Schank (1999) has a similar theory based on current work in artificial intelligence and how the brain functions. Storytelling and listening to stories are critical to encoding information in ways that make it likely to be retrieved and applied in a variety of circumstances. Schank notes that "knowledge . . . is experiences and stories, and intelligence is the apt use of experience and of the creation and telling of stories" (p. 90). He says that a story is useful because it enables the listener to construct linkages to the ideas being presented and provides greater opportunity to map the new information into existing memory networks. Thus, creating dramatic contexts around that which is being taught is both ancient practice and consistent with current brain research.

Practical, Cutting-Edge Pedagogy

Today those on the cutting edge of pedagogy understand the importance of building practical techniques that draw on these new understandings from the various branches of psychology. For example, Jeffrey D. Wilhelm, in his book *You Gotta Be the Book* (2008, p. 85) describes how developing low-performing students' ability to read literature with comprehension involves their "seeing the story world." This approach involves helping students create mental images of a story's landscape. Wilhelm discuses how to use dramatic technique to help students notice cues in the text for visualizing this secondary world.

Ultimately, both ancient experience and modern conceptions of learning all point to the critical importance of using dramatic technique in instruction. As a result, there is now a strong theoretical basis for considering the triggering of students' imagination as a central rather than supplemental part of teaching content. Outrageous Teaching relies on drama and humor to stimulate students' imaginations so that they will generate mental stories, emotions, and images about what is being taught, which in turn will enhance the likelihood that the content will be processed deeply and retained. This is particularly critical for students who generally resist thinking deliberately about what is being taught.

But enough about theory and history. Let's get back to the real world of the classroom and actual teaching and see how and what Dwight is doing. As you read this next snippet from his Outrageous lesson, consider how what he is doing links to the theoretical perspectives just discussed, and in particular how he is continuing to use story, mood, and imagination.

DWIGHT'S LESSON, CONTINUED

When we left Dwight, he had walked into the classroom wearing a disguise, emphatically put a tree stump on the floor, and announced that he was a master stump salesman and that the students needed stumps in their homes.

The lesson continues as follows:

Dwight then talks for five minutes in a manner that imitates a TV car salesman, giving a confident, nonstop monologue about all the benefits of having a stump. He lists about a dozen reasons why the students would want to have a stump. Each reason is more Outrageous than the one before.

> *Suppose you come home and have a terrible itch in your back. What can you do? Why, you can rub your back against the stump. You come home and it's cold and your heater is not working. What can you do? You can burn part of your stump for warmth. For you guys, having a stump is a symbol of manliness, and women look up to a man with a stump. Suppose you come home and find that someone has stolen all of your furniture—you can sit on your stump.*

You can even serve food on your stump. And after you have eaten a wonderful meal, you look in the kitchen for a toothpick, and there are none, and you suddenly remember that you forgot to buy more. What to do? Break off a splinter from your stump and, voilà, you have a toothpick.

Of course Dwight is just getting started. He continues:

In addition to all the ways I have just described that a stump can enrich your life, there is more, much more. If you have a problem, you can confide in your stump, tell it your deepest fears and concerns—it will always listen and never argue with you.

If you do not have enough closet or shelf space at home, you can hang your socks or jewelry on your stump.

Dwight goes on and on and on for a few more minutes about many other uses for stumps, occasionally pounding the stump on the floor for emphasis.

The students laugh politely or give skeptical looks after each reason for needing a stump. Above all, they are enjoying the moment and wondering where things are going, and why their teacher is acting this way. After five to ten minutes of nonstop selling, Dwight finally pauses and says:

I know by now all of you realize that you cannot live without having a tree stump, and that all of you want one.

Of course, even though the students are having a great time, no one wants to buy one. Nonplussed, Dwight continues:

Unfortunately, I cannot sell you this stump because it is my last one until I get my next shipment. However, I have an even better opportunity for you right now, because I am looking to hire one of you to be on my sales team. I want to see which of you can be a great salesperson like myself. This is a chance of a lifetime at a great career.

Questions: What content area is this lesson in and what is the primary learning objective? *Hint:* It is not a business course. The important thing is that just as you are not sure what is going on, neither are the students. The storyline is maintaining a high level of both curiosity and suspense. You will be able finally to figure out what is going on when the complete lesson is presented in the next chapter and I am confident that you will be impressed with the resultant content learning.

SUMMARY

The history of drama use in education has shifted in terms of rationale and approach. It has shifted among the following options:

- Encouraging play to promote child-centered self-expression
- Incorporating drama into instruction to improve the learning of content
- Improving speech
- Encouraging play and spontaneity of expression
- Developing students' dramatic skills and knowledge
- Developing cognitive abilities in ways that transfer to improved learning in other areas

This book's approach to emphasizing dramatic techniques for teaching content is a return to the original progressive conception and it unifies the strengths of both Finlay-Johnson's and Heathcote's conceptions. One approach focused on factual learning, the other on deepening understanding of the content. Outrageous Teaching does both.

Research on transfer resulting from dramatic approaches to content learning is promising, and this book provides further anecdotal evidence of such transfer. In addition, a substantial base of theory from a wide range of fields, such as cognitive psychology, and of evidence emerging from neurology, supports the expectation that appropriate dramatic approaches increase learning.

Conceptions of the role of imagination in rational thought and learning have veered between viewing it as an obstructionist frill to considering it an essential part of conscious thought and learning. It is now increasingly clear that linking learning to students' sense of imagination and culture is not a diversion, but instead is integral to stimulating the desire to learn, increasing retention, and deepening understanding. Research from the HOTS program has shown that when dramatic approaches are linked to Socratic interaction, not only do test scores increases to a far greater extent than results from remedial approaches with children born into poverty, self-confidence and tolerance also increase. In other words, we can use dramatic techniques to increase content learning in ways that also enhance self-expression.

The techniques offered in this book are also updates to the earlier progressive initiatives for teaching content, in terms of both methodology and function. This update is based on advances in cognitive psychology, social psychology, and neuroscience about the nature of the learning process, as well as on my successful large-scale experience in applying dramatic technique to accelerate the learning of disadvantaged students. The result is a more focused and powerful learning environment that can be applied to the initial teaching of content rather than used only as a supplemental tool, and in a way that also enhances thinking and creative expression.

From Discipline to Outrageous Teaching: Classroom Use of Dramatic Techniques

A wide variety of classroom dramatic practices have evolved in response to the many needs of classroom teachers and to the historical evolution of philosophical conceptions of the most appropriate use of such techniques. All successful teachers rely on dramatic techniques to some extent even if they do not think of them as such.

This chapter surveys the landscape of dramatic practices commonly used in the classroom, starting with practices frequently used by the teacher for maintaining discipline and for other elements of instructional management, then moving to practices used as learning tools, including games, role-play activities, simulations, and similar practices. The latter part of the chapter focuses on content instruction—first on techniques for introducing content, then on the subsequent actual teaching of the content, which is the goal of Outrageous Teaching.

The most frequent use of dramatic techniques is to maintain discipline and other instructional management functions. This chapter offers teachers a variety of ideas to support these efforts. When drama is employed as a teaching and learning tool, it is generally used for social or artistic development. Examples of the social uses include using drama to develop skills in conflict resolution, listening skills, self-awareness, tolerance, visualization, self-expression, and movement.

Dramatic technique is also used to teach content. These practices generally include various types of student role-play and are most often used for reviewing content and deepening the learning or understanding of that content. These practices are seldom used as the primary approach to teaching content objectives.

Clearly, all of these uses of dramatic technique are valuable, and they all have their place. Indeed, they have all contributed to Outrageous Teaching. This chapter discusses most of these uses; it skips over the social and artistic uses of drama and the teaching of drama as a subject, because these have been covered extensively in the existing literature on the uses of drama.

Finally, the chapter illustrates Outrageous Teaching by presenting Dwight's entire lesson. It shows how Dwight used this lesson to teach a specific content objective, and it reveals what that objective is. It then analyzes how the other uses of dramatic technique have contributed to the lesson, how those techniques have been extended and modified by the lesson; and the effects of the lesson on the content learning of the students. The contributions of the other uses are critical because teachers already use many of the practices that constitute Outrageous Teaching.

MAINTAINING DISCIPLINE

The most common classroom use of dramatic technique is to maintain discipline. Good teachers with potentially unruly classes establish both rules of order and a mysterious trigger of potentially dire consequences (that is, students who fail to observe a particular trigger action by the teacher will experience "dire consequences"). What makes the technique work is the teacher's choice of dramatic action, and his or her ability to "sell" the idea that a catastrophe will result if students fail to heed the warning.

The most common goals of employing such a trigger are to get students' attention, to get them to quiet down, or both. The teacher's action is usually a simple one, such as slowly counting to three, pulling out a watch and waiting for a prespecified length of time, using a clicker to sound out a prespecified number of clicks, and so on. The most dramatic trigger warning I witnessed was a teacher dragging a piece of chalk across the board in such a way that it made a screeching sound that students hated. All the teacher had to do thereafter was motion as though he was about to scrape the chalk again, and the result would be immediate silence and attention.

When a good teacher dramatically invokes the trigger warning, a sense of urgency immediately engages the psyches of the students and they start to shush one another. The teacher's use of dramatic skill in this action combines body position and facial expression (a horrified, baffled, angry, or determined look helps).

One of my student teachers tried to control an unruly middle school class by outshouting them, yelling to get their attention, and constantly threatening them. Every day she would go home hoarse. I always left her class with an earache. There was always lots of noise, little teaching, and little control. Once middle school students sense that they can get under a teacher's skin, they are merciless. The louder the teacher is, the more boisterous the students get. A yelling teacher is usually interpreted by students as a sign that the teacher is to be ignored and tormented. This student teacher's yelling was accompanied by all kinds of threats, which were totally ignored by students even after several were sent to the principal's office. Indeed, sending students to the principal's office as a tactic to try and restore calm when the class was out of control always made matters worse. The singling out of a student to go to the principal's office always triggered a five-minute episode of "Why me? Everyone else is misbehaving! You're picking on me!" and so on.

I explained to the frustrated teacher that she had to stop yelling and threatening because she could not send the whole class to the principal's office, because all she was doing was contributing to the overall noise level of the class. I explained that she needed to institute a clear set of disciplinary rules, and to use a dramatic signal when she expected the students to come to attention—or else. It would be best if such a signal was both visual and auditory. I asked her to develop a system of explicit rules and a dramatic trigger gesture.

The next time I came to the class, as soon as all the students were seated the teacher waved a banner and blew a note on a small recorder. The students stopped talking and the lesson began. Simple. Whereas previously they had ignored her explicit threats, the implicit threat that something bad would happen if they did not come to order within three seconds of hearing the sound was much more compelling in their minds. In other words, the *implicit* threat, backed by clear rules, and the teacher's dramatic presence supporting a momentary trigger routine were more real and compelling to the students than were the *explicit* threats. It wasn't that the threat had changed, but that the manner in which the threat was delivered had changed to a more dramatic form that caused the students to reinterpret the presence of their teacher. Students now bought into the *sense* of threat to a far greater degree than they had bought into the threats themselves. This simple, dramatic flair probably saved the student teacher's education career. Now she could really teach, and cut back on throat lozenges.

INSTRUCTIONAL MANAGEMENT

In addition to maintaining basic discipline, dramatic technique can also be used to improve other aspects of classroom instructional management. Some of these techniques are conventional and widely used; others are not. Some of the techniques are basic and others are advanced. The following two subsections review the wide gamut of dramatic techniques that teachers can employ to enhance their instructional management skills.

Basic Techniques

Expressive Microbursts   The dramatic technique most typically used to interest students in what is being taught at a given moment is to highlight a key idea by using *expressive microbursts*. These are exaggerated tonal or facial expressions or gestures used by teachers to covey the importance of something that is happening or that has just happened. For example, most good teachers employ a variety of dramatic gestures or voice tones to praise students, to encourage or dissuade them, and so on. Teachers in the early grades are using microbursts when they use energetic tonal changes to exaggerate key words as they read stories to the class. A microburst may be wide-eyed exasperation at something a student has said or done, a high five for a good answer, a change in voice tone to convey excitement at how students are thinking through a problem, or a change in the speed of speech, such as slowing down to highlight the importance of what one is saying. It can be a look of wonder at something you have just read to students or are about to read. It can also be a look of anticipation as students reveal the outcome of an experiment or present some other type of report.

When I was teaching inner-city middle school students, a student would sometimes do something so goofily inappropriate (if there is such a term in education) that I would want to burst out laughing. I would consciously control myself, however, and put on a look of stern disapproval. That was pure acting. In the case of older high school students, I would put on a look of concern or surprise that they could do such a thing.

Expressive microbursts are momentary reactions that are not typical of how a given teacher generally talks or looks. Indeed, good teachers seem to do them unconsciously. Tauber and Mester (2007) offer a number of great tips on voice animation (Chapter 5) and body animation (Chapters 4 and 7). One of their counterintuitive body-animation recommendations is to respond to students' emotional outbursts by being totally inanimate and putting a bored look on your face.

Just as a sportscaster or newscaster develops certain mannerisms or expressions for which they then become known, teachers can consciously increase their use and variety of expressive microbursts. There are moments in all lessons that can benefit from such behaviors. A simple method that teachers can use to improve their use of expressive microbursts is to tape record themselves teaching—yes, start with an audio recording instead of a videotape. Chances are that your voice is flatter throughout a lesson than you perceive it to be. Find instances in the recorded lesson when you could have used your voice in a more exaggerated manner, by changing either your sound level, your pitch, or your pace, to convey your reaction to something that happened or to increase your emphasis on something you taught. Practice and record the more exaggerated way of using your voice. After a bit of practice you will become far more vocally expressive and more frequently shift the level of your voice.

As you shift your voice, your facial expressions will also shift. Videotape yourself and do the same thing with facial expression as you did with your voice. Notice how few or many times your facial expression changes throughout a lesson, then work on increasing that variation.

Warning! A few expressive microbursts go a long way. Watching a person who constantly shifts voice and expression is as painful as watching someone who never changes it.

Changing Persona with Humor and Strangeness   One can carry the expressive microburst notion a step further and create quick shifts of persona. My favorite moment-to-moment expressive microburst as an inner-city classroom teacher in a high-poverty school was to shift my persona quickly whenever a student responded in a passive or wise-guy way—which they did, particularly early in the school year. I would quickly shift from being the typical serious teacher, put an innocent smile on my face, and turn into a bigger wise guy than the student. I would respond in an Outrageous, surprising way—a way in which they had never before heard a teacher respond. For example, whenever students gave me their famous answer to one of my questions, "I dunno, Teacher," I would respond, "But if you did know, what would your answer be?" Eventually, with a bit of patience, most students will indeed make an effort to respond. (I would later tell the student privately that I did not accept a lazy response because he or she was smart and capable of thinking of a good answer if he or she tried. Thereafter, that student will be less likely to try a passive response.)

By providing highly surprising responses I was able to keep students off balance in their efforts to be cool and passive. They began to realize that their tried-and-true methods for distracting and annoying teachers and for getting themselves off the hook only stimulated me to become even more of a wise guy. They quickly learned that they could not get under my skin or get me to back off from expecting an appropriate answer or piece of work, and that I would come right back at them with a weird response, I earned their respect and they became highly teachable. Not allowing students to put forth less than their best eventually won them over. The combination of being a weird wise guy and having high expectations is a far better strategy than false praise or encouragement such as "You will do better next time," "Good try," and so on.

Indeed, humor, both real and feigned, is probably the least used dramatic classroom technique, and one of the most powerful.

Advanced Instructional Management

Dramatic techniques can also be used to address advanced instructional management issues, particular those characteristic of classes with high percentages of children born into poverty or recent immigrants. In high-poverty classrooms, the instructional management issues are more complex and difficult than the issues found in other classrooms and cannot be solved with expressive microbursts alone. They require the use of more elaborate dramatic staging to set a new context for teacher-student interaction. Indeed, such classrooms may provide the greatest untapped opportunities for using dramatic technique to improve instructional management.

Handling the Silent Classroom   An example of an advanced instructional management issue in a high-poverty classroom is that students generally hesitate to verbalize answers to questions. When they do voice answers, they generally give one- or two-word responses, and even those are generally spoken hesitantly and quietly. There are many reasons for this student behavior, but it reflects primarily a lack of confidence. Conscientious teachers will generally encourage such students and ask them to speak up and repeat their answers more loudly. Some teachers will then go even farther and ask the students to expand the answer and put it into a complete sentence, although if the student complies, this response will also be spoken too softly to be heard.

In such classrooms, the teacher is constantly asking students to speak up. Most teachers give up at some point and begin routinely to repeat the students' answers and embellish them. One has only to sit in a high-poverty class for awhile to see this pattern in action. The rationale used by teachers for such repetition and embellishment is that it validates what the students have said and makes them feel better. Although there is some truth to this, knowing that the teacher will do this becomes a crutch for the students. Such a crutch is not a substitute for students voicing their ideas in a confident and proud manner.

(As an aside, the hardest change for good teachers to accomplish during the five days of training in the HOTS program is to *stop repeating students' answers.* Some teachers have likened trying to break this habit to quitting smoking. Indeed, there is no comparable form of human interaction in which one party in a conversation consistently repeats what the other party has said before responding to what was said. A possible exception is if one is talking to someone who is senile. Indeed, try to have a conversation with someone who is instructed to repeat everything you have said before responding. You will quickly find it excruciating.)

At the same time, trying to get reluctant verbalizers to speak up loudly and proudly takes a huge amount of class time without any guarantee of results. This is a significant instructional management problem. When faced with a dilemma such as this in which doing the right thing can cause a critical loss of instruction time, and the typical approach is relatively ineffective, *what is a teacher to do?* Who or what are you going to call on for help? The answer, of course, is *drama.*

Can you think of an unconventional, dramatic way to get students to speak louder consistently without constantly asking them to do so—even if only for one period?

_____

_____

_____

Following is one possible dramatic technique that could be used for this purpose.

The teacher walks into class with a big wad of cotton in one ear. (It helps if you use a red marker to put a spot of simulated blood on the cotton.) The teacher announces in a very loud voice:

I woke up this morning with a very bad ear infection. There was some bleeding and a lot of pus. I went to the hospital and the doctor told me to call in sick, but I didn't want you to fall behind, so I am here. I think the pus has stopped, but I can't hear very well, so I need you to speak up.

After the first few students speak, the teacher slaps his or her ear and says loudly:

I see your lips moving but I can't hear what you're saying. Please speak up.

After a few such examples, the lesson proceeds with everyone speaking loudly. Magic! At the end of the lesson, or the next day, the teacher explains why she pretended to have an earache and compliments the students on how well and proudly they spoke.

Of course the teacher needs to have some throat lozenges handy to do this, and it would be hard to do it all day. However, as with all drama, a little bit goes a long way. After this lesson, whenever the students lapse into their shy, quiet answering voices, the teacher can pull out a piece of cotton and put it in his or her ear or remind the students that they were able to speak up when they thought their teacher was hard of hearing, so obviously they have the ability to do so. At such moments the teacher may also emphasize that the students are smart, that they have a right to be proud, and that one sign of pride is speaking confidently.

I used this technique once with a group of doctoral students. For about twenty minutes they consistently spoke louder than normal. Then they began to suspect that things were not what they seemed to be. I explained that I was deliberately modeling a highly effective dramatic technique that can be used with K–12 students. I am not sure whether they thought I was being profound or absurd.

Handling the Passive Classroom   Another advanced dramatic technique available to teachers is one I have used in an evening graduate-level class. After a day of work the students generally want to settle in and listen, but I want them to engage in lively discussions, regardless of how frenetic a day they may have had. I also want to encourage them to internalize the assigned readings. How do I convey this expectation and gain their cooperation? In the following example, I had a surprise planned for their discussion of the first set of assigned readings.

When the students walked into class they saw me wearing a set of headphones and holding a microphone. I announced to a make-believe audience that this was a national PBS radio broadcast of a discussion of the theories of Vygotsky among a group of experts. I then posed a question related to the assigned reading and handed the microphone to a student to respond. *Forgive me! I forgot to mention that the microphone was a banana.* The banana was dutifully passed around the room and everyone got to participate in the broadcast. When I called out a student's name, the banana would be passed to him or her. There is something about the process of speaking into a banana that makes it difficult not to try to say something interesting. A stiff-stemmed flower also works as a simulated microphone, as does a sneaker (preferably a brand new one), as does a [use your imagination].

What these examples have in common is that, to deal with what would otherwise be a frustrating instructional management problem, I created a fictional context or scenario in which students' could tap into their sense of caring and imagination and good-natured humor.

The bottom line is that there is more than one way to "skin a cat"—to use a politically incorrect expression—when dealing with classroom instructional management issues. Teachers teach many informal lessons in their everyday interactions with students. There are usually ways to address these issues other than constantly preaching, admonishing, or, even worse, looking aside and not even making an effort—highly creative ways that will embed themselves deeply into the psyches of the students and achieve the desired results. All you have to do is identify an ongoing instructional management issue that concerns you, take a step back, think creatively, and ask yourself:

> How can I create a dramatic or imaginary context that will stimulate students to respond in the manner I want them to?

At your next staff meeting, turn the typical gripe session about student behavior into a brainstorming session to identify possible weird dramatic techniques for coping with and improving that behavior, then give it a try.

REVIEWING AND ENRICHING CONTENT LEARNING

Dramatic techniques are most commonly incorporated into instruction across the content areas for the purposes of reviewing, reinforcing, and deepening content that has already been taught conventionally. These techniques typically include games, student role-play, simulations, or similar practices.

Using Classroom Games

Involving students in games and contests can be a fun and effective approach for reviewing, reinforcing, and deepening what has already been taught conventionally. When I was a beginning junior high school teacher of the lowest-performing classes in each of the grades, I dreaded Friday afternoons, when I found it impossible to teach or even to get students' attention. It was as though they felt it was their right to start the weekend early. I reacted in the worst way possible and resorted to giving them worksheets and keeping them late if they failed to finish. Obviously they responded by mindlessly filling in the blanks. No teaching or learning occurred.

I then decided to take the most boring elements of the subject I was supposed to be teaching—in this case, English (even though I was a math teacher)—and hold spelling bees and quiz contests of all sorts to review what the students had learned that week. It worked great. The students and I now looked forward to Friday afternoons, and their performance on class tests the following week improved.

Of course this idea and experience were not original or unique. Teachers commonly use a wide variety of open-ended games to facilitate review across all content areas. Jeopardy and spelling bees remain highly popular. Computers have made it possible to expand the range of games typically employed. They have made it easy to create crossword puzzles and to put on elaborate electronic quiz shows, often modeled after popular TV game shows.

The drama in such games results from the competition, whether individual or team or both. It is always a good idea to award some minor prize to the winning individual or team. A sliding scale of reward can also be applied so that all participants win something. Such rewards can be a healthy snack, or extra credit.

A teacher who is philosophically opposed to the notion of individual competition can add up all the scores and measure whether the combined score of a team's members improved from the prior week. This approach places the emphasis on improvement rather than on winning.

Although teachers can easily develop their own classroom games and procedures for reviewing and reinforcing students' learning, many resources for developing games in a variety of content areas are available, and often free. The Internet is a valuable source of such materials, and a Google search reveals many potential sites and games. A search of Amazon or Barnes & Noble is also useful. In addition, most professional teacher journals and websites have reviews of instructional games.

Research evidence supports the use of games. For example, Ramani and Siegler (2007) found that playing board number games improved low-income children's numerical knowledge.

Student-Created Games

Over the years, most of the classroom games that I have observed over the years have used questions made up by the teacher. The students or teams have had to come up with the answers within the game format. An alternative is to have individual students or teams of students create the questions for one another, or even for other students and classes. Having individuals or teams write the review questions and answers is a particularly valuable approach for underperforming students such as Title I and learning disabled (LD) students, or for any students who are lagging behind in reading comprehension. The act of converting information from a textbook into a different form is a powerful technique for developing reading comprehension skills. In other words, in typical classroom work, students normally use information from their text in a literal way, either to summarize it or to respond to a teacher's question about it. Writing questions or clues for a crossword puzzle, quiz show, or other game requires students to reformulate the information into a different format and is thus a valuable tool for developing reading comprehension skills.

One of the reasons for the major gains in reading comprehension in the HOTS program was that once a month the students would create crossword puzzles or quiz shows on the computer using content they had learned in their regular classes. They would then either play against one another with the computer keeping score or print out the puzzles for the classroom teacher to use for a review lesson.

Having the HOTS Title I and LD students create the content for these puzzles and quizzes was a major contribution to the substantial growth in these students' reading comprehension. In addition, when the teacher used the puzzles with the rest of the class, it was a boost to the HOTS students' self-esteem.

Having students prepare these questions and answers requires two additional steps by the teacher. First, he or she has to review the questions and answers to make sure they are accurate. Second, he or she has to teach the students how to write questions or clues. Uh oh! Although teaching students how to do this sounds simple, it turned out not to be. When I first started advocating this approach to teachers, the workshop would invariably be brought to a halt by someone asking, "But how do I train students to write questions?" Indeed, the standard rule of classroom engagement is that teachers develop the questions and students try to answer them. When you try to change this and ask the students to write the questions, all hell breaks loose. Generally, students born into poverty have no idea how to reformulate content, and teachers have not been trained to help them write questions.

Given these problems and the effectiveness of having students write questions as a means to develop reading comprehension skills, we developed some techniques that teachers can use to train their students to write questions and clues on any text materials they have been assigned in any content class. Exhibit 3.1 describes these techniques.

An advantage of having students give input to games and puzzles is that in addition to helping them review content, this approach can also be used to stimulate their learning of new content. For example, teachers can assign new content for the students to learn on their own, and then have them construct quizzes based on the new material.

Teachers do not need to use software to organize these types of review processes or to have students write questions and answers as described in Exhibit 3.1. Teachers do not even need to buy manual versions of games. They can create their own versions of a wide variety of games and quiz shows. Although computer games can be a bit more motivational and dramatic than manual games, review games organized by teachers work very effectively, especially when rewards are given for success.

Exhibit 3.1
Steps for Helping Students Convert Content into Questions

Assign some content for students to read from the regular curriculum or textbook. After they have read the text, go through the following four steps. Have students work either individually or in groups.

Step 1. Choose a noun from the text on which to base the clue you will write.

Step 2. Answer one of the following questions about the noun:

What does it look like?

What does it do?

What is it similar to?

What is it different from?

What is it made of?

What are its parts?

What does it make you think of?

Step 3. Use only one of the following techniques to turn your answer into a clue:

Write a complete sentence about the noun.

Write a question about the noun.

Leave a blank in the sentence for the noun.

Use a phrase such as "looks like," "sounds like," and so on, as a clue about the noun.

Step 4. Decide whether the clue you have written is a good one.

Is it too easy or hard?

Does the noun fit your clue?

Will other people be able to answer your clue correctly?

For creating some types of activities, such as crossword puzzles, using computer software does make sense, however. The software organizes the clues and answers and quickly produces an elaborate, professional-looking product that students can explore and edit in alternative ways. Appendix B lists a variety of software that can be used to create such games and activities, along with criteria for evaluating such software

A new classroom trend is to use the clicker technology that TV game shows use to poll audience response. Students use a clicker to transmit their responses to quiz questions to a computer program that instantly tallies and tracks the responses and shows the teacher how the class is doing.

Student Role-Playing

Extensive literature exists on the importance of student role-playing to reinforce and deepen learning. Most of this literature on role-playing focuses on reading comprehension and literacy, particularly with younger children. Examples include Hiatt (2006), who emphasizes drama play to bring books to life; Heller's (1996) discussions about using pantomime; Kelner and Flynn (2006), who emphasize the use of interviews with characters and even objects in stories, such as Cinderella's slipper; Jossart and Courtney (1998); and Goodwin (2006). Wilhelm (2008) employed role-playing as a means of developing the reading comprehension of his seventh grade students. He developed the following role-playing strategies, or what he called "dramatic happenings" (p. 132), for helping his students engage more deeply with a story they were reading:

• *Revolving Role Drama.* Pairs of students switch roles that they enact with a partner during a period, and switch partners.

• *Dramatic Play.* Students are given a prompt or situation from the story and asked to imagine and enact what would happen.

• *Guided Imagery.* Students are asked to imagine scenes.

• *Snapshot and Tableaux Drama.* Students physically or artistically freeze scenes in the story and then develop headlines for the expressions displayed and explain why they chose what they did.

• *Analogy Dramas.* Students write and perform vignettes from their own lives that parallel a scene from the story.

- *To Tell The Truth Game.* As in the old TV game show, judges ask questions of a group of students portraying characters from the story and decide who best became the character.
- *Correspondence.* "Students wrote and responded to diaries, postcards, letters, and advertisements, in the role of the story's character" (p. 134).
- *Missing Scene Scripts.* Students develop and role-play scenes that were left out of the story, alternative endings, or both.
- *Newscast.* Students develop a newscast that involves interviewing characters and editorializing about their actions in the story.

Wilhelm convincingly described how, with the use of these role-playing techniques, his nonreaders went from not seeing the point in reading and not going beyond the literal words to discovering how to construct meaning, how to enter the story world, and how to live the story. They came to discover how literature related to their lives. He cited a student, Libby, who observed that it is easier to read and write if you are a character.

Reader's Theater A good bit of work has also been done on children undertaking roles in stories and theater games to develop self-confidence and self-expression. McCaslin (1990) talks about dramatic play and play making, Rooyackers (1998) provides acting games for children, and Cresci (1989) offers creative dramatics for children.

Reader's theater is a movement that was established primarily to develop comprehension and fluency skills by having students do dramatic readings of literature (Black and Stave, 2007). Flynn (2007) has recently extended this movement to an approach she calls Curriculum-Based Readers Theater, which includes the reading of scripts based on classroom content created by teachers and students. Reader's theater is not a full theatrical production; there is no staged action. Rather, it consists of a reading with gestures. Both traditional reader's theater and Flynn's approach have been updated to take into account the need to meet state standards.

Role-Taking Dorothy Heathcote explored the use of student role-playing as a major instructional technique across the content areas. In her conception, students become role-*takers* to solve content-related dilemmas posed by the teacher. In role-taking (as opposed to role-playing), students take on the mantle of "expert" to solve problems using key content concepts. They become responders, decision makers, experts, or to use a cognitive term, sense makers. As individuals placed in the position of trying to make sense of what is going on around them, they become travelers in a strange landscape. Instead of playing a previously discussed role in a story, students are placed as themselves in the position of taking responsibility for figuring something out or for helping solve a problem. So, for example, if they were studying health problems, they could take on the role of public health experts and prepare a report for the city council on the prevalence and causes of asthma or HIV and make recommendations. (Several additional examples of role-taking are presented in Chapter Five.) Wilhelm (2002) describes a process of having students who saw the movie *Fast Food Nation* research and prepare diet and nutrition guides for better eating.

Simulated Experiences

In addition to having students role-play characters in stories and plays, teachers may also have them adopt a variety of other roles in role-playing exercises. These may include political roles, work roles, characters in war situations, tourists, and so on. Students can even become "things," such as atomic particles, numbers, and so forth. In such role-playing activities, students act as they believe or have learned that people and things in these positions actually behave. Such instructional activities are generally referred to as *simulations*.

Using Simulation Units   Teachers do not need to rely on available materials to stage an instructional simulation activity. They can develop their own, which is mostly a matter of using some easily available knowledge and being willing to be daring. For example, Chapter Three of Heathcote and Bolton (1995) contains a wonderful discussion of a teacher going through the process of developing a simulation unit on China and includes the decision making process the teacher went through. Coincidentally, that teacher, like the teachers in most of the examples in this book, was also a student teacher.

A variety of simulation units are also available to help teachers organize role-playing units in which the role-playing activity is extended across a series of lessons. A popular variety of simulation unit at the secondary level is the mock unit in social studies. Such units include mock trials, conventions, and elections. Detailed resources are available to help teachers establish such settings. Appendix C lists state and national sources of materials for conducting mock trials and elections.

Another source of help in finding role-play units and lessons are teacher lesson-plan exchange sites. For example, links to free sources of lessons can be found at http://www.lessonplans.org.

Computerized Simulations A wide variety of simulation software is available for use in most content areas. Students can use this software to play a role in applying the relevant content knowledge to try to succeed at a challenge under the control and guidance of the computer.

For example, in Oregon Trail, students are placed in the role of explorers trying to overcome obstacles while traveling between Missouri and Oregon in the frontier days. In a program called the Pond, students become scientists studying life in a pond. Other available software allows students to be architects designing floor plans in order to understand area and perimeter in math, or to be detectives tracking down imaginary villain Carmen Sandiego as a way to learn about countries around the world or about history.

Appendix C describes additional sources for such simulations. It also discusses problems associated with using computer-based simulation units to enrich content learning, such as the increasing complexity of such software, and why I have turned to developing most of the software used in the curriculum I develop as opposed to using commercially available software. In any case, in the absence of careful, ongoing guidance from the teacher, students tend to treat even the good software as a guessing game rather than as an information-based decision-making exercise.

Limitations of Conventional Role-Playing

Role-playing is a valuable tool for reinforcing and enriching content, but it also has limitations that restrict its use and applicability.

In the vast majority of cases presented in the extensive literature, role-playing of all types is used to reinforce and deepen what has already been taught. In other words, the content is first taught conventionally, then the students engage in the role-playing activity. So, for example, students would usually have first studied the characteristics of our government or judicial system before engaging in a mock election or trial. The more elaborate the student role-playing exercise is, the more content students will need to have been previously taught. In addition, the teacher is usually the organizer of the activity and manages and referees the process as the students role-play. I have seen only one example in the literature of a teacher role-playing. Tauber and Mester (2007) describe a two-hat technique in which a teacher plays two historical figures with very different philosophical perspectives. Each of the figures is distinguished by a different hat, that is, the teacher switches hats to indicate when each person is speaking. Students react to the debate between the two figures.

In general, organizing and managing student role-playing takes a lot of time and puts a great deal of pressure on the teacher. For example, in their conception of using story drama to develop reading comprehension skills, Kelner and Flynn (2006) ascribe the following responsibilities to teachers:

- Select an appropriate text.
- Familiarize students with the text.
- Determine drama and reading comprehension strategies.
- Prepare the students to take on roles by reviewing acting tools and skills.
- Direct the action.
- Facilitate and perhaps narrate the drama.
- Lead the reflection and assessment of the drama.

The problem with this process is that it is highly staged, requiring a tremendous amount of planning time and that all of the content and skills, including the acting skills, be taught conventionally first, and it almost doubles the instructional time (a commodity in rare supply these days) needed to accomplish the content objective.

In addition, Dorothy Heathcote was not convinced that many of the role-playing techniques used in literacy development are in fact drama. She is quoted by Taylor (2000, p. 102) as saying, "Drama is not stories retold in action. Drama is human beings confronted by situations which change them because of what they must face in dealing with those challenges." She accordingly placed her students in situations where they needed to use content to resolve dilemmas.

I would not go quite as far. The acting out of stories, whether in full performance or in dramatic readings, is part of the theatrical tradition. In addition, acting out stories can probably enhance literacy, although it has less use in other content areas. Finally, in Heathcote's conception, the teacher is still primarily a director staging the process. So the process is still not a natural one in which students are confronted with real (to them) dilemmas.

For all of these reasons, the bottom line is that although role-playing is a valuable tool for content enrichment and reading comprehension, it offers little support for the original teaching of new content.

DRAMATIC PRACTICES FOR INTRODUCING NEW CONTENT

A widely used dramatic technique that straddles the boundary between content reinforcement and teaching new content is what I call "creating a mood" or "setting the stage." In this technique, the teacher does something to give students a sense of the topic, moment, or place they will be learning about. For example, if the students are learning about another country, the teacher may come to class dressed in the traditional clothing of that country. Pictures of the country may be scattered around the classroom. Music from the country may be playing as students walk into the room. The tried-and-true practices of creating an elaborate bulletin board or decorating the classroom with relevant pictures and writings may be included in this technique.

Although such embellishments generally help create student interest, the lesson then proceeds in a typical fashion and student interest starts to lag unless you are also providing food from the country being studied as a reward for paying attention. In other words, this technique usually just dresses up a conventional lesson. The curiosity generated in students by the initial dramatic surprise is not built on in the remainder of the lesson or unit, where the actual teaching and learning occur. So, for example, even though the teacher comes to class wearing the garb of another country, the only difference in the way the lesson is taught is how the teacher is dressed.

So, although creating a mood or setting the stage is a dramatic technique associated with the teaching of new content, it is not used to *teach* that new content. Nevertheless, this familiar technique is important because it is a key component of Outrageous lessons. An Outrageous lesson, however, also incorporates additional dramatic techniques and maintains the unconventional dramatic perspective throughout the teaching and learning process.

Teaching New Content Outrageously

Unlike the purpose of all the previously discussed uses of dramatic technique, the goal of Outrageous Teaching is to teach *new* content and to teach it more effectively than would be possible with conventional instruction. So, even though they are based on many of the previously discussed dramatic techniques, Outrageous lessons are the primary instructional mechanism for teaching new content.

The Dramatic Building Blocks of Outrageous Teaching

This chapter has discussed a wide variety of dramatic techniques, including the following:

- Use of props and sounds to get students' attention
- Expressive microbursts
- Manipulation of facial expressions and body animation
- Manipulation of tonal expression
- Use of humor and strangeness
- Creation of persona
- Creation of make-believe contexts and scenarios via role-playing and simulations

Although many teachers do not think of themselves as having dramatic flair, the reality is that all good teachers use some or all of these techniques frequently. This means that there is in fact a dramatic base to their teaching. What is significant about the everyday use of these techniques is that, as the snippets of Dwight's lesson in Chapters One and Two show, they are the building blocks of Outrageous Teaching, but Outrageous Teaching brings all them together in a conscious way to create lessons and units that teach existing content objectives in uncommon and unusual ways.

Outrageous Teaching is also key to advanced instructional management. The cotton-in-the-ear approach, discussed earlier, for getting students to speak up illustrates how an unusual strategy can be used to achieve a problematic goal. Outrageous Teaching thus provides a very different and more effective approach to successfully accomplish problematic content objectives.

Outrageous Teaching creates an alternative, powerful learning environment by combining existing dramatic techniques, and by intensifying and, in some cases, modifying how they are typically used. For example, Outrageous lessons take an unconventional approach to role-playing. In the snippets of Dwight's lesson presented in Chapters One and Two, Dwight role-plays to create an atmosphere of surprise and suspense. The students are in the dark as to what his intentions are, why he is selling stumps, and what the content objective is, but they are curious. So what happens next?

To understand how Outrageous Teaching extends the goals and techniques of dramatic practices, it is time to experience Dwight's complete lesson. In particular, note the difference between the students' roles and the role of the teacher.

DWIGHT'S COMPLETE LESSON

The students file in, and once they are settled, the teacher announces that Dwight is home sick today but a special guest is coming to make them an exciting offer.

Dwight then enters disguised in a bushy white beard, wearing a tall Amish-style black hat, dressed in overalls, and carrying a tree stump. He emphatically puts the tree stump on the floor and announces in a booming voice:

> *I am a master salesman and have heard that all of you in this room have wonderful social skills and would make great salespeople. I am here as part of a national search to find the next generation of salespeople to sell a new, exciting line of products, the next great product, a complete line of stumps!*

By now the students have recognized Dwight and are starting to titter a bit, although they are also curious. Dwight continues:

> *I see that you are skeptical about the importance and sales potential of stumps. Well, let me tell you all the things you can do with stumps and I am sure that in five minutes you are all going to want to know where you can buy one.*

Dwight then talks for five minutes in a manner that imitates a TV car salesman, giving a confident, nonstop monologue about all the benefits of having a stump. He lists about a dozen reasons why the students would want to have a stump. Each reason is more Outrageous than the one before.

> *Suppose you come home and have a terrible itch in your back. What can you do? Why, you can rub your back against the stump. You come home and it's cold and your heater is not working. What can you do? You can burn part of your stump for warmth. For you guys, having a stump is a symbol of manliness, and women look up to a man with a stump. Suppose you come home and find that someone has stolen all of your furniture—you can sit on your stump.*

You can even serve food on your stump. And after you have eaten a wonderful meal, you look in the kitchen for a toothpick, and there are none, and you suddenly remember that you forgot to buy more. What to do? Break off a splinter from your stump and, voilà, you have a toothpick.

Of course Dwight is just getting started. He continues:

In addition to all the ways I have just described that a stump can enrich your life, there is more, much more. If you have a problem, you can confide in your stump, tell it your deepest fears and concerns—it will always listen and never argue with you.

If you do not have enough closet or shelf space at home, you can hang your socks or jewelry on your stump.

Dwight goes on and on and on for a few more minutes about many other uses for stumps, occasionally pounding the stump on the floor for emphasis.

The students laugh politely or give skeptical looks after each reason for needing a stump. Above all, they are enjoying the moment and wondering where things are going, and why their teacher is acting this way. After five to ten minutes of nonstop selling, Dwight finally pauses and says,

I know by now all of your realize that you cannot live without having a tree stump, and that all of you want one.

Of course, even though the students are having a great time, no one wants to buy one. Nonplussed, Dwight continues:

Unfortunately, I cannot sell you this stump, because it is my last one until I get my next shipment. However, I have an even better opportunity for you right now, because I am looking to hire one of you to be on my sales team. I want to see which of you can be a great salesperson like myself. This is a chance of a lifetime at a great career.

Dwight then picks up a shopping bag and pulls from it a series of common objects such as a comb, a large piece of cardboard, and so on. He gives one of the objects to the first person in each row. He then directs that the students in each row should get together as a team and in ten minutes come up with as many reasons as they can as to why someone should buy their object. They are then to elect a spokesperson to present the team's ideas and try to convince the rest of the class to buy the team's product.

The students quickly transition into groups. To my amazement, the loungers start taking leadership in the group discussions. Indeed, the loungers then become the groups' spokespeople.

After ten minutes of preparation, each team does a three- to five-minute presentation. The ideas and presentations are fantastic and imaginative. The former loungers deliver highly creative soliloquies that mimic the tone and nature of Dwight's presentation. In addition, I am amazed at the volume, variety, and creativity of the presentations. (I suspect that for some of these students it is the first time they have volunteered to do something all semester.) The cardboard becomes a megaphone and a sunhat and so on. The comb becomes a backscratcher and a nose picker, and so forth. The hair clip becomes a money clip, a clothes hanger, and on and on.

After all the presentations are completed, Dwight says:

> Before I announce the winner, I want everyone to quickly write down the ideas your team just presented for why someone should buy your product.

The students quickly shift modes and start writing. There is no whining or time wasting, because students are eager to capture their team's ideas on paper.

Dwight then has a few students, one from each team, read back what they have written. Each student reads in a very confident, salesperson-like tone. There is none of the typical reluctance to share.

Then, in the last five minutes of the class, Dwight announces that not only are all the groups worthy of being hired as salespeople, but he is going to give everyone a good salesperson award. He then tells them they have just done something else that is very important: they had just written excellent persuasive essays. He also notes that writing a persuasive essay is one of the major district requirements for promotion.

Dwight then gives them a definition of a persuasive essay and a few characteristics of such writing. He also notes that most students have trouble writing such essays, which is why he is so impressed with the writing they have done and how easy it was for them to do so.

Dwight then ends the lesson by saying in a very puzzled tone:

Hmmm, I don't understand why you found it so easy to write a persuasive essay when most students have so much trouble doing that. I also wonder if the reason is something you can use to continue to develop your essays. Let's try to figure that out in tomorrow's lesson.

WHAT CAN BE LEARNED FROM DWIGHT'S OUTRAGEOUS LESSON?

Dwight made a great choice in picking this Outrageous lesson. He knew it would address a critical topic on which it would be difficult to get students' attention once he announced the lesson's objective, and that it would be nearly impossible to engage students in the ideas. He was facing spending at least half the period dealing with students resisting the content and complaining about it. And he knew that once he got them working on writing a persuasive essay, they would find it to be a highly abstract idea. He might be able to get them to write down the definition of a persuasive essay, and to convince them why it was important, but little else would be accomplished.

In stark contrast, Dwight's Outrageous lesson was not only effective, it was also efficient. In other words, the class accomplished a lot in a short period, including the writing of short persuasive essays. Although the dramatic components did take up some of the time, that time was more than made up for in the time saved in not having to deal with distractions. Finally, the students not only learned the content objective, but they did so enthusiastically and with a high level of thoughtfulness. *Magic!*

Dwight did not repeat this lesson using conventional techniques. It was the sole introductory lesson on persuasive writing. In subsequent lessons in the unit, Dwight continued to use the context of creative selling as the basis for getting students to write more complex persuasive essays. As the sole methodology for teaching this or any other content lesson or unit, Outrageous Teaching does not slow down the curriculum. If anything, it speeds up the learning process and deepens understanding of the content from the beginning. This form of teaching is a not an add-on dramatic practice. Rather, it is a substitute for conventional teaching of the content objective.

It should also be emphasized that although Dwight approached the lesson with the trepidation expected when venturing into the unknown, once he realized it was working he relaxed and had fun. His willingness to stretch his teaching technique to include drama, humor, and imagination was rewarding not only for his students but also for Dwight himself. Instead of going through another tug-of-war period, he experienced a period of deep connection with the students, and they connected with the content.

Personal Reflection: What I Learned from Dwight's Students

Before discussing the structure of Dwight's terrific lesson, I would like to share something I learned from watching it. This lesson, more than any other Outrageous lesson I observed, demonstrated the latent talent, ability, and creativity that reside within some of our most academically passive students. The fact that so many of the loungers quickly rose to the top of the process made me understand why so many self-made people in our society achieved acclaim and riches despite having little formal education, having been dropouts, or having done poorly on conventional measures of educational progress.

Watching passive students come alive and reveal their true underlying abilities made me proud of what my student teacher had accomplished. At the same time I also felt frustrated that we do not make a greater effort to create the alternative, dramatic approaches to teaching that fuel the innate, untapped talent of so many students in our classrooms. What I learned from this lesson was the following:

When teachers apply their imagination to their teaching, it sparks the students to apply their immense sense of imagination to learning.

I subsequently observed other classrooms in the district in which teachers were trying to get students to write acceptable persuasive essays—sometimes for the fifth time—with little apparent success. I also attended some staff meetings at other schools and at district headquarters where everyone was bitching about how hard it was to get students to write reasonable persuasive essays and about how it was a yearlong process. In such sessions I did not suggest the tree stump approach because I feared it would unleash a wild spree of chopping down tress or, more likely, people questioning my sanity. At the same time, the ease and enthusiasm with which students began to write creative persuasive essays in my student teacher's class stood in stark contrast to the difficulty the majority of teachers seemed to be having. This disparity in student work demonstrates that many problems in teaching and learning are often the result of the failure of teachers and curriculum designers to be superimaginative and bold.

Comparing Dwight's Lesson to Conventional Instruction

Looking back at Dwight's lesson, we see that it was similar to a conventional lesson in that it focused on teaching a particular content objective from the school's curriculum. However, the climate of the classroom throughout the lesson was completely different than in a conventional lesson, with students engaged and emotionally invested in the ideas. Dwight was in complete control of what happened. Transitions from one part of the lesson to the next occurred quickly and enthusiastically.

Another similarity to conventional lessons is that the content learning objective was stated to the students. In conventional teaching, however, the content objective is usually stated at the start of the lesson and may even be written on the board so that it is visible as students walk into the room—an immediate dampener of student energy. In Dwight's lesson, the content objective was given only at the end of the period. The students had no inkling of what the content objective was or that there even *was* an objective until after they had mastered it. All they knew was that they were having fun and that the activities were natural to them and that they could do them well. This is the power of Creatively Authentic instruction. In addition, Dwight does not revert to the role of teacher and use conventional teaching techniques until the last five minutes of the period, when he explains the formal content objective and why he behaved so Outrageously.

Comparing Dwight's Lesson to Other Forms of Dramatic Practice

Analyzing Dwight's lesson, we see that he incorporated many of the dramatic techniques discussed earlier in the book, especially those used in discipline and instructional management: change in persona, props, expressive microbursts, and voice and body animation. He also used extensive role-playing. In one sense there was nothing new here, which again means that most teachers have used some of these techniques.

What was different here is that all of these techniques were used together, and they were used in a "bigger" fashion than in traditional instruction. In other words, the change in persona was exaggerated. Indeed, in this case the teacher was not even a teacher. And instead of the prop being a whistle or a flag or a piece of chalk, it was a tree stump. Finally, all of the dramatic elements were tied together by the element of surprise—a surprise entrance and a disguise.

Another difference in Dwight's lesson was the nature of the role-playing. Dwight was not supervising the role-playing. He was role-playing himself and using it to create a context for the students' role-playing. As a result of the scenario, the students' role-playing evolved naturally. (Indeed, what the students were doing was more playing and role-taking than role-playing.) The only element that Dwight's lesson had in common with the role-playing teacher tasks listed by Kelner and Flynn (2000) was "Lead the reflection." In other words, Dwight's approach to role-playing was far more efficient, engaging, and Creatively Authentic than conventional student role-playing. No time was used up by organizing the students to role-play and explaining how to do it. Instead, the students were drawn in role-playing by having suddenly to react to the strange things their teacher was doing. In addition, the purpose of Dwight's role-playing was not just to set the stage or to create a mood for the lesson; it was the lesson.

Probably the biggest difference between traditional and Dwight's use of dramatic technique was that Dwight's lesson replaced conventional instruction for teaching the two content objectives: having students understand what a persuasive essay is, and having students write a persuasive essay. *This Outrageous lesson was the means used, and the only means used, to teach these content objectives.* Subsequent lessons in the unit would convince students that selling ideas is like selling a product; and even though the subsequent lessons in the unit on persuasive essays would be taught largely conventionally, the context created by this Outrageous lesson would serve as a link from the first lesson to all of the subsequent instruction.

Did Dwight's Pragmatic Lesson Compromise Progressive and Dramatic Ideals?

As noted in the previous chapter, many theater advocates have argued that the use of dramatic technique for the pragmatic, prosaic goal of teaching content creates "dramatic illiteracy" (Taylor, 2000, p. 206), stifles creativity of expression, is limited to lower-order skills, is a diminution of art, and so on. In Chapter Two I argued that these claims were red herrings. Now you can begin to judge the validity of these claims on your own, in the context of examining Dwight's lesson, and form an opinion as to whether creativity, thoughtfulness, and self-expression flourish in Dwight's Outrageous Teaching.

I suspect that most readers would agree that Dwight's lesson was highly creative and involved a high degree of self-expression and thinking on the part of both teacher and students. The fact that students also learned something critical to a much greater extent than they would have under conventional instruction is a plus. So we have a win-win situation. Of course this lesson may be an exception, so the discussion of whether both creative teaching and highly efficient learning improvement are possible simultaneously will be rejoined after additional examples of Outrageous Teaching are presented in Chapter Five.

How Does Dwight's Lesson Link to Theories of Learning?

Chapter Two listed some of the theoretical bases for using dramatic technique. Dwight's lesson illustrated the application of most of these theories. It used story to enable students to construct a mental image of what persuasive writing is. The learning occurred within a compelling social process and play that triggered thoughtful discussion. The lesson tied the learning objective to students' imagination of how they might succeed in life. In other words, it was Creatively Authentic, which means that the students will continue to view persuasive writing as important and "cool."

All of the techniques used not only captivated the students but also aided their learning and increased the probability that what they were learning was embedded in their memory. I suspect you could ask them two years later what a persuasive essay is and they would remember it. If you were to ask them, "What do you remember about Dwight as a teacher?" they would probably tell you, "He was the dude that came in with a tree stump." And if you were to ask, "Do you remember what he was teaching that day?" they would probably say, "Yeah, something about a persuasive essay." And if asked, "How was he as a teacher?" they would likely say, "He was great! He really cared about helping us learn."

The Aftermath: Was Dwight Reprimanded for This Lesson?

No! Quite the contrary. The supervising classroom teacher, a master teacher herself, was blown away by the lesson. She shared it with her colleagues. The lesson was the talk of the teacher's lounge for weeks, and the supervising teacher had the stump put into the teachers lounge for several weeks as a symbol to her colleagues of what is possible in education when creative approaches are used.

Indeed, there is no reason that Dwight should have been reprimanded. He taught the assigned lesson, and the students achieved the content objective at a high level.

Was There a Method to Dwight's Lesson?

At one level, Dwight's lesson for jaded high school students looked spontaneously creative—like a lesson born of individual insight and daring, produced by a uniquely and highly talented individual, that another teacher could never duplicate. It certainly was a highly creative lesson. However, Dwight was not a superstar. He was a typically good, conscientious student teacher. In addition, his creativity was not spontaneous but resulted from the considered application of a formal lesson-planning methodology that anyone can use to equal effect. The methodology for designing Outrageous lessons, which I refer to as the Dramatized Content Planning Method, is described in Chapter Four.

SUMMARY

This chapter has reviewed the variety of ways that teachers incorporate dramatic technique in their classrooms. All of these uses are valuable, whether for maintaining discipline, improving instructional management, or teaching content. In addition, many of the techniques, with a few notable differences, form the basis of Outrageous Teaching. The fact that all good teachers already use some of these techniques suggests that all teachers can indeed successfully develop and teach Outrageous lessons.

Outrageous Teaching integrates all of the dramatic techniques discussed in this chapter and takes some of them a step further in order to create lessons and units that can serve as primary instruction for teaching specific content objectives. Outrageous Teaching is not designed to replace the other uses of dramatic techniques. Rather, it is meant to open up new, untapped opportunities for using dramatic techniques as central tools in the effort to improve student learning, reduce the learning gap, and improve the performance of failing schools or classes. It can also open up new horizons for practice, for expanding teachers' toolbox of techniques, and for enriching their professional lives.

Dwight's lesson exemplifies how any topic, no matter how boring it may seem to students, can be turned into an engaging lesson that produces high levels of learning. In addition, although Dwight's lesson may seem like a phenomenon unique to him, that other teachers could never replicate, it was in fact produced by following a specific planning methodology with wide applicability across the grades and across content areas. In other words, whatever student emotions teachers have tapped into so far, they can go even further in accelerating content learning and heightening student interest—even if they never use a tree stump.

Outrageous Teaching is a professional pleasure that need not be a guilty one or deferred to the next life. A whole frontier of the profession and practice of teaching has largely gone unexplored, so let's begin the exploration!

How to Design Outrageous Lessons: Essential Steps

This chapter describes how to apply the planning method that Dwight used to developed his Outrageous lesson: the Dramatized Content Planning Method. All of the steps in using this method to systematically develop your own lesson plan for an Outrageous lesson are presented.

The strength of the Dramatized Content Planning Method is that although it is practical, it does not stifle creativity. Quite the opposite! It enables all teachers who are willing to apply a few basic principles to develop highly creative and original Outrageous lessons. Indeed, all of the diverse examples of Outrageous lessons in Chapter Five were generated by teachers using this planning method.

DESIGNING OUTRAGEOUS LESSONS: THE DRAMATIZED CONTENT PLANNING METHOD

The Dramatized Content Planning Method can be used to design Outrageous lessons for teaching virtually any objective in any content area (except maybe long division), regardless of how prosaic it is. Additional examples of Outrageous lessons in the next chapter will show how this planning method has been used across grade levels and content areas.

Although the Dramatized Content Planning Method is practical, it does require more thought and preparation than the typical lesson-planning process. This is why you should be strategic in choosing the lessons to which you initially apply these techniques. It is suggested that you initially focus on those lessons that you dread teaching because you know that either students will be totally bored or there is no way to present the content in a way that will make sense to students.

For example, as a math teacher I used to dread having to teach word problems and the multiplication of signed numbers. How do you get students to understand how to put English and math together, or why a minus times a minus is a plus? Every teacher has some such topic or lesson that she or he does not look forward to teaching during the course of the year. So rather than plow through it with the typical prompts such as, "I am teaching this because it is on the test" or "You will understand why this is important when you become an adult," view this lesson as an opportunity to try a totally different approach, one that is Creatively Authentic, that is, one that taps into how students view the world and their role in it. In such cases you have nothing to lose, because even if it does not work, you and the class are no worse off. Of course, when it does work, everyone will be much better off.

As you gain confidence in your Outrageous lessons, you may then decide to extend your use of the Dramatized Content Planning Method and develop Outrageous lessons for content objectives that are particularly meaningful to you and that you want to make a deep and lasting impression on your students.

Following is a blow-by-blow—sorry, I mean a step-by-step—description of how to apply the Dramatized Content Planning Method to develop a plan for an Outrageous lesson, hereafter referred to as a Dramatized Content Lesson Plan.

COMPONENTS OF A DRAMATIZED CONTENT LESSON PLAN

There are many ways to characterize the key elements of drama. The following components emerged as critical to enabling my student teachers to create Outrageous lessons for teaching content. Each lesson should contain the following components:

- Surprise
- Characters
- Disguises, both costume and voice
- A setting that incorporates as many media and senses as appropriate
- A storyline or scenario with a dilemma, fantasy, and humor
- Props
- Eliciting of an emotional reaction (such as empathy)

- Transition to the students' learning activity
- Content materials
- Debriefing of students on the content objective of the lesson

This chapter describes each of these components in a general way, as well as how to incorporate them into a lesson plan; Chapters Five and Seven provide lots of concrete examples of assembled lessons. Finally, a lesson plan template for assembling the components is presented.

The most important thing to keep in mind as you put together the creative and weird components of a Dramatized Content lesson plan is that the most important element remains the delineation of the content objectives to be taught and learned. The objectives to be taught remain conventional and unchanged. What is different is the method of teaching the objectives.

Planning the Surprise

The most important dramatic component of an Outrageous lesson is *surprise*. Something needs to happen that shocks students out of their comfort zones, makes them sit up and take notice, and makes them wonder what is going on, why things are different, and what is going to happen next. Sometimes the surprise will occur the moment they walk into the classroom; other times it will occur shortly after the period starts.

Think of the Outrageous lesson as an experience in the theater, when the curtain rises for the first time and you see something you have never seen before. When the students walk into the classroom, they are entering your theater and they need to experience something they have never experienced before—something totally unexpected. You may be in disguise as someone else, you may be hiding, you may be acting strangely—for example, singing—or you may not even be there. Sometimes the surprise is that there is no surprise right at the beginning, but then early in the lesson something totally unexpected happens; For example, you may start foaming at the mouth (using fake foam) and pretend you do not notice anything different.

Sometimes you may recruit an accomplice from the school to help you spring the surprise. You can have a fellow teacher or an administrator start your class by announcing that no one has seen you today and they do not have a substitute, so the students will be expected to sit quietly the whole period. Once that person leaves, after about thirty seconds you pop out of the closet, or wherever you are hiding, and explain you do not want anyone to know you are here today, because (fill in the blank).

_____

_____

_____

Alternatively, the other accomplice can start the class and announce that although you, the teacher, are not there today, at any moment a special visitor should be arriving—a visitor invited by your teacher to be in class today to (fill in the blank).

_____

_____

_____

Then you walk in, in disguise, and the accomplice leaves—hopefully while maintaining a straight face.

Dwight's lesson clearly started off with a big bang in the surprise department.

Developing a Character or Persona

In this lesson you are generally not going to be yourself. Who are you going to be? How is this character going to behave? If you remain in the role of teacher, then your behavior has to change in a dramatic, surprising way so that in effect you are a different you. In one of the examples in the next chapter, the teacher remains herself but manifests a dual personality in which her persona changes abruptly several times during the lesson. In most Outrageous lessons I have seen, however, the teacher has chosen to assume some other role.

For many teachers, the hardest part of Outrageous Teaching is to assume the role of another character. For a lesson to work, you may have to become a general or a street person or an escapee from a mental institution or a visitor from the past, and so on. In all cases, you have to develop a new persona for the lesson.

Another effective technique is to anthropomorphize yourself into a thing. You may become an electron or a plant or an animal, and so on. You could be the world's first talking dog or the world's second talking horse. (The creators of the old TV show *Mister Ed* beat you to the talking horse character.)

Imagine yourself as a plant for a lesson designed to teach students about photosynthesis. You can create a scenario in which you are trying to get them to understand how you feel because no one else cares—and everyone knows that plants have feelings. Worst of all, no one understands what it is like when you go through your cycle of Photosynthesis Making Syndrome, more widely known as PMS. It is terrible that no one makes appropriate allowances for your mood swings, but because your students are an exceptionally sensitive group, you are going to let them in on how to better understand the demands that photosynthesis places on a plant's emotional well-being. (Think of what a grand surprise entrance you could plan for this scenario. For example, someone could announce that you will be late because you had to go to the nurse's office to get a checkup because you were not feeling well, and then you walk into the classroom with large patches of green on your face, branches sprouting out of your back, and so on and so forth.)

Disguise: Costume, Voice, Mannerisms

To reinforce the element of surprise and to become the other character or persona, you will usually, but not always, need a disguise. The disguise will usually consist of some sort of costume or voice change or both. The costume does not have to be elaborate. Some simple elements can be used to hide your face, such as a wide-brimmed hat or lots of cotton in strategic places on one's face. Other simple ways to change your facial features include wearing an eye patch, or stuffing a big wad of chewing gum in the corner of your mouth, and so on.

To pull off the disguise, you will usually want to change the tone, pacing, or emotion of your voice, or some combination thereof. For example, you may turn into a hyperactive person who speaks quickly, or someone who speaks in a hushed tone because you are fearful. Your voice is a powerful tool for expressing and reinforcing the emotion of the theatrical setting that your classroom will become. Placing a bit of cotton in one nostril is sometimes an effective way to change your voice, or perhaps you will become someone who can no longer speak.

You may also want to add one or two mannerisms to your character's style. For example, he or she may periodically spit, cry, or trip (Comedian Chevy Chase made a career out of the latter), or you may want to give your character a silly laugh.

You can even give mannerisms to things. If you are a plant in a room with a window, you may want to occasionally step up to the window and plaster yourself against it to get as much sun energy as possible so that you can continue to explain yourself to the class.

At the same time, do not overdo your character. A little bit of disguise and mannerism change goes a long way. Subtlety can be very effective. The best disguise

I ever saw was a teacher who walked into the room with a slightly modified nose (that is, it was not a snout). She started to teach normally. At first the students acted normally too, but slowly they began to realize that something was different, yet they were not quite sure what. Frowns began to appear on the students' faces. They stopped paying attention to what she was saying because they were all trying to figure out why she looked different. About four minutes into the lesson a group of students started shouting, laughing, pointing, and saying things like, "Teacher, what happened to your nose?" Then everyone laughed. The teacher at first pretended to be embarrassed, but then asked why a different nose made them laugh. The students responded that it was funny because it was unexpected. Of course at that point she had them in her hip pocket. This lesson was the introduction to a unit on humor writing, which she described to them as writing in which unexpected things happen.

This lesson shows how a little change can go a long way in stimulating student curiosity and attention.

A Setting That Incorporates as Many Media and Senses as Appropriate

Your classroom needs to be a setting that is consistent with and reinforces the element of surprise and the character you have created. In some cases, the classroom will remain the classroom, but one in which you will to create a different-than-normal mood. In other cases, the classroom will no longer be the classroom. It may become an outpost near a battlefield, or even the battlefield itself. It may be a different place in a different time.

Simple use of a variety of media is very effective in creating in students a feeling that they are in a new setting. The adjustment can be as simple as playing appropriate music to establish a mood as students walk through the door. Other sounds may also be appropriate. For example, if the room is to become a battle observation post, you will want to hear the booming of guns. Web sites such as http://www.soundeffects.com offer sound effects that you can purchase if you are unable to improvise them on your own.

Manipulating lighting is another effective technique. The room can be dark as students walk in, with a single lamp turned on to illuminate you. Smells are also an effective way to convey mood and setting.

There is also the old standby of posting appropriate pictures and posters around the room.

A Storyline or Scenario with a Dilemma, Fantasy, and Humor

There is an expression, "With a good story, anything is possible." You can be in a bar in a strange country at 1:00 A.M. or in a classroom at 11:00 A.M. and in both cases, if you have a good story, those within earshot will gravitate to you. The key to the success of an Outrageous lesson is to tell a good story. The lesson is then geared to developing Creatively Authentic moments, that is, interactions that are consistent with the imaginary story you have created.

Once you have decided on the content objective or objectives to be taught in your first Outrageous lesson, the next step is to develop the storyline or scenario. The storyline or scenario describes what is going to happen during the lesson and why. It is the foundational inspiration for all the other elements, and the conceptual glue that holds everything together. It is the method behind the madness that converts the overall experience into a learning event.

Usually you will start the lesson-planning process with a general idea for the storyline or scenario. For example, you may decide to be an explorer searching for a new land. Then you can add elements of humor and fantasy. Perhaps you are a blind explorer who needs help reading a map. Perhaps you have a peg leg and can no longer get around, so you are going to train a new generation of explorers. Perhaps you are a famous explorer with amnesia and cannot remember the lands you discovered and how you discovered them. Perhaps you are an explorer who never got credit for the lands you discovered and you complain about how Columbus and others hogged the credit.

The storyline or scenario describes how the premises you have created link to the content objective. The first scenario is appropriate if you are trying to teach map-reading skills. The second scenario is appropriate if you are trying to teach orienteering skills. The third scenario is appropriate if you are trying to get students to read about the history of the explorer. The fourth scenario is appropriate if you want students to read and learn about several explorers from a given period.

Of course, what is an explorer from four hundred years ago doing in the classroom? This question prompts you to continue to add fantasy and humor elements. You can pretend to be the oldest person on earth, with an appropriate disguise, costume, and mannerisms, such as shaking hands, a cotton floor-length beard, and so on. You can pretend to be very frail and hard of hearing and constantly nod off every time students start to say something. You can speak using Old English expressions and pretend not to understand some of the modern English words your students are using.

You can wear a colonial waistcoat or some other form of easily recognizable old clothes. (One such item is sufficient.)

You can be the ghost of the explorer, who has returned to the living to claim the credit for the explorer's discoveries that others have wrongfully claimed. In such a case, you would probably want your face to look blue, which you might accomplish with body paint, blueberry juice, and so on.

You can tell a tall tale of how you were exploring in Alaska and the last thing you remember is falling into a crevice, and the next thing you remember is starting to swim for your life this morning. Why? You mutter something about how the ice put you into suspended animation and preserved you. Then something they call global warming melted the ice and somehow you floated into this classroom. Of course, if you use this approach you may want to consider walking into class looking like a wet mop and wearing galoshes that squish whenever you take a step. You could also add the mannerism of occasionally shivering, and say that you are still suffering from the effects of having been frozen for four hundred years. You can then add some humor by insisting that under no circumstances should anyone talk back to you by saying "chill out," or you can say you need to be microwaved to warm up and ask whether anyone knows where you can find a large microwave machine.

Of course you may decide you would rather be a pirate than an explorer, and add the element of hidden treasure, which can be a bag containing some healthy snacks.

In any event, once you set the basic premise of the storyline or scenario, it is easy to add lots of additional humor and fantasy elements to create an even taller tale and an even more bizarre scenario. The funnier and more bizarre the storyline or scenario is, the better!

If you have decided to be a plant, you will need, it has already been suggested, to periodically interrupt what you are saying to go to the window and flatten yourself against it to get some more rays of sun to build up your energy. What are some other elements you could add?

_____

_____

_____

How about periodically drinking some water, shedding flower petals, complaining about fertilizer with prunes in it, and complaining about being pruned because of how much it hurts, and so on.

Finally, the heart of any drama is a dilemma that needs to be resolved. The storyline or scenario needs a dilemma to spur further action. Heathcote (1984, p. 91) refers to being "trapped, a state from which one can escape only by working through the situation," as a tool of drama. Resolving the dilemma, or getting out of the state of being trapped, is the key to converting the students' emotional response into learning.

In most cases, the dilemma will be a problem your character is facing in the storyline that you need the students' help to resolve. For example, in the sample scenarios just discussed, the dilemma might be that the explorer with amnesia has been selected for a lifetime achievement award at the Kennedy Center and has to make a speech summarizing his or her accomplishments. She or he then asks the students to help write the speech. This request in turn creates the need for the students to read about the explorer, then write and perhaps perform a speech.

Indeed, the dilemma is the key dramatic mechanism that converts the fun and fantasy into student learning. In the example just used, the reasonable request of asking students to write the speech, given the explorer's amnesia, produces the learning activities needed to achieve the content objective.

Therefore, as you develop the storyline or scenario, think of a possible dilemma that can be incorporated. The dilemma should help shape the overall scenario, provide the basis for adding humor and fantasy elements, and most important, lead to the creation of a problem the resolution of which produces the desired learning activities.

In other words, instead of students role-playing what has already been learned, they are role-playing to learn it in the first place. This process has the dual advantage of not requiring extra learning time to accommodate the role-playing, and that the desired content is learned more effectively to begin with.

Warning! If your storyline or scenario does not make you giggle when you think about it, give it some more thought. Solicit ideas from others.

Props

To support the storyline and your character, you will probably need to incorporate some props. For the preceding explorer scenarios you will probably need some maps, perhaps a bag of treasure to be discovered, and so on. You may also want to find a picture of an ancient explorer that you can pretend is a picture of yourself as a young person.

If you are a plant, you may want to make a plant hat and put a piece of fruit under it, which you can reveal when you describe the results of the photosynthesis process. Also, a green face and green hands and clothes would also be appropriate, and as already suggested, a branch or two growing out of your back.

Eliciting of an Emotional Reaction

A Creatively Authentic storyline or scenario will probably depend on your getting students' cooperation by tapping into some fundamental emotions, such as their sense of fairness, their desire to help and empathize with the downtrodden (which will probably be you), their desire to show off and act goofy, and so on. Due to their unprecedented access to entertainment, young people today generally feel very comfortable participating in a fantasy setting as a way to learn. Your storyline or scenario will be designed to provide a Creatively Authentic reason for students to engage in the planned learning activity. Students' emotional response then becomes the spur for their willingly engaging in the planned learning activity. This is a far better approach than the conventional way of simply telling the students to get to work. You request their help rather than demand that they do something.

Transition to the Students' Learning Activity

The hardest part of the storyline or scenario to get right is the transition from the opening surprise elements to getting the students engaged in the formal learning activity that will support the content learning objective. It is relatively easy to develop an engaging scenario for starting the lesson, but then it is time for the formal learning to occur. How do you manage that transition?

The tendency is to revert to the role of teacher and direct the learning process from that point on as you would normally do—telling them what to do, asking them questions about the reading, urging them to pay attention to what you are telling them, and so on.

This is the critical moment in an Outrageous lesson. If you revert back to being simply the teacher, then all you have done is provided an entertaining opening to the period. This is a "creating a mood or setting the stage" teaching strategy. *It is not an Outrageous lesson!*

To be an Outrageous lesson, the storyline or scenario and the role-playing need to provide a rationale for the students to engage in the intended formal learning activity *while you remain within the character you have created*. In other words, there needs to be a fantasy-based reason for you to ask students to engage in the formal learning activity. This reason usually derives from the dilemma your character is facing.

You can usually develop a storyline or scenario in which the students need some specific knowledge in order to resolve the dilemma your character is facing, or they need to practice a specific skill to enable your character to provide them with a wonderful, once-in-a-lifetime opportunity.

So, for example, in the case of the explorer with amnesia who is receiving the lifetime achievement award, you may ask the students to review your achievements and help you write the acceptance speech. You could even ask them to get into teams, look up the information, and write the speech for you. They could then read their ideas back to you and select the winning story.

If you are a plant, you may indicate that you are lonesome by yourself and want to have babies but you do not know how to do that. Can the class help you figure that out? If students ask why you cannot read the book yourself, you can respond in an exasperated manner, "Everyone knows that plants can't read!"

Content Materials

These are the formal content materials you will use for this lesson. They may include a chapter from a textbook, content handouts, other materials for students to read or write on, and so on. *These are the same materials you would use if you were to teach the lesson conventionally.* Now, however, students will engage in the learning because it is their role in the storyline or scenario.

Content Debriefing

During the last few minutes of the lesson period, you will step back into the role of the teacher for the purpose of formalizing the lesson and the learning objectives. Without such a debriefing, there is a danger that the students will not realize what they have learned and achieved. The debriefing contains several important elements.

Summary of Content Learned   *Summarize what the students have learned in terms of the formal content objective of the lesson.* You may also choose to in some way extend the knowledge gained, for example, by adding some additional information, explaining why the knowledge is important, and so on.

This debriefing is critical to making sure that the students understand the content objective of the lesson.

Confession   *Explain why you acted as you did, and reassure the students that you were just acting and have not taken leave of your senses.* You can also ask them whether they enjoyed this way of learning. This quick conversation ensures that when students talk about their day at home that evening, instead of saying that one of their teachers flipped out, they will talk about the very creative lesson they experienced, about how much they learned, and about how they enjoyed learning in that way. Maybe their parents will then demand more of this type of teaching.

In addition, without this confessional element in the debriefing, it can be argued that Outrageous lessons constitute lying to the students and misleading them. (I prefer to think of it as pretending rather than lying.) Although one can take comfort in the expression that "all is fair in love and war, and in getting reluctant learners to learn," the reality is that over the course of such lessons the teacher is not being honest with the students and is deliberately misleading them. Today's students have grown up surrounded by entertainment media of all types and, as a result, feel very comfortable learning through drama and fantasy. It is critical that in the debriefing you explain that you were performing a role in order to help them learn something important, but what they learned was real. Students will then view the process as your having fooled them—or as your having *tried* to fool them, because they will never admit that they were fooled—rather than as your having lied to them.

If you still have ethical problems with this type of lesson, I suggest you recommend that your children, grandchildren, and students not watch Sesame Street, not read fiction, not go to the theater, and so forth. It's all lies!

At the same time, there is always the concern that manipulating students' emotions through the storyline will cause them to worry about the teacher. For example, if the teacher walks in looking blue—or when it was announced that Dwight was at home sick—some students might worry that something is actually wrong with their teacher. This concern can be mitigated by incorporating humor so that the students quickly figure out that this is make-believe, or by having another adult in the room acting as though nothing is wrong. It is also ethically critical that as soon as possible the teacher reassure the students that he or she was pretending and is completely OK, and then apologize if he or she caused any worry.

Praise *Take a moment to compliment the students on how they expressed themselves, and on the quality of their participation and learning.* Indeed, in many cases this will be the first time some of the students participated in class with enthusiasm and insight. It is worth recognizing and reinforcing their behavior.

Sshhhh—Please Do Not Tell! Finally, if you plan to use the same lesson later in the day, ask the students to keep quiet about what you did in the lesson. Ask them not to reveal the way you taught the lesson and not to give away the surprises you have planned. Of course, chances are they will spill the beans, but they will likely do so in a way that makes you look like a superteacher, and the next group of students will arrive with a sense of anticipation. *There is simply no way to keep a great, magical lesson a secret!* Indeed, if you do not do the lesson the same way, the other classes may complain that you are being unfair to them.

DWIGHT'S PROBLEM IN PLANNING HIS LESSON

Dwight struggled with the problem of how to stay in his role throughout the lesson in a way that made sense. His initial storyline was inadequate for maintaining his role into the students' learning activities. His preliminary idea for his lesson on teaching persuasive writing was to start the lesson as a TV pitchman trying to sell students a used car. Then he would explain persuasive writing and ask the students to think of an experience they had had trying to convince someone to do something, and then write about that experience.

I reacted to his plans by telling him that his idea of pitching something was a great entrée into teaching persuasive writing. However, I also told him that his initial approach was half a loaf. He was only starting the lesson creatively and then, after the initial spectacle, was reverting back into a teacher giving directions. Chances are that the students would have been amused by the spectacle and might have done a little better at the initial persuasive writing task than otherwise, but it is unlikely that it would have sparked enthusiastic writing.

We went through the Dramatized Content Lesson Planning template (Exhibit 4.1) and I challenged him to create a scenario in which he could stay in the role of visiting salesperson throughout the lesson and provide a Creatively Authentic reason for the students to engage in a persuasive interaction experience. To do so he would have to think of a scenario or reason why the pitchman would want to ask the students to engage in persuasive action that could translate into writing. He then came up with the idea of recruiting students to be salespeople.

Bingo! He had a way to transition naturally from his role-playing to the students' role-playing/taking, and thus keep the process of learning from the storyline going up to the end of the period, when he debriefed them on what they had done relative to the content objective of the lesson.

Indeed, Dwight got so caught up in the notion of creating a sense of surprise that he refused to tell me what changes he had made to the lesson. He wanted me to be as surprised as the students, and he was confident that he had come up with an idea that would let him remain in character throughout the lesson. So when I watched the lesson I was as amazed as the students were when he walked in with a large tree stump.

So, Dwight's experience illustrates that it is pretty easy to come up with a great initial idea for the fantasy basis of the lesson and for one's initial role. The trick is to develop a storyline or scenario that sustains the lesson beyond the initial spectacle into the students' learning as role-players/takers. At the same time, it took just one initial insight—to have the students compete to become product spokespeople, something they see all the time—to sustain the drama throughout the lesson. In other words, once you have come up with your own initial ideas, it usually takes just one more hook in the storyline to complete the lesson plan.

In addition, as Dwight enhanced the storyline, he built up the humor. Being a car salesman became being a stump salesman. That scenario was funnier and more surprising, and enabled him to transition into having students sell common objects that existed in the room.

(By the way, I forgot to ask Dwight where he got the tree stump, so if you want to replicate this lesson you will have to figure that out on your own. I suppose you can ask Google. In any case, I am confident that if you want to replicate this lesson, you will be able to figure out where to get one.)

APPLYING THE DRAMATIZED CONTENT PLANNING METHOD: KEY STEPS

The first step in the Dramatized Content Planning Method is to select the content around which you want to create an Outrageous lesson. Again, this is content you would normally teach. Your purpose is to develop a novel approach to teaching the content, not to teach novel content. Then select the content materials to be used in the lesson.

Once you have established the content-specific details, the fun starts. Have a few drinks, or whatever else you do to relax or to stimulate your mind. Developing an Outrageous lesson is really a state of mind, a willingness and mindset to think differently.

Try to think of a weird storyline or scenario for getting the students involved in learning the content. Chances are that the first storyline you come up with will be on the right track but not sufficiently elaborate to support the entire period, as was the case with Dwight's original plan. It will probably be enough to get the period started, but will not have enough depth or weirdness to provide a reason for you to stay in character while the students transition into the formal learning activity you have planned. Keep building on your ideas and elements, and develop a creative dilemma.

Once you have a beginning storyline or scenario, develop your character. Who are you? How is your character going to look? How is your character going to behave?

Talk to friends about your initial ideas. Brainstorm with them. Your weird friends and relatives are likely to be the best source of additional ideas. Everyone has at least one weird relative they try to avoid. In this case, seek that person out and pick his or her brain for ideas.

You can also go to the theater during this creative process to see a play. Focus on how the playwright and actors create character and setting in support of a storyline that delivers an intended lesson, albeit indirectly. If you have a chance to see a good comedy in the theater, all the better!

Keep on thinking about how to make your storyline or scenario, character, and dilemma bigger, broader, and funnier, but also more sympathetic. For almost all of the teachers I have worked with, their initial idea for a storyline was fine and did not have to be changed. It merely needed embellishment.

At some point you will figure out how to shape and extend the storyline or scenario so that you can sustain it through the transition to the formal learning part of the lesson. As already noted, Dwight had to extend his storyline from one in which he was merely a salesperson to one in which he was a salesperson recruiting additional salespeople. Keep on building the elements of the storyline or scenario, the character, the setting, the surprise, and the dilemma. Dwight realized that trying to persuade the students to buy a stump was funnier and more surprising than trying to convince them to buy a car. Even when you think you

Exhibit 4.1
Dramatized Content Lesson Plan Template

Content Objective:

Props and media	Content materials
Who are you? Visitors/conspirators?	**Disguise elements**

Opening surprise and setting

Storyline or scenario and method (such as role-playing, anthropomorphizing, and so on)

Transition to student learning activity phase (the what and why of the assigned work, such as students' expert advice is needed or they are trying out for something)

Ending discussion (debriefing and completing content objective)

have the lesson nailed, continue to try to think of elements to add, and of more elaborate versions of your existing ideas.

Now you are ready to put your lesson on paper and perform it. Exhibit 4.1 is a lesson plan template for summarizing your ideas.

ASSESSMENT

The good news is that no special assessment is needed to evaluate Outrageous Teaching and lessons. Whatever assessment the teacher, school, or state is using is applicable. Because the goal of Outrageous Teaching is that it be used as a substitute for conventional instruction to teach targeted content objectives, the only question that needs to be asked is whether students learned the content better, regardless of how that outcome is conventionally measured. In addition, even if only one lesson in a unit is taught Outrageously, and even if it is the first lesson, it is reasonable to ask if students did better on the overall unit. (Chances are that teachers continue to use the imagery, context, and experience of the Outrageous lesson as a referent and to ground the subsequent lessons.) Indeed, the next chapter provides several examples in which teachers taught an Outrageous lesson to one group of students and taught the same lesson conventionally to another group, and then gave both groups end-of-unit tests.

Although traditional assessment techniques are sufficient for validating the use of Outrageous Teaching, it is likely that an assessment comparing a conventional lesson to an equivalent Outrageous lesson would probably be even more revealing of differences in students' performance and engagement. It is hoped that such research will be conducted in the future.

ACHIEVING SELF-FULFILLMENT

Although planning a lesson using the Dramatized Content Planning Method does take more time than planning conventional lessons and requires more daring and personal investment, the payoff for both teacher and students goes far beyond the single lesson. Such lessons provide a basis for motivating and deepening student learning over the course of the unit, even when the remainder is taught conventionally. Even a single Outrageous lesson creates a powerful bond between teacher and students, and leaves an indelible impression that goes beyond the immediate content being taught—an impression that can be used to build an ongoing interest in learning, not only for the current unit but for subsequent ones as well.

Chances are that if another teacher had applied the Dramatized Content Planning Method to the same content objective that Dwight taught, that teacher probably would have developed a different dramatic context for teaching it, and chances are that it would have been equally effective. The Dramatized Content Planning Method is highly flexible and encourages the teacher to use his or her own imagination and experience to create the dramatic context. You may have chosen a different lesson and unit to teach Outrageously because you previous had success in teaching this content objective, or you may have taught Outrageously in a different content area. In any event, there is a sensible way and time, based on need and opportunity, for each individual teacher to teach Outrageously.

Overcoming Trepidations

At this point you may be thinking that developing an Outrageous lesson is overwhelming because of all the details that need to be worked out, and that you cannot think of the weird ideas that such a lesson entails. Teachers often express to me that it is not their personality to think or act that way in front of anyone, let alone their students.

In fact, you probably do not normally act this way. So what? Actors typically do not act in their off-stage lives the way they act on stage. Many are severe introverts. So think of yourself as an actor and develop a new persona for your performance. You can revert back to yourself the next day—if you want to.

Indeed, many of the things we do as teachers are well-ordered routines. However, although orderliness is desirable in many respects, it is not all there is to good teaching. I have never known anyone who said they went into teaching so they could implement well-ordered routines.

Yes, there are a lot of details to be worked through in developing a Dramatized Content lesson plan. And yes, preparing to teach an Outrageous lesson does require more work than a conventional lesson. And yes, applying the Dramatized Content Planning Method does take a very, very, very different thought process than preparing the typical lesson, when all you have to worry about is presenting the content. However, this type of lesson is used only very occasionally, and a little bit of Outrageous Teaching goes a long way.

Outrageous Teaching also calls forth the fear of the unknown. How will the students react if I give up my position of authority and try to intrigue them with surprise, character, and storyline? But you had the same trepidations when you taught your first lesson as a student teacher, and when you walked into your own classroom for the first time. Would the students listen to you? You overcame those temporary feelings of insecurity. Such feelings normally accompany all growth and new experience.

Big secret: *Designing and teaching an Outrageous lesson will be a ton of fun for you! And you will be successful!* All you have to do is be willing to act divergently one day a semester, and have the attitude that you are willing to do whatever it takes to spark interest and learning on the part of your students. The result is incredible satisfaction, and success in the *act* of teaching (an unintended but apt pun).

SUMMARY

This chapter has described the Dramatized Content Planning Method for developing Outrageous lessons and lesson plans. (As you will see in Chapter Seven, the method can also be extended to develop Outrageous units.) The method provides a practical base of support for teachers to design their own lessons. At the same time, the idea of developing and teaching an Outrageous lesson is still a bit abstract given the few snippets of suggestions and examples provided so far. It is also hard at this point to understand just how powerful such lessons can be. To help make the approach more concrete and relevant to your teaching, the next chapter contains sample lessons that I witnessed being taught across a variety of content areas. These lessons will enable you to see how powerful and unique the resultant learning experience is for students.

As you read the next chapter, please keep in mind that seven of the nine lessons were developed and taught by my student teachers. (I developed the other two.) In other words, you do not have to be a highly experienced master teacher to pull off what I think you will agree were masterful, unique lessons.

Hopefully you will find the sample lessons both fun and motivating.

Outrageous Lessons:
Examples from the Classroom

This chapter describes a series of Outrageous lessons taught across a variety of content areas and grade levels. Most of these lessons were created by my student teachers over the years. All of the names are fictitious.

OVERVIEW

Each lesson in this chapter (highlighted with a gray screen) is described from beginning to end. For most of the lessons some background information is provided about its development, as well as about the nature of the teacher-student interaction that existed under conventional instruction. A debriefing about each lesson's effect on the students and the teacher is also provided. Students' reactions to the lesson are discussed, as well as the advantages of having taught the content Outrageously rather than conventionally.

Each lesson is then analyzed in terms of the planning process described in Chapter Four. Tables 5.1 and 5.2 compare the lessons in terms of how the Dramatized Content Planning Method was implemented. Finally, plans for each lesson are provided in Exhibit 5.1 and Appendix D.

The first eight lessons (including Dwight's) were developed by my student teachers; I developed the last two. Nine of the lessons were observed at a high school or middle school, and the tenth at an elementary school.

Although these lessons were taught at the high school and middle school levels, I know from my experience with the HOTS and Supermath programs (see the Preface) that these techniques work equally well from fourth grade on up. The fourth grade is critical because that is where the heavy emphasis on content learning generally begins and intensifies, and it is where disadvantaged students start to fall behind, even if they made progress at the earlier grade levels.

Suggestions for Reviewing the Lessons

The temptation for the reader will be to look only at lessons in your content area or at your grade level. It is suggested that you review all of the lessons to see the whole gamut of creative ideas that were generated and tried. This hopefully will spark your creative juices.

The early lessons focus on various aspects of language arts and social studies. These content areas are the most obvious candidates for Outrageous lessons. There are also examples from math and science. Some of the scenarios can be applied to other content areas.

Adaptation of the Lesson Ideas

You may not be able to consider implementing the lesson exactly the way it is written here because some of your circumstances will be different. For example, some of the lessons refer to something the supervising teacher did, usually at the start of the period. You will not routinely have another teacher in your room. However, you can adapt these lessons by inviting one of your fellow teachers or an administrator to come to your class for a few minutes at the start of the period to perform that function.

JULIE'S LESSON (LANGUAGE ARTS, MIDDLE SCHOOL)

Julie is an excellent student teacher working in one of the better middle schools in the district. She has not told me anything about her planned lesson, but I have driven to the school in anticipation of seeing a wonderful Outrageous lesson in her English class. However, once the lesson starts, I am disappointed and wonder if I got the date and time right.

The Lesson

Julie spends the first five minutes reading a boring story about monkeys in a jungle in a monotone. The students are fidgeting—and so am I.

Then all of a sudden Julie stops, looks around, slaps her forearm, and complains that she has been bitten by a bug. She pauses silently for a few seconds, then starts reading the story again in a highly animated fashion, gesturing wildly and imitating the animals and what they are doing in the story. She does this for a few minutes, then suddenly stops, puts her head on the table, and acts as though she has fainted. When the students approach to see if she is OK, she asks them:

What happened?

The students respond that she had been bitten and then acted wildly for a few minutes. Julie acts horrified and at first denies the students' reports. She starts reading again in a monotone, and then repeats the sequence. This time when she awakes, Julie exclaims,

I know what happened. I got bitten by a powerful bug called a Story Bug. Yuck! They are gross!

She then continued, saying:

I need to rest for a few minutes to recover from the effects of the bite. In the meantime, I would like everyone to get into groups of four. I want each of you to write a one- or two-paragraph story about what you do right after you get up in the morning.

After about fifteen minutes of dutiful but unenthusiastic work, Julie stops them. She tells the class that she has fully recovered and asks the students to read their stories to each other. The typical story is about how they go to the bathroom, wash their hands and brush their teeth, and so on. As the students share unenthusiastically, they are still not sure about the mental state of their teacher. After only a few have read, Julie loudly exclaims:

Look out! Oh no! There is a swarm of story bugs flying into the classroom. Watch out! Don't let yourself get bitten while reading your story!

Of course everyone then pretends to have gotten bitten, and the class becomes filled with animated, twirling students reading their bug-bitten stories. Normally placid students are suddenly alive and trying to out-embellish each other. It is incredibly noisy but the students are totally into it.

Julie then interrupts and asks:

Who would like to come to the front of the room and do the before and after versions of their story?

I am amazed as virtually all of the shy students raise their hands. Julie calls on about five students. Each in turn does an appropriately boring reading and then improvises a very animated version of the story. What fun!

The students do not notice that their teacher is writing down some of the words they are using.

With about five minutes left, Julie compliments the students and asks them to pay attention. She writes on the board some of the motion and emphasis words that students used to embellish their stories, such as *quickly*, *grabbed*, *excited*, *beautiful*, *foaming*, and so on, and then says:

> You have just discovered how actions and choice of words can make even a boring story exciting. These are some of the new words you used in the revised versions of your stories, plus some additional ones. These are words that add motion and emphasis in writing.
>
> An important part of creative writing is to use words that indicate motion and add emphasis to even simple actions.

For homework Julie asks the students to remember the bug-bitten version of their story and to rewrite it the way they had performed it.

She ends the lesson by saying:

> You have discovered that you are all very creative storytellers and I hope you get bitten by the story bug frequently.

Julie follows up the next day with a conventional lesson about the different words they had used to incorporate motion and emphasis into their revised stories. She then analyzes a piece of literature to examine where and how the author had conveyed motion and emphasis, and then had the students continue to elaborate their writing.

Exhibit 5.1 contains the plan for Julie's lesson. (The plans for the other lessons are included in Appendix D.)

Comments on Julie's Lesson

On a personal note, I think that this lesson has one of the best elements of surprise I have seen because it totally fooled me into thinking I was seeing an example of awful teaching by a good teacher who was having a bad day. When the drama subsequently unfolded, it was as surprising to me as it was to the students.

Exhibit 5.1
Julie's Lesson Plan

Content objective: To learn how to write expressively, and the types of adjectives and adverbs typically used in such writing.

Props and media	Content materials
None	Story about the animals in the forest from the class reader

Who are you? Visitors or conspirators?	**Disguise elements**
I remain myself	None

Opening surprise or setting

The opening surprise is that there is no surprise other than selecting some particularly boring passages to read. The main surprise is when I pretend that I am bitten by a bug that causes me first to faint, then to awake in a hyperactive state, and then to go back to sleep momentarily.

Storyline or scenario and method (such as role-playing or anthropomorphizing, and so on)

Play the role of pretending to get bitten by a bug, which produces first sleepiness, then highly expressive euphoria. The main initial surprise is pretending to get bitten, then putting my head on the table for a minute or two, then jumping up and down as I reread and reparaphrase the same passages with far greater expressiveness.

Transition to student activity phase (the *what* and *why* for the assigned work)

Have the students develop a boring story then get bitten by the story bug. There is nothing more boring than getting up in the morning.

Ending discussion (debriefing and completing content objective)

Introduce the elements of expressive writing. Create a list of action and expressive words the students used to make their revised stories expressive.

The content objective of the lesson was to introduce students to the concepts of incorporating motion and emphasis in stories. It was also the introduction to creative writing.

Not only was the element of surprise powerful, but it was also delivered without creating a new role—that is, the teacher remained the teacher throughout—and without props or disguise. The surprise was carried out through the acting and guts of the teacher. I say guts because during the simulated fainting spells the teacher took her eyes off the students. (Today, because students have cell phones, simulated fainting might not be a good idea, because some students may dial an emergency number. Perhaps just getting a strange, paralyzed look on one's face would suffice. An alternative would be to have another adult in the classroom to assure students that Julie will wake up soon.) The only additional factor was that Julie asked her peer in the adjoining classroom for permission to do the lesson, because of the expected rise in noise level for about ten minutes of the lesson.

The dilemma in the scenario—Julie's needing to recover from the bug bite—was tied to the subsequent activity, which seemed like a make-work assignment. Under normal circumstances, asking students to write a boring two-paragraph story would have elicited protest and whining. In this case, they got right to work.

This initial writing task led directly to the main content goal of the lesson, expressive writing. While the teacher discussed the content goal briefly at the end, all the students got the point. Deep learning occurred.

The learning in this lesson was far deeper than if the teacher had first told the students the goal, then given them the rules and asked them to write something creative. Only those students predisposed to creative writing would have responded to such an approach. In addition, trying to explain a concept as abstract as creative writing to middle school students is very difficult. In this case, the learning occurred spontaneously, and all of the students participated and had their notion of what it means to write changed. They also learned the power of word choice when telling or writing a story.

After this lesson, whenever the students complained that they could not think of something to write, the teacher reminded them what creative storytellers they had proved themselves to be in this lesson. It was also now a peer norm in her class that writing creatively was cool. Whenever students would get stuck, she would ask them to pretend to get bitten by a story bug and to act out the bug-bitten character for a minute.

All in all, this lesson was an incredible introduction to creative writing, and the content objective was achieved in a way that was deeply meaningful to the students; that is, it was a Creatively Authentic lesson that catered to how middle school students think and behave.

DEVELOPING SOCIAL STUDIES LESSONS

Social studies is probably the easiest subject around which to construct Outrageous lessons. History contains so many dramatic moments. The most obvious opportunities for Outrageous lessons are probably when students are learning about famous battles and wars. The students in one Outrageous lesson I observed had read information about events leading up to a Civil War battle, as well as about the events of the first day of the battle. In the lesson, the teacher had the students reenact the battle right outside the school. He provided each student with either a grey or blue sheet of paper to wear to identify which side they were on, and with signs to indicate locations on the "battlefield." After the reenactment, the teacher brought the students back into the classroom to write letters about the battle and about what they thought would happen the next day. Several students then read their letters in class. They were very poignant.

I marveled at how much had been accomplished in a single period: moving outdoors, reenacting, moving back to class, writing, and presenting their writing.

Needless to say, after that experience, the students were eager to learn about what happened in the following days of the war. The next day they continued reading about the subsequent battles, always discussing both the historical facts and how the soldiers on each side would have been feeling.

In a different but somewhat related vein, when a class was reading about two famous generals, the teacher became a woman from the past who had dated both men. She asked the students to tell her what they knew about the generals. She told them they knew hardly anything. She then gossiped about the generals and talked about how they had both asked for her advice many times. She complained about being left out of the history book, and she wanted to know why all of the personal details she knew about the generals were not included.

There are many other types of dramatic moments in history on which Outrageous lessons can be based: the discovery of new lands and new peoples, elections, bold actions by leaders, moments of crisis and triumph, and so on.

TAMARRA'S LESSON (SOCIAL STUDIES, HIGH SCHOOL)

The best Outrageous social studies lesson I ever observed was taught by an elegant African American woman whom I will call Tamarra. She was very fashion conscious and was always impeccably dressed and coiffed. (No, I am not being patronizing! There is a reason for mentioning this that will become clear as you read about her lesson.)

I had previously observed several of Tamarra's lessons in the class that was giving her the most trouble. Tamarra was having a major problem with class management, particularly with getting students to transition from the opening class discussion to reading their textbooks or writing. This transition would normally take her ten to fifteen minutes because the students were very hyperactive and loved to socialize and complain. Tamarra continued to improve, but it seemed that any transition with this particular class still took at least five minutes. I therefore suggested that she do an Outrageous lesson with this class.

Tamarra decided to do her Outrageous lesson on the origins of unionization in the coal industry in Appalachia. Here is what she came up with.

The Lesson

As the students file in, the cooperating teacher tells them that Tamarra is not present today and there is a substitute teacher, but they need to be very quiet because the substitute teacher is not feeling well. Indeed, the "substitute" teacher is dressed strangely and has her head down on the table, and her face is covered by her hands. The lights are out, the room is dark, and blues music is quietly playing.

The students go to their seats and wait quietly. After a minute or so, the "substitute" teacher raises her head. She has black splotches all over her face, her hair is a shambles, and her blouse is tattered. She partly raises her head but does not look directly at the class. She coughs and cries and says:

> *The doctor tells me that I have tuberculosis and my lungs are clogged with dust, and I don't have food in the house for my children, I have a fever, and I am soooooo tirrred. I work so hard scraping out some coal everyday, but now I have trouble breathing. [Cough, cough.] I don't know how I can go on, how I can work, how I can feed my children. [Sob, sob.] I work fifteen hours a day and at the end of the day I am paid $2 for the whole day. My boss doesn't care even though I have*

worked here forever. If I do not work I will be thrown out of my shack. I don't even have the strength to beg.

Tamarra goes on in this vein for about ten minutes, slowly and painfully. All this time the blues music is playing quietly. She finally looks directly at the class as the cooperating teacher turns on the lights. She is seemingly surprised to see them and says:

I do not know who you are or what you are doing here but all of you look well fed and educated. How did you get that way? You probably do not believe how bad things are from me.

She then hands out some pictures of the period she is representing. As the students circulate the pictures, she asks:

Is there any way you can help me? No, I do not want charity. I want advice. Can you figure out something that I can do to make sure that others do not have to live as wretched a life as I have, and something that will give me hope that my children will have a better life?

She then points to the supervising teacher and says between coughs:

This man here says that maybe there is something in your book in Chapter Eight that will help me, but I cannot read. I know this is a lot to ask but could you read it and tell me if you find something that can help me and give me advice?

Tamarra then puts her head back on the table and covers it with her hands. There is absolute silence as the students transition to reading.

Within thirty seconds the entire class has their books out and are quietly reading the chapter. Not a sound can be heard in the room other than the blues music. Some of the students quietly and respectfully start to discuss with each other the significance of what they have read. There is no joking or socializing, just quiet, respectful discussion.

With about ten minutes left in the class, Tamarra raises her head and again looks at the students and asks:

Did you find out anything that can help?

One of the students blurts out that she should get into a union. Tamarra responds by asking:

What is a union?

After several of the students explain, she gasps, or rather wheezes, in amazement and asks:

Is this possible?

As the students explain, she acts crestfallen and says:

Although I appreciate your trying to help, my boss is mean and would never allow this.

The students rush to explain the struggle to form the union, and its history, and so on. She lets them go, fueling the discussion with the occasional appropriate question.

With about a minute left in the period, Tamarra thanks the class for giving her the idea of forming a union and says she now feels there is hope for her children and she will talk to everyone about forming a union. She then puts her head on the table, the lights go out, and the music rises.

The students are spellbound, and when the bell rings they are not sure what to do. Some go up and pat her on the shoulder. They linger. When she finally leaves the role and stands up, they crowd around her looks at the makeup she put on and asks her questions about how she created the look, where she found the tattered shirt, and so on.

Comments on Tamarra's Lesson

This was a very gutsy lesson. The two hardest parts in creating this lesson were to figure out a scenario to bridge the opening dramatic monologue with the rest of the lesson so that Tamarra could stay in the role and provide a reason for students to read the assigned chapter, and to teach most of the lesson without looking at the class—her most difficult students. The latter was the harder and gutsier decision. Would she lose control of her rambunctious class even more than normal by teaching with her head on the desk for substantial parts of the period? It takes a great leap of faith to try and control a class without looking at or speaking to them, while trusting that they will respond with curiosity and respect.

The response of the students amazed even Tamarra's veteran supervising teacher. No one had trouble finding their book. No one had a need to go to the bathroom. No one had a need to flirt or annoy someone else. Not a single reprimand was uttered the entire period.

From that day forward, Tamarra never had a problem getting the class to make quick transitions. A different type of bond had been formed between teacher and students.

SHIRLEY'S LESSON (LITERATURE, HIGH SCHOOL SENIORS)

Shirley was a tiny, young student teacher. She ended up in the lowest-performing high school in the Tucson Unified School District. The previous year only one senior from this large school had gone on to college. An English teacher, Shirley was assigned the classes that no one else wanted to teach—senior-level remedial classes. Indeed, she was assigned the class of students who had already failed remedial English and were repeating it.

I probably empathized with her more than with any other student teacher I ever supervised. The first time I visited one of her remedial senior classes I was amazed at how much taller than her the students were, how unmotivated they were, and how low their skill level was. In the beginning of the semester, the students constantly refused to read out loud or do any writing. They complained whenever she tried to get them to do anything. She practically had to beg them. In addition, they were constantly disruptive. (Shirley's cooperating teacher was never present, preferring to hang out in the teacher's lounge, in violation of district policy and state law.)

Shirley had a major struggle on her hands. To her credit, she was tough, stubborn, and energetic. She not only did not give up, she also kept pushing them to read and write, always telling them they would improve if they tried. The first time I visited the class, she spent more than half of the period trying to get a few of the students to read, while they made excuses or outright refused. Little actual reading occurred. The typical exchange would be that she would ask a student to read and the student would say something like this: "I read two days ago. Why are you asking me to read again? You are picking on me."

Shirley would persuade and encourage, saying something like, "This is a small paragraph and your reading is getting better."

Shirley was undeterred. Each visit there would be slightly more reading and a bit less complaining as the students saw that Shirley really cared and was not going to back down. So, whereas at the beginning of the semester she had to call on four students to get one to read, the ratio fell to having to call on only two students before one would read. However, even late in the semester it was still a constant struggle, with much time lost to students complaining and refusing, Shirley coaxing, and so on.

Shirley did not give me any clue as to what she was planning for her Outrageous lesson. She said she wanted to surprise me. I arrived about five minutes late on the day of the Outrageous lesson. Here is what I saw.

The Lesson

I look through the door window before entering the class. The students are seated around a table, miraculously seeming at attention. However, I do not see Shirley or any other adult. As usual, the supervising teacher is not present. Strangely, there is no riot going on. Quite the contrary, the students are sitting attentively, but attentive to what or to whom? The scene seems surreal.

As I enter the room and take a seat in the back, I still do not see Shirley. I hear a whisper and a student starts to read. When the student finishes, I hear another whisper. Another student starts to read. No argument. I cannot hear what is being whispered. Another whisper, another reading.

What is going on? I have no clue!

I then spot Shirley hunched under the table dressed in a hooded raincoat and wearing sunglasses. One of the students notices my puzzlement and whispers to me that someone is stalking her.

I sit back puzzled and listen to the students reading. They are caught up in the story. The reading is flawless. The story is very dramatic. It is about the Irish conflict and it ends with a sniper in Dublin shooting one of the "enemy." When the sniper comes down to make sure the individual he has shot is dead, he discovers it is his brother.

With about ten minutes left in the period, Shirley emerges from under the table and tells the students she now feels safe. She asks them what they thought of the story. They discuss their feelings about how moving and surprising the story was.

She then asks:

What is the same about a sniper and a stalker?

After several students respond, she asks the critical question:

> *What was the same about how the author got you to care about the sniper and how I got you to care about my situation?*

The students give some thoughtful answers. They also explain the moral of the story. They do not sound like senior remedial students. Shirley then explains:

> *I appreciate your caring about my situation. However, I wasn't really being stalked. When I told you that and dressed like this, I was being an author creating a mood, just like the author of the story you read. Authors create a mood to get you interested in the characters and situation. What are some of the words and sentences the author used to create a mood?*

Again, thoughtful responses. Shirley continues by saying:

> *Tomorrow we will read another short story and I want you to analyze how the author creates a mood.*

Shirley ends the period by complimenting the students on their reading and discussion and then says:

> *I appreciate the concern you showed for me. I hope you understand that I also care about how you do in school because I know you are all capable individuals who have a lot to offer and who can do much better academically.*

The students file out with smiles on their faces.

Note: The short story the students read was "The Sniper," by Liam O'Flaherty.

Personal Reflection

I did not visit the class again for another two to three weeks. I was curious about what I would see when I did return.

On my next visit, the students were reading and discussing with little prompting needed. There were no discipline problems. The students' reading had improved dramatically. Because this was my last visit to the class, I was moved to do something I had never done before. Just before the end of the period I asked Shirley if I could address the class. She said it would be OK.

I told the students that in all my years of being a professor I had never seen a class make so much progress in such a short period, and that if they continued to work on improving their academic skills they would be able to achieve whatever they wanted in life. I also told them that if they continued to make the same level of improvement, there was no reason they could not make it to the university.

They thanked me as they walked out of the room with smiles on their faces.

Comments on Shirley's Lesson

In the part of the lesson I did not see, Shirley established the scenario from the very beginning. She arrived in class a minute late. She wore a raincoat with the hood drawn over her face and wearing sunglasses. She looked worried. She told the students that she thought someone was stalking her but she did not want to miss class, so she would hide and teach from her hiding place. She then got under the table and asked the students to be very quiet. She asked one of them to see if there was anyone outside the room, and when he reported there wasn't, she started the lesson from under the table.

The mood of shared concern that was created by this scenario mirrored the foreboding mood of the story. It should be noted that this lesson occurred prior to the shootings at Columbine. Obviously the lesson would have to be modified in today's world of school shootings and lockdown policies. However, this example is still indicative of a creative use of drama that had powerful and enduring effects. The lesson generated a breakthrough in the willingness of the students, who had not experienced much academic success and who had been written off by the system, to believe in the education process and that they could improve.

The work that Shirley did that semester was to my mind the best and most courageous job of student teaching, or any type of teaching, that I have ever seen. In addition to her sheer determination, it was clear that the Outrageous lesson was a major turning point in Shirley's relationship with her students. By linking reading to the students' sense of compassion, the Outrageous lesson convinced them that they could develop their reading skills and that there was value in reading literature. Of course it would have been preferable if the students had been provided with such a lesson prior to their becoming seniors. At the same time, the major lesson from this experience is that imaginative teaching can transform even the most hardened and jaded of students. (Too bad the regular classroom teacher did not get to see this.)

VIERA'S LESSON (LITERATURE, MIDDLE SCHOOL)

Viera was having a tough time with one of her middle school classes. It was a low-performing seventh grade, and one of the most hyper group of students I had ever seen. In addition, many of the students were English Language Learners. It was difficult to keep them in their seats, to get their attention, and above all, to get them interested in reading English literature.

Viera decided to turn the introduction to the final and most difficult book of the semester into an Outrageous lesson. She did not tell me the title of the book or what she was going to do, other than that she was going to let it all hang out.

The Lesson

At the start of the lesson, when the students walk into the room, only the supervising teacher is there. She settles the students, to the extent that they are ever settled. She then says she has no idea where Viera is and that it this a problem because they are starting a new unit and she does not know what they are supposed to be doing. At that moment, the assistant principal walks into the room and whispers into the teacher's ear. The teacher looks surprised and concerned.

The assistant principal leaves and the teacher turns to the class and says:

I have just gotten some terrible news. Your teacher had a mental breakdown last night and was taken to the hospital's mental ward. Then she ran away this morning and no one knows where she is.

At that moment, Viera bursts into the room. She is breathless. She is dressed in a hospital gown a tunic that looks like a straitjacket, and some sort of hospital head covering. She indeed looks like an escaped mental patient.

She runs to a corner of the room and says:

Don't tell them I'm here. They think I'm crazy. They want to lock me up. I'm not crazy. Do you think I'm crazy?

The students are generally shocked and not sure how to react, and some hesitatingly answer no.

I am not crazy!

She puts her hands over her ears and says:

They say I am hearing things in my head that are not there.

She slowly walks around the room and in one of the aisles between the desks she stops and shrieks:

Oh no. There it is again!

She gets on her knees and puts her head on the floor as if she is listening. She stands up, looks into the eyes of the nearest student, and asks:

Do you hear it? Do you hear it?

The flustered student responds by saying:

Hear what, Teacher?

Viera runs to another part of the classroom. She repeats the process in several other places on the floor, with several other students. She encourages some of them to put their ears on the floor and listen, and she asks if they hear the sound. Other times she puts her hands over her ears and asks the students to make the noise stop.

As she circles the room, she continually asks the class as a whole or individual students whether she is crazy. She then goes back to the corner and puts her ear to the wall and says:

I hear it in here too.

She calls to the supervising teacher and asks if she hears the sound. The teacher indicates that she cannot.

I don't understand why no one can hear the sound.

The class is quiet and confused. The students are not sure what to make of the behavior of their teacher. They have never seen a teacher behave this way and they are starting to get worried. Viera turns to the class and says:

I know that once they find out I am here they are going to come and get me and take me away to the mental ward. Only you can save me. Only you can figure out what is happening and explain it to the people if they try to take me back to the mental hospital. I know the secret is in the book on your desk. Please help me by reading it.

She then leaves the room, saying:

I'm going into hiding so they can't find me until you have figured out how to explain why I'm not crazy. Please read the story as quickly as you can.

The students are still puzzled by what they have seen, but they quickly open their books and start to read.

There is no further discussion, yet the students continue to read quietly until the end of the period. They occasionally ask the supervising teacher the meaning of a word.

This Outrageous lesson was of course an introduction to the story "The Tell-Tale Heart," by Edgar Allen Poe.

As the period ends and the students are leaving, Viera appears by the door to assure them that she is really OK and that she wants them to figure out from the story why she acted the way she did.

Comments on Viera's Lesson

I was not present the rest of the week, but Viera reported that the next day she again came late but dressed normally. The supervising teacher started the class by asking the students to continue reading. When Viera arrived, she asked the students what they had read so far. She challenged them to try and figure out what in the story had made her act the way she had the previous day. The students quickly got back to reading the story.

Viera had set up this Outrageous lesson as an experiment. She had taught her other seventh grade class conventionally. When she tested both classes, she reported that the class with whom she had done the Outrageous lesson did better, even though to that point they had been the lower class.

I should not admit this but I was quite skeptical that these students would in fact be able to read the story, because they were reading the original version with its somewhat arcanc language, not some simplified version. In the end, these low-performing, literature-resistant, highly squirrelly students eagerly persevered in reading this story, with high levels of comprehension.

Once again we see the power of surprise in stimulating student curiosity, and the dramatic increase in learning and improvement in behavior that result from provoking such emotion and from the kindling of students' sense of compassion and opportunity to help someone.

The notion that a low-performing, squirrelly class could be controlled by the teacher putting an ear to the floor is completely counterintuitive. Once again, this lesson demonstrates the immense untapped learning potential that exists in the typical low-performing class—or any class. It also demonstrates that when teachers take creative chances, rather than losing control of the class, they have the opposite effect. Indeed, after the unit, whenever the class got too boisterous or inattentive, Viera would put her hands to her ears, shake her head, and announce,

There is so much noise in this class that I may go mad!

This would immediately quiet the class.

The scenario that Viera chose could have been elaborated on in any number of ways. Can you think of any alternative scenarios she could have used to help with her "madness"?

_____

_____

_____

For example, she could have asked the class to become her lawyers and defend her in court, or she could have asked them to become her psychiatrist and treat her instead of relying on the hospital, and so on.

In the end I found it amazing that a class with low reading skills could read and understand this story. It renewed my faith in the power of great teaching, and in the ability of all students to learn at higher levels with the right form of instruction.

SERENA'S LESSON (POETRY, HIGH SCHOOL)

The current popularity of rap music provides endless opportunities to turn all manner of assignments, from book reports on any topic to test responses, into a rap music contest, with the one rule being that the rap must be based on the content knowledge.

The following lesson uses a different approach. It uses the element of surprise to bring students out of their shell and lets their instinct to be demonstrative take over—all in the interest of letting the poetry speak.

Serena decided to reinforce her students' interest in poetry by recreating the beatnik poetry reading scene of the late 1950s and early 1960s in Greenwich Village, New York City. She went all out and transformed another classroom into a coffee shop. She covered the window with a large sign—Nick's Coffee Shop—below which, in smaller letters, was written, "No one can *beat Nick's* coffee shop"—pun intended.

The Lesson

The supervising teacher announces that Serena is absent and that she does not have the lesson plan, so instead of keeping them in the classroom with nothing to do, she will give them a special treat by taking them to the new coffee shop on campus to meet its owner.

The students line up and wonder what is going on. They are led to a room down the hall whose window is covered by the large sign described earlier.

When the door opens, the students are led into a dark space filled with coffee aromas, candlelight, and quiet music. Large cloth banners cover the windows and parts of the walls, and one hangs over the door. One big sign says "1959" and another says "Greenwich Village, New York City."

A dimly lit figure wearing a beret, sunglasses, and a (painted-on) goatee and sitting cross-legged on the front desk quietly says,

> *You are now in Greenwich Village, New York City, in 1959. My name is Allen Ginsburg. Welcome to my coffee shop, fellow beatnik poets.*
> *Help yourself to the best coffee brewed this side of Seattle. The only rule is that you must read a poem and show proper respect for each reading that moves you by clicking your fingers.*

(Note: The coffee served is actually fruit juice.)

Allen/Serena turns on a light in front of the room that casts shadows and proceeds to reads a poem with great expressiveness. When the reading is over, Allen/Serena waits for the finger clicks.

Once students get the idea and click their fingers, Allen/Serena thanks them for their expression of approval.

Allen/Serena then asks for a student volunteer. On one side of the room is a list of poems they have read that year, and Allen/Serena asks the volunteer which poem he wants to read. Once the student has made a selection, the coffee shop owner gives him the text. The student reads with great expressiveness, followed by finger clicks from the other students. The process is repeated twelve to fifteen times.

The students read with great passion. I am impressed by how they are able to capture the essence of the meaning and the lyricism of the words. After a while I stop admiring the lesson and start listening to the poetry.

With about ten minutes left in the period, Serena praises the students' poetry reading and how they captured the emotions embodied in the poems' words. She reviews some of the emotions they portrayed. She then talks about the period of beat poetry and its influence on American poetry.

Serena ends by thanking the students for patronizing her coffee shop and says she hopes they will come back, if not to this shop then to other public poetry readings. The students have a few minutes to enjoy their "coffee" and socialize. This is a coffee shop after all.

I would note that this was the only transgender Outrageous lesson ever put on by one of my student teachers.

Additional Ideas and Thoughts

If Serena had wanted to do a follow-up lesson to reinforce the concept of poetry reading and the nature of poetic expression, she could have done an interesting comparison of poetry readings in the beat period and more modern poetry readings, both those put on by literary groups and those of the hip-hop culture, such as poetry jams and slams.

As an aside, the HOTS program had an annual poetry contest. Students would submit poems about historical figures (other than athletes) and my staff would pick a winner. One year we had enough funds to fly the winner, a female African American middle school student from inner-city Stockton, California, to Tucson to appear at the annual Tucson Poetry Festival. She was given a spot on the program and read her poem just before the performance by the featured poet, who happened to be a Nobel Laureate. I still have the picture of the two of them shaking hands, the student holding a teddy bear. When we explained to her what a Nobel Laureate is, she was dutifully impressed but still thought her poem was better.

A source of hip-hop culture poetry readings is the Russell Simmons Def Poetry Jam series on HBO, which is available on DVD. I particularly recommend seasons one and two, which include many of the performers and performances from the amazing Def Poetry show on Broadway. Although many of the performances are not appropriate for classroom use, some are funny, others are poignant, and all are clever. My favorites are "Money" and "KKK." The latter laments the current reincarnation of the old racist movement, which is now sapping the energy of the African American community in the form of Krispy Kreme Kakes.

JOSE'S LESSON (SPANISH, HIGH SCHOOL)

I somehow ended up supervising some Spanish language student teachers even though I do not speak Spanish and much of the instruction they did was in Spanish. One of the student teachers, who I will call Jose, was extremely taciturn. He would never smile while teaching or use any facial expression other than extreme seriousness. As a result, he never looked truly comfortable in front of the class and had trouble communicating his passion for knowledge and learning. I told him he was going to become a good teacher but he had to learn to relax in front of the class and use a variety of expressions and emotions while teaching.

He made little progress in those respects throughout most of the semester. As a result, I felt he would benefit the most from doing an Outrageous lesson. I realized, however, that such a lesson was so contrary to his fundamental personality that he probably would not give it a try.

I was pleasantly surprised when he agreed to do an Outrageous lesson.

The Lesson

Jose is late to class. The supervising teacher announces:

Because Jose is not getting paid for his teaching, he has to work as a waiter at night to earn money for himself and his family. This morning his boss called and told him he needed to work this morning. I just got a call from Jose and he said he just got off from work and will be here soon. Unfortunately I do not have today's lesson plan, so we will have to wait for him to come and teach, and hope that he gets here soon.

At that moment Jose bursts into the room. He wears a black jacket, white shirt, and black bowtie. He has a white towel over his arm. He apologizes for being late and immediately gives everyone a menu. The fact that the students are arranged as normal, seated around tables, facilitates his treating the classroom as a restaurant.

Jose asks the students to look over the menu and get ready to order. The menu is entirely in Spanish. Although the students know a few of the words, most of them are new ones.

Jose then goes to the first table and starts to take orders, beginning with appetizers and proceeding to dessert. If the students try to answer in English, he pretends not to understand. If they choose steak for the main course, he asks whether they want it cooked rare, medium, or well-done. All the discussion is done completely in Spanish.

Jose is completely animated. He uses lots of expressions and hand gestures, and pantomimes to convey meaning. The combination of the students being familiar with ordering in a restaurant and already knowing some of the Spanish words enables them to figure out many of the new Spanish words Jose uses from context.

Jose moves from table to table, going through the same routine at each one. His deliberate repetition of words and expressions increases the students' familiarity with them. As he progresses around the room, he expects the students at each table to respond to him using more of the new words than the students at the previous table used. Whenever a table completes an order, he congratulates the students with a smile.

Jose is nonstop animation as he goes around the room. He seems excited as the students start to get the idea of how to incorporate the new words into their orders. As he gains confidence that the lesson is working, he even incorporates some humor and acts like a clumsy waiter. At one point he trips, and another time he goes back to a table pretending to have forgotten their orders.

By the time he has gone through all six tables there are only five to ten minutes left in the period.

Jose then uses the overhead projector to display a list of all of the new words they have used. I am amazed to see that thirty-four words are listed. Because it was all done in Spanish, and I had not seen the lesson plan, I had no idea that he had incorporated so many new words. He then asks the students to write down the words. Once they have done that, he leads a discussion about what the words mean. He gets through about two thirds of them. Just before the bell rings, he asks the students whether they prefer to learn new words this way or the typical way, that is, receiving a handout and then trying to memorize the words and write sentences. The students universally respond that they prefer to learn this way.

Jose tells the class he is proud of all the good learning they have done, and as they head out the door, Jose high-fives the students, who enthusiastically high-five him back.

Comments on Jose's Lesson

I knew going into the lesson that the objective was for the students to learn key words for ordering a meal in a restaurant. After the lesson I told Jose that I was surprised at how many new words he had taught. I asked him if that was typical for a vocabulary lesson. He said he had never tried to incorporate so many new words into a single lesson before, but all of these words were needed in order for the students to put together a meal order. He said that normally he would have spent two to three days introducing all of the words in a conventional lesson.

After I complimented him on a terrific lesson, I asked how it felt to teach with such energy and enthusiasm, and what effect he felt it had had on the students. He told me he was tired and relieved but it had been a terrific experience. He was pleasantly surprised that the students at all the other tables paid attention as he was discussing the order with a given table. He was also pleasantly surprised by how much more learning occurred than during a conventional lesson, and he enjoyed the interaction with the students. I told him the students equally enjoyed the interaction with him.

Jose told me he wanted to try the Outrageous lesson to introduce new vocabulary for ordering in a restaurant because he thought that the unit on introducing new vocabulary was the hardest type of lesson to get students interested in and in which to maintain discipline.

When he came up with the idea of being a waiter, he immediately focused on how he would dress for the role. I prompted him to think of himself as an actor and asked him how he could embellish the role of the waiter, to give the waiter a personality. The discussion produced the idea of an earnest, eager-to-please, inexperienced, bumbling waiter. We talked about using some comedic elements, such as tripping, running out of pen ink, and so on.

Can you think of some other comedy elements to add?

_____

_____

_____

Following are some ideas we came up with that he decided, probably wisely, not to incorporate:

• After all of the students had completed their orders, he would tell them he was going to the kitchen to bring out their food, then he would go into the hall and come back with a covered dish for each table, filled with what he thought they had ordered. Each dish would contain a treat that had nothing to do with what they had ordered, such as a bag of nachos or a bag of M&M's, and he would act surprised when they said it was not what they had ordered and then offer to take it back.

• He would go out into the hall with the orders, wait sixty seconds, then come back and announce that the chef had gotten food poisoning and had to go home so the restaurant was closed.

The point is that once you have gotten a basic idea in your head, you can always come up with additional elements and other ideas to embellish the mood and scenario.

At the same time, a few pieces of clothing and a few comedic ideas go a long way. The comedic ideas that Jose used were important because of the importance of maintaining an element of surprise in order to keep the students focused on the repetitive discussions. The students stayed focused as words and phrases were repeated because they did not know what the "waiter" was going to do next.

Postscript

Jose taught the same lesson to another class in a conventional manner. He reported that it took twice as long to cover the same materials, and when he tested both classes, the class that had been taught using the Outrageous Teaching approach did much better.

I saw Jose teach one more lesson after that. He was indeed looser—in a good way—and more expressive in front of the class. He was no Robin Williams, thank goodness, but he had learned that being expressive was an important part of teaching and something he would continue to work on.

The bottom line is that, once again, an Outrageous lesson proved to be both an efficient and effective way to teach content. Much more was accomplished than would have been accomplished using a conventional approach. More words were introduced and learned. Retention was also better as the comparative test results showed.

A BRIEF EXAMPLE OF ANOTHER SPANISH LESSON

I had a similar experience with another male Latino student, Pedro. His teaching was very stilted and he was working with unmotivated students in a low socio-economic status (SES) school. He was getting very frustrated with his students.

He agreed to do an Outrageous lesson. Like Jose, Pedro wanted to use the lesson to introduce a new vocabulary unit. In his case, it was to teach the Spanish words for parts of a cow.

If you have read all of the examples presented thus far, you can probably guess the scenario that was used.

Pedro decided to pose as a butcher. The goal was to get students to learn the words by grossing them out.

He walked in dressed in a bloody (red ink) apron and a butcher's hat. He announced that he was a certified butcher and that a person could earn a lot of money in that profession, and he was going to train them in how to do it. He had arranged several cuts of gross-looking meat (spoiled liver is particularly gross) on labeled pieces of cardboard. He had obtained the meat by convincing a local butcher to give him some unsold pieces.

He told the students that the first challenge was to be able to identify the parts of meat and where each comes from on a cow. He provided a diagram of a cow for them to refer to.

The only rule was that the students could not pass on a piece of meat to the next student until they had learned the word for it. Because the students were grossed out, they quickly learned the names.

It was a successful lesson.

MATH AND SCIENCE LESSONS

Usually teachers can readily see opportunities for teaching Outrageous lessons in language arts and social studies. But math and science—nah! People tend to think of math and science as dry, technical, very matter-of-fact subjects that do not lend themselves to Outrageous lessons. Nothing could be further from the truth. Over the years I have seen a great variety of interesting Outrageous lessons in these subjects.

One useful dramatic technique to use in math and science is to anthropomorphize the concepts, that is, to have the students act out the concepts. Examples of anthropomorphizing key concepts would be to have students play the role of atoms or signed numbers, acting out the characteristics of these concepts and their relationships with each other. So, for example, some students could be neutrons, some could be positrons, and others could be electrons. Students could then be asked to form relationships based on the properties of the particles they have read about. Wilhelm (2002) provides an example of discussing chemical reactions and equations in terms of individuals and couples coming to a party and the nature of their social interactions. The same thing could be done with signed numbers, fractions, and so on. A related concept is to build on the fact that much of math and science describes motion or things in motion. So using motion in Outrageous lessons is a great way to teach concepts from these subject areas. For example, one of my students used *Saturday Night Fever* dance steps to illustrate procedures for the division of polynomials. (These techniques also work for teaching grammar. I may be dating myself but I think grammar is still taught in some schools.)

You can also create a wide variety of logic games. One teacher devised a murder mystery and a logic game in which students were to identify behind which door the cookies were hiding, to illustrate indirect proofs.

In addition, the history of math and science discoveries is full of dramatic moments that lend themselves to Outrageous Teaching. Brian Greene (2008) characterizes science as "the greatest of all adventure stories, one that's been unfolding for thousands of years as we have sought to understand ourselves and our surroundings. Science needs to be taught to the young . . . in a manner that captures this drama." He further characterizes science as "a language of hope and inspiration, providing discoveries that fire the imagination and instill a sense of connection to our lives and our world."

Science and math are full of dramatic stories of repeated failures culminating in triumph, accidents, and great ah-ha moments that have led to discoveries that have produced major improvements in the quality of life, or in other cases, produced disasters (such as Hiroshima). Math and science discoveries have led to new ways of looking at the world (such as probability theory) and to new ways of viewing ourselves (such as psychology). Recreating these historic moments and events is a good way to provide a dramatic context for teaching related technical concepts and for heightening the interest of students in the importance of those concepts.

Following are examples of Outrageous lessons in math and science that used some of these techniques.

JOHN'S LESSON (SCIENCE, MIDDLE SCHOOL)

John was among the worst student teachers I ever had. He had no confidence that he could teach or get students to learn anything or even pay attention to him. He was very self-conscious and had no skill in communicating his love of science to his middle school low-SES students. He focused strictly on trying to get the students to learn the definitions in the textbook. (A top science education scholar once called U.S. science textbooks little more than illustrated dictionaries.) His students clearly were not interested and constantly acted out. When he was trying to teach, they would largely ignore him and have conversations with each other, and even turn their backs on him. Most of the period was lost to his trying to get them to pay attention.

During the semester in which I worked with John he made some improvement. I constantly challenged him to think about why students should be interested in what he was teaching, and how he could make the content important and meaningful to them. I posed these questions to him when he was teaching them about stars, for example. He was stymied. With some additional probing, he volunteered that all matter in the universe was generated from exploding stars. I asked him again, *So what does that have to do with the students?*

He thought for a few minutes, a smile finally lit up his face, and he said, "That means they were made from the stars."

Bingo! He finally had a Creatively Authentic way to link star formation to his students in a way that would make them sit up and take notice.

When the students responded positively to this idea, it built up his confidence a bit. He was finally able to operationalize Brian Greene's conception of science education as "transporting them beyond the stars" (Greene, 2008). This insight is also a good example of the ongoing, momentary, dramatic micromoments that good teachers constantly bring to the teaching of science and math.

John remained plagued by self-doubt, however, and his teaching remained mostly borrrrring. Although he was very reluctant to try an Outrageous lesson, he realized that it was his last chance to try and figure out how to derive some pleasure from teaching.

The Lesson

When the students walk into class, John is not there. The supervising teacher says he has no idea where John is. The students then hear a loud boom, and John staggers in. His face is smudged and he is wearing an old-fashioned pilot's hat and goggles. The hat and goggles are askew. He sits down, muttering about how he is a total failure. He pretends not to notice the students. He has his back to the class. Finally he says:

> *I am a failure. Our plane just crashed. We are out of money. It was foolish of me and my brother to think we could build a flying machine. It is impossible. I guess the people who said if God wanted man to fly he would have given him wings were right. It is time to be realistic and give up.*

John then turns around and seems surprised to see the students. He says:

> *Who are all of you? Why are you all dressed so strange? No one dresses like that where I come from.*

He notices that someone has a Walkman (the lesson was done in pre-iPod days) and asks:

> *What is that?*

As the student starts to explain that it plays music, John says in a startled tone:

> *That is impossible.*

The student demonstrates, and John acts shocked. John then picks up one of the student's other gadgets and repeats the cycle. He then says:

> *You are indeed special people with magical gadgets. Where did you come from? Where are we? This does not look like my time.*

After the students explain the year, John looks shocked and says:

> *I think that somehow the crash put me forward in time. What are your names?*

After a few students respond, someone asks what his name is. He points to the name tag on his coveralls and says:

Orville Wright.

Then he says:

Perhaps you can share some of your magic with me. I am trying to build a machine that flies. I know this sounds like a stupid idea. I had decided to give up. However, perhaps you can share some of your magic tools or knowledge with me.

He picks up the science text.

What is this?

He briefly thumbs through it and then says:

This book seems to have some of your special secrets. I see there is a chapter about flight. Would you do me a special favor and read it and then explain it to me while I rest and bandage my wounds?

The students quickly pull out their textbooks and read the relevant chapter in hushed silence. After about ten minutes of fiddling with his bandages, "Orville" looks up and asks the students to tell him the secret knowledge they have uncovered.

After the students explain the strategy that enabled the Wright brothers to come up with their successful design, "Orville" looks excited, stands up, and walks out the door, saying:

Let me try to use these ideas and rebuild my flying machine.

"Orville" is out of the room for what seems like five minutes. Every thirty seconds or so the clanging of metal is heard. Amazingly, the students are quiet and remain in their seats, wondering what is going on. Will their teacher come back? If he comes back, what is he going to do?

All of a sudden "Orville" bursts through the door yelling:

It works, it works! I can fly!

He starts "flying" around the room. His arms are outstretched and covered with wings he has fashioned from brightly colored paper held in place by a light piece of wood that runs the whole length of his outstretched arms. He runs around the room and between the rows of student desks, yelling all the time:

It works! I can fly!

"Orville" runs around the room like a wild man for several minutes. Just as the students overcome their surprise and begin to enjoy the show, he suddenly runs out of the room. More clanging sounds are heard. "Orville" comes back into the room and says:

Thanks for sharing your magical science knowledge with me. I have just built a time machine so I can get to my time and share your knowledge with the world. Who knows, someday someone may use this design as a the basis for building an even larger flying machine that can hold hundreds of people and fly even faster than I did today.

After the students assure him that it will happen and that he will be famous, "Orville" walks out the door.

Thirty seconds later, John walks back in as himself. He has shed his coveralls and flying hat and goggles. He is out of breath and says:

I'm sorry I am so late but I have been stuck in traffic. Did your substitute teacher come in time? Did you behave? Did you learn any science?

The students laugh in a good-natured way and play along, telling him about the visitor from the past.

John pretends not to believe them but asks the students what science knowledge they shared with the strange visitor. After they explain, he ends the period by saying:

You shared the right knowledge with the visitor from the past, and you are right that the scientific breakthrough made by the Wright brothers led to the development of the modern airplane. This shows how some of the knowledge in your textbook, and the right science knowledge and ideas in the hands of the right people, can change history. So the science in your book is more than words on paper. It is the story of how people figured things out, and by doing so made our lives better. Hopefully someday you will use the knowledge you learn in school to discover and make something new, or something better, or someone happier.

The bell rings.

Comments on John's Lesson

I will always remember the look of sheer bliss on John's face as he raced around the room, "flying," and realized that he had captivated his students. It was as though he was shedding the entire weight of his doubts about himself and his ability to teach. When we discussed the lesson right after the period ended, he was as high as if he had taken amphetamines. He was pure adrenaline. He was talking a mile a minute about how great it felt that his lesson had worked, and how wonderful the students were. He could not stop laughing and smiling at the memory of what he had just done.

I have never seen anyone's personality be so completely changed as a result of a successful teaching experience.

The lesson used a visitor-from-the-past scenario to create a reason for the students to learn about the breakthrough realizations that enabled the Wright brothers to be the first to design a machine that could fly. The lesson was not just about the history of the development of the airplane, however; it was also about the importance of scientific knowledge and the spirit of discovery.

This lesson, with its series of entrances and exits, reminded me of the great British comical play *Noises Off*. This play has been made into a movie, but it is best seen in a live performance. The madcap comedy features a group of actors making a series of entrances and exits, with the action getting zanier and zanier as the play proceeds. Who would have thought that a teacher could maintain discipline and interest in a hyperactive middle school classroom by walking out of a room and making some sounds outside the room with the door closed.

It was amazing to see how enthralled the students were over the suspense of whether the teacher would return and over what would happen if he did. This was the first time ever that I saw someone establish discipline and high levels of interest by running in and out of the room.

The lesson also made great use of a few sound effects, that is, different types of clanging and a crash.

The lesson changed the relationship between John and the class. He became a bit more relaxed when teaching, and they started to respect him as a teacher. In my last meeting with John I urged him to continue toward his goal of becoming a science teacher, but always to bring a piece of "Orville" with him to class every day. Then he would be successful.

STAN'S LESSON 1 (MATH, GRADES 5 TO 10)

As a former math teacher, I have always dreaded teaching certain concepts because I have known that the students either would not be interested or would have a superhard time learning. In most cases it was very difficult to get students to truly understand and apply the concepts or to visualize them in their minds. For example, how do you get students to understand how to solve word problems, which bring together the symbol systems of math and science, particularly students who are already having trouble using these systems independently? I dreamed of one day designing a better way to teach these concepts. The advent of computers and the receipt of a grant from the National Science Foundation enabled me to design Supermath, a program for teaching key pre-algebra units.

In designing the Supermath units, I incorporated elements of drama into the use of technology to teach those math topics and objectives that are the hardest to get students interested in or to understand. These are the topics that are hardest to teach in any way other than as a series of arbitrarily mandated rules and by relying on the old standbys of "You need to learn this because it will be on the test" and "You will understand the importance of this when you become an adult." During the years when they are developing pre-algebra skills, students are also rebelling against adult conventions. Telling such students that they will understand the importance of these concepts when they become adults does little other than reinforce that math is not part of their world, and to some extent that perspective is correct. Other than when shopping and making change, kids can do quite well without math skills. Indeed, it is hard to come up with examples of using math in everyday life that are relevant to them—which is one of the reasons that teachers revert back to using examples from the world of adulthood.

For example, how do you make decimals and word problems interesting to students so they will want to invest mental energy in them, that is, to reflect on their fundamental properties and engage in problem-solving activities that use these concepts?

So, the approach I chose for Supermath was to tap into the students' heightened senses of fantasy and fairness. I created fantasy scenarios in which mathematical principles were important to being successful in the imaginary environment.

For example, I had students learn about how to determine the relative size of decimals by trying to capture the evil decimal Carmen San Decimal by searching through different levels of a "'hood" where the addresses consist of decimals. As the search moved from larger to smaller entities (that is, from building entrances to alleyways between buildings to garbage cans in the alleyways to holes between the garbage cans), the addresses consisted of more decimal places. By engaging in the search and eventually capturing the archvillain by solving the address clues provided by the computer, students learned how to determine the size of decimals regardless of the number of decimal places by linking them to imaginary physical locations. The students were then able to reflect on the activity and come up with original math insights about the nature of decimals by using the "'hood" as a mental model and by relating the properties of decimals to physical locations, and the increasing size of decimals to going uptown.

In another example, students learned to solve word problems by communicating with a space creature that had crash-landed inside their computer and could not get out. The creature sent a signal to the students that it was lonesome and requested a story. The students wrote stories for the creature to read to keep it company. The stories, which were constructed with helpful prompts from the computer, turned out to be math word problems. Artificial intelligence techniques provided the creature with the ability to understand the students' language and to respond mathematically to the stories. By seeing and analyzing the math solutions that the creature provided in response to their stories, the students constructed and internalized a sense of the link between language and mathematics.

Although most of the units used the computer to establish the fantasy settings, one of the units—the one on how to multiply signed numbers—did not. On the surface this seems like an easy concept to teach: a negative number times a negative number is a positive number. Simple, right? Not really. Why does multiplying a negative number by a positive number result in a positive number? I defy you to come up with an explanation that makes sense to students. It is pretty easy for students to see why -5 plus -5 is -10; i.e., if you owe \$5 and then borrow an additional $5, you owe $10. So the rule for adding signed numbers is fairly intuitive. But why does −5 times −5 result in +25?

Following is the Outrageous lesson I designed to enable students to infer the rules for multiplying signed numbers on their own. The lesson is presented as though you, the reader, were teaching the lesson.

Note: This Outrageous lesson assumes that the students have first learned the rules for adding signed numbers.

The Lesson

When the students walk into the class, they see either a number line written along the complete length of the blackboard, or a banner of a number line hung along the front of the room. The center of the line is labeled *0*. Units are marked off with tick marks on each side of the *0*, spaced as far apart as about the distance of a small step, that is, one to two feet. There is a plus sign at the left end of the number line (as you face it), and a minus sign at the right end.

On the left wall of the room there is a big plus sign. On the opposite side wall there is a big minus sign.

If you were teaching this lesson, here is what you would do:

When the students enter they sit down and the lesson starts conventionally. You announce, The objective of the lesson today is that we will continue to study signed numbers. Please open your books to page [fill in the blank].

Of course the students respond lethargically. Once everyone has opened their book, however, you suddenly announce:

Uh oh!

The students wonder what is going on. You stand up and say:

I have an uncontrollable urge to dance.

With that, you twirl around the room, waving your arms. After a few moments of this, you stop in front of the *0*. Breathing hard, you say:

That was fun. Sorry, but at times something comes over me and I just have to dance. Look, I am right by the number 0. Given what 0 usually means, what can that number indicate in terms of dance?

The students give a variety of answers, such as "a starting point," "an ending point," "a resting point," that is, "no motion," and so on.

> *Good! Being here next to 0, which is my favorite number, I simply want to dance. I tell you what: If you promise not to tell the principal or your parents, we will forget about math today and just dance. Okay?*

Of course the students agree.

> *You may not know this but I am a professional choreographer. Who knows what a choreographer is?*

After the students respond, you ask:

> *Who here thinks they are pretty good at learning new dances?*

You ask the six to eight students who are the most confident about their dancing prowess to come up to the front of the room and pair them up into teams of two each. Clear some space for the dancers. Then say abruptly:

> *Assume the position.*

When they look confused you say:

> *No, that does not mean that you are under arrest, just that I want you and your partner to line up a certain way. One of you should stand right behind your partner across from the zero mark, and everyone else should face this side of the room. Let's call this the zero position.*

You have all of the dancers face the wall of the room that has the plus sign on it. Then you say to the rest of the class:

> *Ladies and gentlemen, you are indeed fortunate today. You have the wonderful opportunity to watch these terrific dancers dance to some of the hottest music of the day. Let's see which team is the best.*

You have the two-person teams line up so that one team member stands behind his or her partner, with each person facing in the same direction, parallel to the number line. Team A should be next to Team B, and so on, so that all of the teams are lined up across from the zero, with each team, and

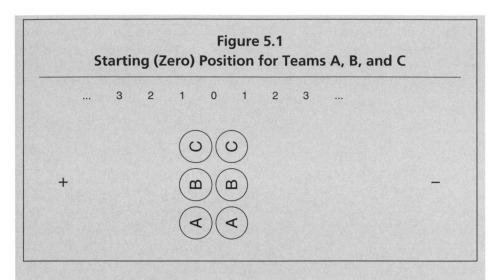

Figure 5.1
Starting (Zero) Position for Teams A, B, and C

team member, facing in the same direction, parallel to the number line, that is, facing the wall that has the plus sign on it. (See Figure 5.1 for a bird's-eye view of three teams in the zero position.)

Now for some hot music!

You put on some old-fashioned music, such as Guy Lombardo or Lawrence Welk, and when the students start to groan you say:

Sorry, wrong music.

Then you put on some contemporary music that you know the students will like, and say:

Let's see some of your best moves.

You wait for a minute or two and then say:

Pretty good. Now I am going to teach you a new dance for this music. You may have heard of the moon walk. The new dance I'm going to teach you is called the Jupiter walk. It's a much more fun dance. You will be the first in the school and the whole neighborhood to know this dance that will soon be sweeping the nation.

The Jupiter walk is done by taking small steps. Dancers, assume the zero position.

You wait until all the teams are correctly lined up as before, that is, until each team stands next to another team, across from the zero, with everyone facing the same way (that is, facing the side wall with the plus sign on it as shown in Figure 5.1), with one member of each team standing behind the other member. You then give them the following dance directions *quickly!*

It is critical to speak fast so that you confuse the students. The directions are purposely confusing and meant to cause the students to wander around bumping into each other rather than actually learning the steps of the dance. (The reason for this will become apparent later in the lesson.)

> *Here are the steps. Everyone face the side of the room, then take two sets of three steps backwards, then take four sets of three steps forward, then turn around and take three sets of five steps forward, then take three sets of three steps backwards. At this point, you simply repeat the entire process—here we go!*

You then turn on the music. When the students do not know what to do, stop the music and innocently ask:

> *What's the problem?*

The students complain that the instructions are too complicated. You act perturbed and say to the dancers:

> *OK, I will explain it again. I know you are good dancers, so get ready to dance. Listen carefully.*

You repeat the cycle, that is, you explain the steps quickly, then turn on the music. The students continue either to stand around confused or to bump into each other. Then you say:

> *OK, I know a way to make the dance easier to learn.*

You take out the following poster:

Jupiter Walk

Move	Direction to Face	# Sets of of Steps	Direction to Step	# Steps per Set
First	−	2	−	3
Second	−	4	+	3
Third	+	3	+	5
Fourth	+	3	−	3

You point to the number line and say:

I have converted the directions for the steps into numbers and signs to make them easier to learn. You can use this chart and the number line to help you.

Point to the chart and say:

The first sign tells you which direction to face at the start of the move. Dancers, turn around and face the negative direction of the number line as indicated by the minus sign on the side of the room. The first number tells you how many sets of steps you are going to take. The second sign tells you whether to walk backward or forward. The second number tells you how many steps are in each set of steps.

Dancers, get ready to do the first move. You must stay with your partner and continue to face in the same direction. Remember to stay on your own toes, not your partner's, and just do the first move.

(See Figure 5.2 for a view of three teams at the start of the first move.)
You instruct the students to begin. They start by turning to face the side of the room with the minus sign and take six steps backward. After they do the first move, which takes them to six on the plus side of the room, you stop them and ask:

Wait a minute, if you are taking two sets of three steps, how many steps are you taking all together, and how did you figure that out?

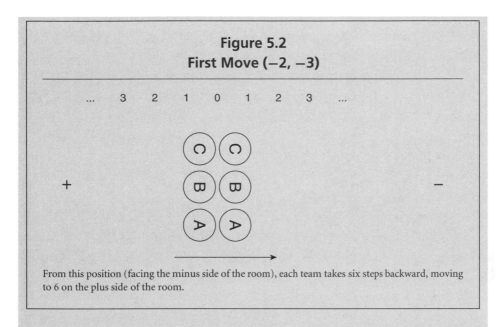

Figure 5.2
First Move (−2, −3)

... 3 2 1 0 1 2 3 ...

+ −

From this position (facing the minus side of the room), each team takes six steps backward, moving to 6 on the plus side of the room.

The students respond with "Six" and "by multiplication." You compliment them, then say:

> *Sorry for that little bit of math. Let's get back to dancing. Now that you know how to figure out by multiplication how many steps to take in each move, make each step about the size of the units on the number line. All right, go back to the zero position and let's try again.*

After the teams position themselves, again at the zero position, have them repeat the first move. After they complete the first move you say:

> *Dancers, now do the second move.*

(See Figure 5.3 for a view of three teams at the start of the second move and a description of how to carry out the second move.)

There may still be some confusion. If so, you have the dancers slowly repeat the first move, and then the second move. Then you have them add on the third and fourth moves in a similar manner. They move in the following manner:

Move 2: −4, +3. The students face the minus side of the room and do four sets of three steps forward.

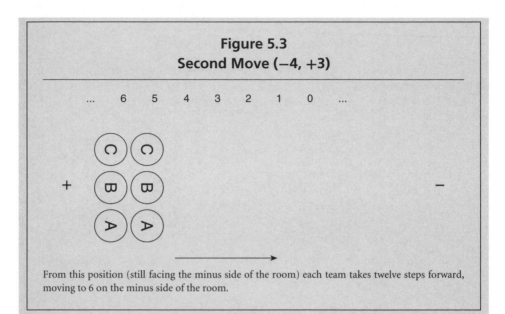

Figure 5.3
Second Move (−4, +3)

... 6 5 4 3 2 1 0 ...

+   −

From this position (still facing the minus side of the room) each team takes twelve steps forward, moving to 6 on the minus side of the room.

Move 3: +3, +5. The students turn and face the plus side of the room and do three sets of five steps forward. (See Figure 5.4 for their position at the start of the third move and a description of how to carry out the third move.)

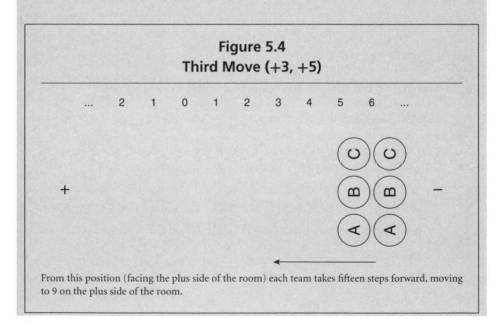

Figure 5.4
Third Move (+3, +5)

... 2 1 0 1 2 3 4 5 6 ...

+   −

From this position (facing the plus side of the room) each team takes fifteen steps forward, moving to 9 on the plus side of the room.

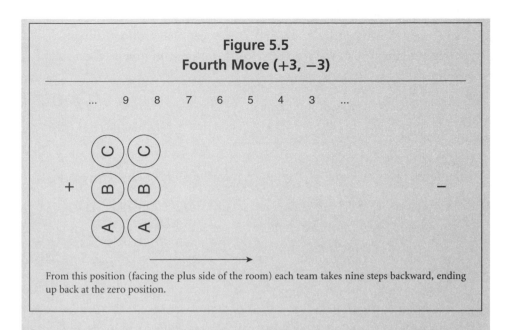

Figure 5.5
Fourth Move (+3, −3)

... 9 8 7 6 5 4 3 ...

From this position (facing the plus side of the room) each team takes nine steps backward, ending up back at the zero position.

Move 4: +3, −3. The students face the plus side of the room and do three sets of three steps backward. (See Figure 5.5 for their position at the start of the fourth move and a description of how to carry out the fourth move.)

When the students have successfully completed all four moves, you turn on the music and say:

> *Let's try to do all four moves to the music, staying together with your partner. I will call out the moves for you. Try to move to the beat of the music. Remember to take steps that are the same size as the units on the number line.*

You turn on the music and call out the four moves in turn at a reasonable pace. The students end up close to the zero position. There is still some bumping, tripping, and moving apart of partners, but there is also a team that does it reasonably well. You then say to the class:

> *Now you get to judge the best pair.*

You turn the music back on and try to get the group through a few repetitions of the dance, and if possible you get more volunteers. Then you say:

> *Let's give all our dancers a big hand.*
>   *Well, that's enough fun for today. We have some time left, so let's do some math. We know that −2 plus −3 is −5. How much is −2 times −3?*

Some students may say −6. However, regardless of the answer, you say:

> *I am not sure if that answer is correct. Have we done anything else in today's class that involved multiplying signed numbers?*

The students realize that they just did it when they were dancing. Then you say:

> *Can you use the dance to come up with the answer for multiplying −2 by −3? Feel free to get up and dance. When you think you can demonstrate the answer, call me over and tell me what your reasoning is.*

Solution: The students should realize that starting from 0 and performing the dance step, they will end up at 6 on the plus side of the room, that is, the number line. Therefore the answer to −2 x −3 is +6.

> *What general principle did you just discover for multiplying signed numbers?*

The students realize that the general form of what they discovered was that a negative number times a negative number is a positive. You then ask:

> *Do you think you will always get a positive from multiplying a negative by a negative? Why?*

Yes. Using the dance idea, the first negative sign means you will be facing the negative direction of the line. The second negative sign means you will be moving backward, so you will always arrive at a positive number when starting from 0 on the number line.

> *What other rules will we have to figure out to know how to do any multiplication problem with signed numbers?*

The students should realize that they need a rule for multiplying a negative number by a positive number, a positive number by a negative number, and a positive number by a positive number. You assign different groups to study each of these three types of multiplication problems. Then you say:

I will now give each team five minutes to use dancing rules to figure out the rule for their type of problem, and be ready to prove it.

After five minutes, you have the teams studying the same problem see whether they have reached the same conclusion, and then you call on a team spokesperson to demonstrate that conclusion through dancing. Then you say:

Take a few moments to write down these rules in your notebooks. I hope you had fun today. This was much better than math—right?

The students will ultimately note that what they did was math.

I guess you are right. I guess you learned how to relate dance moves to mathematics, or mathematics to dance moves.

You then ask:

What was the advantage of using numbers that made it easier than the directions I first gave you to understand my brilliant choreography?

The students should respond by saying something like, "With numbers and signs we had to process less information."

You conclude, *if you dare*, by saying:

Numbers are indeed very efficient ways to communicate a wide variety of information. I am sure you know the expression: A number is worth a thousand words. I call using numbers to give dance directions "Math Choreography." Indeed, you may have heard of line dancing in country and western music. Now do you know why it is called line dancing? It was obviously developed by cowboys or cowgirls who were mathematicians and who loved number lines.

Compliment the students on how they used dance to discover math rules, and for figuring out how to follow "math choreography."

Postscript

I first presented this lesson's approach to a former president of the National Council of Teachers of Mathematics, a mathematician who had written a leading school math text. I was sure he would think this approach was silly. To my pleasant surprise, he indicated that it was the best way he had ever seen to present the extremely difficult idea of multiplying signed numbers. Cool!

The lesson I learned from him was that it is OK to be bold and have fun with numbers and mathematical principles. Indeed, most mathematicians enjoy being playful with numbers and creating games based on mathematical principles.

Conversely, when I show this lesson to math educators, that is, those who train math teachers, the response is more mixed. The humor is often lost on them, and they do not like the notion of the teacher suggesting that they take a day off from math. To these people my advice is, *Lighten up!* Our job is not simply to present information but to get students to reflect mathematically. The only important issue is how students react to the approach. They are much more likely to become interested in the math concepts and to learn them deeply through this humor-fantasy approach than through any technique currently being taught to teachers. Using a Creatively Authentic approach in pre-algebra is better than authentic teaching in almost all cases.

Does this lesson work? The first time I watched a teacher do this lesson in an average class in an inner-city school setting, it worked like a charm. Indeed, the students got so intrigued that they extended the idea of math choreography into an original, more involved class line dance that they performed at a school assembly.

In any event, this lesson demonstrates to students the value of using numbers to convey information concisely and efficiently. It also demonstrates how a dramatic scenario can be used to enable students to infer complex mathematical principles.

STAN'S LESSON 2 (MATH, GRADES 4 TO 5)

One of the curriculum development techniques I use to make mathematics Creatively Authentic to most students is to make up historical stories about the concepts—in this case, the origin of fractions. Although some math purists will reasonably object to the use of this technique, the reality is that the real mathematical origins of fractions is way too complicated for most students to comprehend. At the same time, creating stories about mathematical concepts is a great way to get them interested in and curious about the properties of those concepts. Following is a successful lesson I developed to introduce the concept of what a fraction is and how it evolved.

The Lesson

As the students arrive, an adult other than the teacher has them line up outside the room. After everyone has arrived, the students are then led into a darkened room. Some form of drum music, or other music that conjures up a jungle scene, is playing. A large poster or two of a jungle scene are posted in the room. There is also a poster of a mastodon or some other large, exotic-looking animal. A two-foot by three-foot (or larger) box on the floor holds enough sand to allow sand drawings to be visible. (If a sandbox is unavailable, you can use a large sheet of black construction paper to simulate the floor of a cave and white chalk to make scratch marks on it.) The windows are covered with black paper and the teacher's desk is in the far corner of the room.

As the students walk in, the teacher is sitting or lying on the floor. The floor around the teacher is clear. The teacher is wearing a headdress or has some feathers in his or her hair. (A grass skirt would also be nice.) The teacher's hair is superunkempt; a messed-up wig works, and for a man, facial hair is appropriate. Once the students are settled, the teacher says:

> Welcome to my cave in the jungle in prehistoric times. You are safe here. If you go outside, however, you have to be very careful. There is danger everywhere. Although there are no drug dealers or bullies, what do you have to worry about when you go outside this cave?

The students speculate about getting eaten by a wild animal, being attacked by another tribe, and so on. Then the teacher asks:

> What do you think you would eat for lunch—hamburgers and fries?

The students suggest nuts, grains, meat, and so on. Then the teacher says:

> Boy, thinking of this delicious food is making me hungry. Yesterday the tribal hunting party killed a huge mastodon. I happen to love steak. Here's some fresh mastodon steak and nuts.

The teacher pulls out a large piece of brown clay or a large piece of liver (I prefer the latter) or some other raw meat and plunks it onto the floor. As the students get grossed out, the teacher says, "Yummy!" The teacher then brings out a bag of peanuts. Then the teacher points around the room and says:

> *Our tribe is in trouble. This is all we have to eat for lunch and dinner, and I am very hungry.*

The teacher assigns someone to be the wise Chief Bumba and invites that student to sit next to him or her. The teacher then gives that student an ID card (a piece of cardboard on a string that the student can put on, with the name Chief Bumba on it). Then the teacher says:

> *As the wise chief, you are in charge of sharing. This is all the food there is to eat in the cave. How do you think others will react if you do not give the same amount of food to everyone wise chief—and why?*

Chief Bumba responds that they will get angry because that doesn't seem fair.

The teacher then assigns five other students to be members of the hunting party and gives them the following identity cards to wear: Mongo, Grok, Tobo, Shuma, Denna. The teacher has them sit in front of Chief Bumba.

> *As you know, the tribal hunting party that killed the mastodon gets to come first to the chief for their fair share of food.*

The teacher has the students wearing the ID tags come to the chief, then turns to the character named Mongo and says:

> *Mongo, I want you to pretend that you don't think you and the rest of the hunting party have gotten enough food and you want to know why you haven't gotten more—although you do trust your wise chief and don't believe in violence.*

As Mongo starts to say something, the teacher interrupts and says:

> *Oh, I forgot one detail. Language has not yet been invented. Because I am from the future, I am the only one allowed to talk. OK, Mongo, go ahead and try to find out why you got only so much of the delicious steak.*

After the student gestures appropriately, the teacher says:

> *Now, wise chief, Mongo looks very unhappy. Explain how you have decided how much of the food Mongo and the other hunters should get in relation to the other ?? members of the tribe [?? is the number of students remaining in the class].*

The teacher points to the box of sand, gives the chief a stick, and then says:

> *All you have is this stick and the floor of the cave that is represented by this box of sand. I would encourage the rest of you to watch the wise chief closely, because the rest of you are also hungry and don't want Mongo and the other five hunters to get all the food.*

The teacher does not let the chief say any words. The chief can use fingers, make marks in the sand with the stick, and so on. If the chief starts to write numbers in the sand, the teacher tells him or her:

> *By the way, numbers haven't been invented yet.*

If the chief is stumped about how to proceed, ask others to help. Alternatively, the teacher lets the students brainstorm in groups for about five minutes, then has them share solutions to the problem. If the teacher gets lucky, the students will come up with a suggestion that involves making two sets of marks, one that represents all the members of the tribe, and another that represents all the members of the hunting party. Then the teacher says:

> *You have just discovered how and why some early tribes began to develop ways of representing parts of things. They discovered that in order to share things fairly, they needed to make two sets of marks. As people got tired of making long rows of marks, other ways of representing parts of things were tried, but none of these methods were very convenient until some special numbers were developed. What is the advantage of numbers over scratch marks on the floor of our cave?*

The students realize that numbers are easier to write. Then the teacher says:

> *Numbers are much better, especially if you have a big tribe. What is the advantage of writing numbers over writing words?*

It is much easier and shorter. Then the teacher says:

> *In the future your descendants will continue the tradition you started of making two sets of marks to represent parts of things, and as you predicted, they will switch to numbers once they are invented. In addition, they will write the numbers one on top of the other, and they will use it for more than just sharing food. They will call it—*

The teacher puts a puzzled look on his or her face and says:

> *I cannot quite remember what it is called. Does anyone know?*

Fractions.

> *That's right. Luckily, because I am from the future, I can teach you how to work with fractions now. Aren't you lucky? We will be learning about how to use fractions over the next several days.*

Then the teacher gives out peanuts or another treat to the members of the tribe, that is, the class members, and tells the students:

> *This has been a good day for our tribe.*

Comments on Stan's Lesson 2

This lesson is different from the previous math lesson in that no specific math procedures are taught or inferred by the students. Little mathematical reasoning is involved. Rather, this lesson implants the importance of fractions by making fractions Creatively Authentic through appealing to students' concern for fairness. On the surface this linkage between fractions and a sense of fairness may not seem like a big deal—but it is. It can make all the difference between students engaging in subsequent lessons about fractions. Indeed, I suspect the reason girls start turning off to mathematics at these grade levels is because they are more mature and understand that the reasons teachers give for why math works as it does makes no sense as far as they can tell. Indeed, Seymous Papert (1980) has noted that you do not do anything interesting in math until you reach calculus, because then you can describe motion. Of course we have to get students interested long before then, and maintain their interest. Hence the importance of a lesson such as this.

This is more than just a hokey lesson, however. The teacher can now build on the construct of fairness throughout the remainder of the unit. So, for example, instead of the typical textbook example "Are 5/10 and 10/20 equivalent?" the teacher can paraphrase the problem as follows:

John is given five of the ten slices of a pizza, and Maria is given ten of the twenty slices of a different pizza of the same size. Is that division fair for both?

Instead of merely asking which fraction is larger, 5/10 or 4/9, the teacher can ask,

> If John is given five of the ten slices of pizza and Maria is given four of the nine slices of a different pizza of the same size, is that fair for both people? If not, who is getting cheated?

Students will quickly realize the need for a procedure to answer these questions, and the teacher can then show them the "trick," that is, the mathematical procedure, to tell who is being cheated.

In other words, once a Creatively Authentic approach is developed, it can enrich the subsequent conventional teaching of the remainder of the unit. All the teacher needs to do is change the wording of the textbook examples.

COMPARISON OF THE LESSONS

The Outrageous lessons presented in this chapter represent a broad range of ideas spread across subjects and grade levels. They encompass a wide gamut of creative scenarios that can be used as models for lessons that you create. In most of the lessons, the teacher remains himself or herself but undergoes a surprising transition, such as going mad, reacting strangely to an imaginary bug bite, being suddenly moved to start dancing, being stalked, and so on. In other lessons the teacher is disguised as a visitor to the class, for example, as a beat poet, as someone from the past, as a persuasive salesman, and so on.

The scenarios and learning objectives covered in the lessons are summarized in Table 5.1.

Table 5.1
Learning Objectives and Scenarios for the Sample Lessons

Teacher	Level	Content Area	Learning Objective	Scenario
Julie	Middle school	Writing	To learn the elements of expressive writing	Teacher and class are bitten by a "bug" whose bite causes unusual, extreme behavioral swings.
Dwight	High school	Writing	To learn the definition of persuasive writing and begin writing a persuasive essay	Visitor is a pitchman who is trying to recruit master salespeople for a special product line of wood stumps.
Tamarra	High school	Social studies	To learn the history of early efforts to unionize coal miners	Sad visitor is a weary, sick, exploited worker who has appeared from the past to ask for help because no one in her present will help her.
Shirley	High school seniors	Literature	To learn why and how authors create mood in stories	Teacher is being stalked and is hiding under the table, thereby creating a mood that sets a different tone for her interaction with the class and creates a context that mirrors the mood of foreboding in the story being read.
Viera	Middle school	Literature	To get students to read and comprehend Edgar Allen Poe's "The Tell-tale Heart"	The teach creates a context related to the story being read and provides a reason to read the story by pretending to have escaped from a mental institution and asking the students to try and figure out why she is hearing noises in the floor and wall.
Jose	High school	Spanish	To learn thirty-four verbs and nouns related to ordering in a restaurant	Teacher is a bumbling waiter who takes the students' orders in Spanish.

(continued)

Table 5.1
(*Continued*)

Teacher	Level	Content Area	Learning Objective	Scenario
Serena	High school	Poetry	To learn how to appreciate poetry and read it expressively	A beat poet is starting a coffee shop in the school and students are invited to the grand opening.
John	Middle school	Science	To learn about the design of the first successful flying machine and the basic principles of flight	Strange visitor is a failed inventor who is always crashing and who, after his last crash, is somehow transported to a classroom of the future, where there is secret, magical science information.
Stan	Middle and high school	Math 1	To infer and understand the rules of multiplying with signed numbers	Teacher is a choreographer with an irrepressible urge to dance and to teach new dances.
Stan	Grades 4 to 5	Math 2	To learn about the importance and structure of fractions	Chief Bumba needs to divide a mastodon steak equally among members of the tribe.

In most cases, the disguises need not be overly elaborate. All that is needed is something to partially cover the face, an accent, and some clothes. The costume can be as simple as combining a painted goatee, beret, and sunglasses, or a bushy white cotton beard and overalls. Costuming the character can also be as simple as wearing a white shirt, bow tie, and dark jacket. It can get more elaborate, like the example of the escaped mental patient.

For men, facial hair is a very effective disguise, as is a wide-brimmed hat, and so on. For women, sunglasses, a wide-brimmed hat, or a change of hairstyle combined with different makeup is effective. However, less done well is better than lots of stuff.

The setting can be as simple as the regular classroom, or as complicated as a simulated coffee shop. Finally, the props most commonly used in these lessons were music and lights.

Table 5.2 describes the props and media, the characters, and the disguises used in each lesson. In six of the ten lessons, the teacher took on the role of a different character. In the other four lessons, the teachers remained themselves

Table 5.2
Props and Media, Character, and Disguises Used in the Sample Lessons

Teacher	Content Area	Props and Media	Character	Disguise
Julie	Writing	None	Teacher as herself	None
Dwight	Writing	Large bag containing a series of common objects, large tree stump	Super salesman	Old-fashioned stovepipe hat, large and long bushy white cotton beard, coveralls
Tamarra	Social studies	Blues music, turning lights on and off, one lamp used as a spotlight	Sick, dispirited coal-mine worker	Tattered blouse, hair askew, smudge marks on her face
Shirley	Literature	None	Teacher as herself	Long raincoat with hood, sunglasses
Viera	Literature	None	Teacher as herself	Hospital cap and blouse, straitjacket
Jose	Spanish	Overhead projector with list of new words used	Bumbling waiter	Black bowtie, white shirt, black jacket, small towel
Serena	Poetry	Text of about twenty poems, coffee essence, candles, quiet mood music, swaths of cloth to hand out, signs with the name of the coffee shop and slogan, sign that says "1959" and another that says "Greenwich Village, New York City," dark juice to simulate coffee, cups	Beat poet	Beret, sunglasses, painted goatee, Nehru-like jacket from a thrift store would also be cool

(continued)

Table 5.2
(*Continued*)

Teacher	Content Area	Props and Media	Character	Disguise
John	Science	Several pieces of metal to clang together to make sounds outside the classroom door, something to make a boom or crash sound, long piece of cloth or paper attached to a balsa wood frame to simulate a wing frame that can be lifted above one's head	Failed inventor	Goggles, old flyer hat, smudges of black on face
Stan	Math 1	Two CDs or other music source with old-fashioned "boring" music on one and contemporary music on another, large + and − signs to tape to the walls, and possibly a number-line banner	Teacher as herself	Perhaps ballet slippers
Stan	Math 2	Several posters of a jungle and another of a mastodon, jungle music, sand box with a stick	Teacher as visitor from the future in a prehistoric cave	Lots of unkempt hair, long fingernails, feathers in the hair, primitive-looking clothes

and a new persona or different behaviors emerged. These included almost dual-personality type shifts in behavior, from narcolepsy to hyperactivity; fear of a stalker; mental breakdown behavior; and singing and dancing around the room. My two favorites in this category are Julie's and Shirley's lessons—Julie's because she suckered me into believing she was doing a normal lesson, and the different behaviors did not emerge for five to ten minutes into the lesson; Shirley's because I could not figure out what was going on and why students in the most difficult class I ever observed were acting like angels and reading out loud without hesitation. The latter group is probably the only class in the history of education that was ever taught from underneath the teacher's desk.

Finally, it should be noted how simple the lessons look on paper. (See Exhibit 5.1 and Appendix D.) In other words, you do not need to write elaborate scripts in Dramatized Content lesson plans. Clearly the key is how you execute the details that you have thought up. The actual script is in your mind, as it is for any lesson. Once you have the basic ideas on paper, the specific words you say to students come naturally.

SUMMARY

I hope you enjoyed these sample Outrageous lessons. They represent a wellspring of diverse creative ideas applied to a wide range of content areas, traditional learning objectives, and age groups. Keep in mind that they were developed not by professional playwrights but by relatively inexperienced teachers. Except for the lessons I developed, the content objectives chosen and the basic storylines came from the teachers, all using the Dramatized Content Planning Method. If they could do it, you can do it. If the techniques worked with the lowest-performing and most jaded high school seniors, they can certainly work with highly impressionable younger students.

chapter SIX

Suspense and Surprise: Why Outrageous Lessons Work

Although each lesson presented in the previous chapters represents a separate and unique instructional act, each of which differs from the others in a wide variety of ways, there are also some commonalities, in terms of both the nature of the lessons and their impact on students. This chapter goes from the specific examples of the lessons to their broader, general implications.

The main message that can be drawn from the sample Outrageous lessons is that even a single lesson can produce substantial increases in content learning, and this can occur across the curriculum and grade levels. Such gains happen because the laws of student-teacher interaction that operate during Outrageous lessons are very different from those that occur during conventional instruction.

THE PHYSICS OF OUTRAGEOUS LESSONS

The physical world seems to operate under two separate sets of rules. One set operates for large objects, such as planets and the universe itself, and for large distances. A different set of rules, called quantum physics, operates for the infinitely small subatomic particles and for tiny distances. Modern physics has not yet been able to reconcile these two sets of rules. The hunt for the universal theory that can unite them continues. In the meantime, both of these almost opposite sets of rules are accepted as valid and are taught side by side.

The world of education needs to do the same. Two sets of rules govern student-teacher interactions. One set governs what happens during conventional lessons, the other set governs teacher-student relationships and conditions for producing learning in Outrageous lessons.

Of course accepting diametrically opposed sets of rules as equally valid and important is difficult. Even Einstein could not accept the laws of quantum physics, because they were so different from the laws he had developed for large masses and distances, and they seemed so counterintuitive and random.

What are the laws that govern student-teacher interactions during Outrageous lessons and how do they differ from the laws that govern conventional instruction?

THE NEW LAWS OF TEACHER-STUDENT INTERACTION

All of the sample lessons in the prior chapters showcased excellent teaching and teacher creativity—and the students responded. All of the Outrageous lessons produced success in terms of student interest, attention, and learning, far beyond the teachers' expectations.

The sample lessons demonstrate the powerful effects of the use of Outrageous Teaching. Much like a powerful magnetic field can change the properties of even the hardest steel, the special properties and techniques of Outrageous lessons produce major dividends in terms of both students' learning and their interest—even in lessons taught by inexperienced teachers. The lessons completely changed the classroom rules of engagement between teacher and students, and among the students. The lessons made new and unexpected forms of deep learning possible, along with new teacher-student relationships. Once the students were captivated, all things became possible. Passivity became participation, unruliness became cooperation, and disinterest became curiosity.

MAINTAINING DISCIPLINE

All of the rules on how to maintain discipline reversed polarity during Outrageous content lessons. The rules for how to maintain discipline during conventional lessons no longer applied. In all cases, there was far better discipline during the Outrageous lessons, along with far superior class management, than when the same teachers taught conventional lessons. What were the new discipline management enhancement techniques used during the Outrageous lessons? The teachers put their heads on the desk and did not look at the students for extended periods, they left the class, they talked to themselves, they hid in the room, and they ran and danced around the room. Clearly, in a conventional lesson such teacher behavior would have caused all hell to break loose. Indeed, in all cases the teachers feared they would lose control of the class during their Outrageous lesson. Although such fears were understandable given the general unruliness of the classes involved, they not only turned out to be unfounded, but the techniques resulted in substantially better student behavior and cooperation.

Creating high levels of student curiosity and interest is the best way to improve student behavior.

Increasing the Efficiency of Learning

The sample lessons were not only effective in increasing student interest; they were also highly efficient in teaching the content objectives. *This is completely counterintuitive.* How is it possible that Outrageous lessons could increase the efficiency of the teaching and learning process given the significant class time spent setting up the dramatic context? It turns out that the time lost to setting up the dramatic context was more than made up for by the reduced amount of time needed to maintain discipline, organize activity transitions, and get students' attention. In the lessons I saw, teachers saved as much as 25 percent of the total class time by not having to deal with mundane classroom management problems, student whining, and so on. There was no need to admonish students or urge them to pay attention, face forward, stop talking, and so on. And yes, requests for bathroom passes were virtually nil during such lessons. (Perhaps Outrageous Teaching represses kidney function.)

So, instead of being able to organize only one to two transitions per period in conventional instruction, many of the Outrageous lessons had seamless multiple transitions, from listening to the teacher to reading to writing to then reflecting.

In effect, students learned the content more quickly. What might otherwise take most of a period to absorb, and only after repeated urgings, threats, repetitions, and multiple examples, were incorporated and applied in a matter of minutes. Students, even low-performing ones, quickly delved into the assigned tasks and performed at high levels. It is easy to talk about high expectations, but it is hard to get students, particularly at-risk students, to actually perform at high levels. In the observed lessons, not only were the degrees and levels of learning by at-risk students impressive but in many cases they performed at the highest levels and exerted leadership in group tasks.

Increasing the Depth and Retention of Students' Learning

Students learned more deeply and were more likely to retain material learned in Outrageous lessons. Whenever teachers did a comparison, teaching the same content to one class Outrageously and to another conventionally, the students taught Outrageously did better at the end of the unit, even though dramatic technique was usually used in just the opening lesson of the unit.

Although Outrageous Teaching benefited all of the students, the impact was particularly noticeable for the low-performing, reluctant learners. The Outrageous lessons enabled new students to emerge as the stars of the class.

Although such findings are anecdotal at this point, they are promising and warrant further research.

Why Learning Increased Students found ways and motivation to harness innate talent to learn what would otherwise have been obscure, difficult material. Observing a low-performing class talking eloquently about the alliances leading up to World War I (see Chapter Seven) and analyzing why and how they came about, and hearing low-performing students discuss Edgar Allen Poe were inspirational moments to me as an educator. Alas, these small successes also mean that *in the typical lesson and classroom we are tapping only a small fraction of the intellectual talent and potential of students, especially in high-poverty classrooms.* Seeing teachers tap into that potential brought home how far we have to go, and how far we can go, to improve education and reduce the learning gap.

A Single Outrageous Lesson Can Produce Substantial Learning

Heathcote felt that producing significant learning through the use of drama required a sequence of lessons or a unit (Heathcote and Bolton, 1995). The sample Outrageous lessons presented in this book demonstrate that it is indeed possible to produce powerful learning outcomes from a single lesson—outcomes that show up on classroom assessments at the end of a unit. This is a testimony to the efficiency of the Dramatized Content Planning Method.

Going Beyond Engaging Students to Producing Content Learning

There are times when engagement is a valuable end in and of itself, e.g., building school spirit, self-concept, etc. However, in most cases, engaging students is not the end but rather the means to the end of increasing learning and the appreciation of learning.

It is easy to engage students. Use computers, show a video, throw a party, act goofy, and so on. Indeed, teachers working with "difficult" classes will often settle for simple engagement. However, engagement does not automatically produce learning. The reality is that while it is hard to improve the performance of reluctant learners without engagement, it is also hard to convert such engagement into actual learning.

For example, although it is clear that computers engage students, it is hard to find evidence that computer use has increased learning. HOTS is one of the few examples where the use of computers produced substantially greater academic growth than conventional approaches. It did so by combining computer use with creative curriculum elements and teaching strategies in a highly systematic way guided by theories of cognition. The resultant learning environment converted the use of computers into sophisticated Socratic learning.

Similarly, much of what I read in terms of ideas for using drama seems to focus on engaging students and being playful without concern for producing specific content learning. Sometimes that lack of concern is deliberate because of philosophic predisposition, and other times it seems to underestimate what it takes to in fact convert engagement into content learning. Indeed, probably 70 percent of the mental energy involved in developing an Outrageous lesson is spent on learning how to use the Dramatized Content Planning Method to design a way to build the initial engaging surprise into a comprehensive storyline that is capable of producing content learning.

A strategy teachers often use to engage students is to create new add-on units that build on students' interests. So, for example, a teacher may present a unit on dinosaurs instead of an existing unit on grammar. However, why not take this engagement idea a step further. The philosophy of Outrageous lessons and units would suggest developing a dinosaur-based approach to teaching grammar, or dinosaur grammar, so as to use an engaging context as an opportunity to teach existing content objectives more effectively. One strategy would be to give students an obviously incorrectly written description of different dinosaurs, and if they can correct the description they get pictures of the dinosaurs, or, or … Indeed, as you will see in the next chapter, one teacher, the Pig Lady, figured out how to use a different context that she knew would be of interest to her special education students to incorporate a year's worth of existing content objectives.

Building Rapport with the Students

Outrageous lessons deepen the student-teacher bond. In addition to providing teachers with new insights into the latent talent of their students, Outrageous lessons nurture in the students a newfound respect for the teacher. Whenever I or the teacher subsequently asked students what they thought about an Outrageous experience, the students generally responded that the lesson showed that "our teacher really cares about us" or that "our teacher is willing to go the extra mile to help us."

Teachers are then able to build on this new relationship and deeply shared experience on an ongoing basis. From that point on, whenever a student did something notable in her class, Serena, who did the lesson on poetry, would simply snap her fingers in appreciation and everyone would know what that meant. If her students got too noisy or inattentive, Viera, who acted as an escapee from a mental institution, could always clasp her hands to her head, shake it, and say, "there is so much noise in this room that I am starting to go crazy again. I am hearing things again." The students would then start shushing one another.

Expanding Teachers' Repertoires

Outrageous Teaching provided the teachers in the sample lessons with another tool for teaching content under conditions where conventional instruction was likely to fail or be painful for all concerned, and where other conceptions of best practice were likely to meet the same fate. In addition, in using the principles of Outrageous Teaching, the teachers were simultaneously engaging in other progressive practices such as discovery learning and constructivism, and students were also engaging in an expanded repertoire of classroom learning styles and behaviors, including self-expression and role-taking. These were not the end goals, however. The end goal was the learning of the content in an enriched and efficient way—and that goal was achieved.

The sample lessons also highlight the tremendous amount of untapped creative potential that lies within the typical teacher—if only she or he would put his or her mind to it. I feel fortunate to have witnessed these and many more examples of great teaching that reflected the idealized image we had of what our classrooms would be like when we decided to become teachers. Alas, this ideal fades as practical pressures intrude—but it does not have to. On those days when they taught Outrageous lessons, these teachers experienced that same idealized adrenaline rush, the joy of having their students in the palms of their hands, and the feeling that their every word and action was impacting their students. I wish others had the same opportunities to witness this type of teaching and its amazing effects on both students and teachers. Hopefully you will have such experiences in the near future.

Teaching Inside a Reshaped Box

Clearly, Outrageous lessons are very different from conventional lessons, and the examples presented in this book represent very high levels of creativity. However, these sample lessons represent not "teaching outside the box" but *teaching in a very different way inside the box—a way that is so powerful that it reshapes the dynamics of the box.*

It is indeed legal to teach this way! It is legal to incorporate humor, weirdness, and fantasy into the teaching of content—and for this generation of students it is probably essential.

CREATING A NEW PHYSICS OF STUDENT ACHIEVEMENT

For all of the above reasons, when you use intensive forms of dramatic technique systematically, even for only a short time, it changes what students are able to achieve. Vygotsky (1978) developed the notion of "the zone of proximal development." Although most instruction is geared to where students are thought to be developmentally, Vygotsky proved that when you gear instruction consistently above that level, students achieve at higher levels (even though they may lag initially). In other words, it is possible to create instructional circumstances in which students perform at levels higher than what would otherwise be expected. The same is true for intensive use of dramatic technique.

When I was developing the HOTS program, we always pushed the boundaries of what we thought was reasonable to expect Title I students to be able to achieve. Every time we started to develop a new unit we would ask ourselves whether we could actually get Title I students to accomplish this—and then we would hold our breaths. There were times when we tried things at which I was sure they could not succeed given their "limited" skill base. Yet they always succeeded. Indeed, we got them to succeed at tasks that highly educated adults initially fail at.

We were always questioned about the grade level to which the language was geared. I had no idea and still do not, and do not want to know. That is too limiting a concept. It is old physics. I do know that the students loved to learn to use big words, and the more the better.

One of the reviewers of this manuscript indicated that the lesson in Appendix E could not be used with second graders and that it was geared to a fourth grade level. Can it be used with second graders? I do not know. We will not know until someone tries it. My suspicion is that a good teacher could make it work at the second grade level. The skeptical reviewer was using the old physics laws of what students can be expected to achieve. He or she was using Euclidian geometry to describe the universe of achievement, and I was using the theory of relativity.

In other words, we generally have too limited a conception of what students are able to achieve, and we limit ourselves to what we can generally get them to do under conventional instruction. But why limit ourselves and our students this way? I would rather try the lesson in Appendix E with second graders and be wrong than assume from the beginning that it is geared for fourth graders. If I do not try, then we lose an opportunity to stretch the minds of second graders.

After working with the HOTS program for twenty-six years, I still do not know what the limit is to what we can get Title I and learning disabled students to achieve. We know what their learning problems are. For example, we know that they typically have trouble generalizing what they have learned beyond the immediate context. But this characteristic is not immutable. For example, after two years of HOTS, when a teachers asked her fifth and sixth grade Title I students, "How many ways are a hamburger and a roller coaster the same?" they came up with ninety-six valid answers. Who knew they could do that, that is, generalize at such a high level? What I have learned is that whenever they failed at something we gave them, it was because our approach was not imaginative and Creatively Authentic enough.

Simply stated, Outrageous Teaching enables all students to achieve at unexpectedly high levels. *The physics of student achievement is changed.*

UNIQUENESS OF THE DRAMATIZED CONTENT METHOD

The Dramatized Content Planning Method for designing Outrageous lessons differs from most other conceptions of the uses of dramatic technique in terms of its primary goal, which is to teach specific content objectives more effectively, especially to students who would otherwise have trouble learning the objective to their full potential. Like all other uses of dramatic technique, Outrageous Teaching seeks to fascinate and inspire students, but in this case it is in the pragmatic service of increasing the learning of specific content objectives. This dual mission of developing a bold, imaginative, and creative approach that will engage students and simultaneously serve a pragmatic leaning outcome affects how Outrageous lessons are organized, and the way in which they shape the learning environment.

Centrality of Storyline, Suspense, and Fantasy

In most uses of dramatic technique that focus on content, students know the content they will be working with and what their roles are. Conversely, the Outrageous approach relies on surprise and suspense to create a mood of expectation in the students. The students have no clue about what is happening, and they do not find out until the last five minutes of the lesson what the content objective of the activities was and what they actually learned. This is a counterintuitive way to teach content. It goes against all pedagogical instincts. *Look at all the time that is wasted in the opening segment of the lesson while the teacher is role-playing and establishing the storyline for the lesson.* But it is not wasted time. Rather, the suspense causes students to switch mood, to turn on their imagination and curiosity, which creates a mind-set of expectation and cognitive processing. Their defenses are down. Their teacher's incongruous behavior sets a mood that makes deep and efficient learning possible.

It is also counterintuitive that fantasy-based storyline can be used to teach real content. But that is the heart of Creative Authenticity: enabling the teacher to tap into students' own conceptions of reality and interests and to link the content to those instincts. The effectiveness of the sample lessons demonstrates the validity of the theoretical perspectives discussed in Chapter Two and the effectiveness of the Dramatized Content techniques. This effectiveness shows that using a storyline to link the learning of the content to an emotionally moving experience indeed deepens learning while also increasing interest—even though less time is spent "teaching" the content. An additional benefit of an Outrageous lesson is that there is no need either to enrich this learning experience or to remediate students because the lesson was learned richly from the beginning.

Although the Dramatized Content Planning Method does put extra responsibility on the teacher to create the storylines, it also provides many rewards in terms of experiencing new forms of expression and attitude on the part of their students as they unleash their imagination and creativity. In addition, five teachers in different schools could be teaching the same content objective using five different storylines, and all generate the same result. Instead of being on the same page as with scripted conventional instruction, they are on the same wavelength.

The Approach to Role-Playing

Clearly the use of general role-play is a long-established tradition, and it is a critical element of the Dramatized Content Planning Method. In an Outrageous lesson, however, role-play is generally employed differently than in the typical lesson or unit. As previously noted, most uses of role-play envision the students as playing out the roles, with the teacher organizing and supervising. In the Dramatized Content Planning Method, however, the teacher is the primary role-player. The teacher's role-playing sets the context for what the students do. Sometimes the students also role-play and sometimes they do not. Most often they role-take.

Student Role-Taking versus Role-Playing and Playing Although the students in the sample Outrageous lessons were not simply a passive audience, they also were not usually role-playing. The only lesson in which students role-played was Julie's, when they pretended to be stung by story bugs, and in Dwight's, when they pretended to be sales trainees. Rather, they were usually engaged in Heathcote's conception of role-*taking*. In this conception, as discussed in Chapter Three, students become responders, decision makers, experts, and sense makers. The students are individuals who have been placed in the position of trying to make sense of what is going on around them. They are travelers in a strange land. This uncertainty naturally causes them to behave differently and to engage in a different learning process. So, although they are still students, they have undertaken greater responsibility in order to help the teacher figure out something or solve his or her dilemma.

In several of the Outrageous lessons students took on the mantle of expert when they provided expert advice to Tamarra about forming unions, and they provided expert advice to John on how to design the first airplane. In the majority of the sample lessons, however, the students engaged in other forms of role-taking. For example, in Shirley's lesson about the sniper and in Viera's lesson about the "Tell-Tale Heart," the students undertook the role of protecting the teacher. Conversely, in Jose's lesson, the students became perplexed diners trying to figure out how to place an order. In this lesson and several others, the students were active voyagers.

In addition, even in Dwight's and Julie's lessons, where they came closest to engaging in what would be considered role-playing, the students' behavior was not like the classic conception. In reality, the students' activity was more playing than role-playing. It was more of a theatrical self-expression exercise. The students had no idea why the teacher had asked them to play, or what the purpose of the activity was.

In other words, both teachers and students undertake a much richer variety of roles in Outrageous lessons than is generally recognized in the literature on role-playing. So the best rule is no rule. Let the storyline dictate what roles students and teachers play and take.

Sequence of Role-Playing   Another difference in the use of role-play in an Outrageous lesson is the order in which it is used. Typically, role-playing is a student activity that follows conventional instruction. That is, the content is first taught conventionally, and then students role-play under the direction of the teacher to reinforce the learning. However, such student role-play, as valuable as it is, takes additional time; it essentially doubles the time it takes to teach content. The Dramatized Content approach is more efficient in that the teacher takes on a role at the start of the lesson and maintains that role throughout the lesson until the last five minutes. The lesson ends with a few minutes of conventional instruction to formally link the role-playing experience to the content objective. In other words, having the conventional instruction follow the role-playing activity, instead of vice versa, means that both can be done in a single lesson—a more efficient approach than the traditional sequencing of role-play activities. In addition, this sequence of having conventional instruction follow the role-playing also increases the amount of learning both in the Outrageous lesson and in the subsequent conventional teaching of the next set of related content objectives.

The advantage of teachers playing a role to introduce new content is best illustrated by the sample lessons for teaching literature. In most traditional uses of role-play in a literature lesson, the story would first be taught conventionally, and then students would act out the story as a way to better understand the motivations of the characters. The teacher would choreograph the process.

Contrast this approach with the sample lesson done by Viera to introduce "The Tell-Tale Heart." In traditional uses of role-playing, the students would first read the story, then act out what was going on. In her Outrageous lesson, on the other hand, Viera role-played being insane at the very start of the lesson. Why?

The answer is that the traditional approach to role-playing would have been very inefficient as a teaching and learning device. First, it would have taken a lot longer to teach the unit. Second, the traditional role-play strategy would not have solved the instructional problem that Viera was facing, specifically, that the students were reluctant readers, and she would have had to struggle even to get them to want to read the text and not be intimidated by it. Third, even after they had read the story, it would have taken quite a bit of time to organize a role-playing activity. Conversely, Viera's role-playing caused the students to read the story with more interest and effort from the very beginning, and to participate more fully in discussing the reading. There was therefore no need to add a student role-playing process to enhance their understanding. The Outrageous lesson was thus not only effective but also efficient in the use of time. Viera's lesson saved time because the original teaching took less time and because there was no need for subsequent role-playing. Even better, the students learned the material better than those who were taught conventionally.

This was the same experience that Shirley had by hiding underneath the desk to avoid detection by a imaginary stalker in order to teach "The Sniper" as an example of how authors create mood. The students read the story far more quickly and with far deeper understanding than they would have under a conventional approach. The increased learning in what was a difficult class to teach resulted from the Outrageous scenario inducing changes in student behavior. What would have otherwise taken several days was done in a single day, with greater comprehension and deeper appreciation on the part of the students for both the author and the teacher.

In other words, the way an Outrageous lesson actualizes role-playing is designed to speed up the learning process and to accomplish multiple objectives at once. Indeed, even when the students also role-play, the lesson is very efficient. When Julie asked her students to pretend they had been bitten by the story bug, they imitated in their own way the role-play that the teacher had done. In this case, having the students role-play worked because they were being asked to create something original and individualistic—a story with highly expressive language. So, asking students to transport themselves to imaginary circumstances was a very efficient way to get them to incorporate highly expressive language into their stories, even though they did not realize at the time that this is what they were doing. As far as the students were concerned, they were just being encouraged to be exhibitionists—something that the YouTube generation finds fulfilling. In addition, establishing the role-play did not require significant time because everyone was playing the same role—one that the teacher had already modeled so it did not have to be organized. So, in this case, student role-playing was both valuable and efficient.

Incorporates More Elements of Drama into Each Lesson

None of the elements of a Dramatized Content lesson are unique relative to other conceptions of how to incorporate dramatic technique. What is different is that instead of focusing on one or two of these elements, the Dramatized Content Planning Method brings them all together in a systematic way, and each is tweaked to optimize the effectiveness and efficiency of the instructional process. This comprehensive systematization makes it easier for teachers to design Outrageous lessons, and for schools and districts to organize in-service workshops. It also makes it possible to teach the technique in preservice education courses. It also increases the probability that the resultant lessons will be powerful ones that teach the content objective more effectively than conventional approaches. This systematization of the process of combining the dramatic elements clearly did not stifle creativity in the development of the lessons presented here or in the subsequent teaching of those lessons. Rather, the Dramatized Content Planning Method provides a stable base from which to "riff" one's imagination.

DEVELOPING AN OUTRAGEOUS LESSON IS A STATE OF MIND

Developing an Outrageous lesson is a conscious switching of gears in how you think about designing and teaching a content lesson. It is a willingness to suspend the rules of classroom engagement and lesson planning as you normally practice them. It is a rethinking of how to teach something for the first time, regardless of whether the lesson is for high school seniors or kindergarteners.

Embracing Being Weird

Applying the Dramatized Content Planning Method's techniques involves embracing a process of being imaginative and weird in your thinking and planning, and then reaching for yet another, even weirder gear in your mind. It is a recognition that even though you have some basic ideas, if you push your mind, it will come up with additional dramatic and comedic elements. It is a willingness to think and act differently, even if only occasionally.

Building Up the Drama—Making It Bigger

Consider, for example, Dwight's lesson on persuasive writing. His initial idea was to link persuasive writing to a sales pitch. He then extended the idea to having students audition to be salespeople in his company. This enabled him to stay in the role of salesperson as the students transitioned into the formal learning process. He added the disguise, the voice, and the mannerisms of a TV used-car salesperson. He found the everyday props around which the students could build a creative, persuasive case.

The result was a brilliant lesson. Could he have made it even more dramatic? Sure!

For example, instead of just saying that he was looking to hire salespeople, he could have said something more compelling, such as the following:

> Alas, I have not been able to find talented salespeople. If I cannot find some soon my company will go out of business. I am here because I have been told that you are a very talented group, and you are my last hope.

This statement would have extended his neediness and desperation, and cast the students as his savior. At the same time, did he really have to expand his neediness in order for his lesson to be great? No. It was a great lesson without that.

In other words, even though you should always be on the lookout for additional elements to further build up the dramatic effect, you need not obsess over them. Put in all the dramatic elements that you have time to think about before teaching a lesson for the first time. It will be successful. Then, as with all lessons, think about how you can build it up even further the next time you teach it. Finding out how far you can push the drama envelope is something you really have to learn by doing. You will discover, however, that continuing to build up your initial ideas is a fun and rewarding process—and at times you will amaze yourself. When that happens, you will dazzle your students.

Courage

The final aspect of the state of mind needed for Outrageous Teaching is courage. Teachers' willingness to take a chance is critical, particularly the first few times you attempt an Outrageous lesson. The teacher-student dynamic is so different during such a lesson that you have to be willing to give up your comfort zone of routine and plunge into the unknown. You will have to teach a few Outrageous lessons before you can start to feel confident that your students will react the way you hope they will. Again, it is like an actor performing a play for the first time in front of a live audience and no one quite knows how the audience will react. In the case of an Outrageous lesson, however, the odds of a very positive audience response are much higher. *I have never seen an Outrageous lesson not work!*

Of course it is easy for me as a writer to reassure you that your efforts will work. In the interest of complete honesty, however, you always need to muster courage every time you teach a new Outrageous lesson for the first time—regardless of how many such lessons you have successfully taught in the past. Consider the following example from my own teaching that occurred as I was writing this book. (I try continually to practice what I preach.)

Stan's First Lesson on Quantitative Analysis: Going from Yawn to Fascination

My university had just started a new doctoral program in educational leadership. I had a great deal of influence on its design. The first cohort was beginning the second semester, and one of their courses was the dreaded quantitative techniques course. Most teachers and administrators remember their statistics courses with dread. I had fought at two institutions for the right to teach this course in a different way, one that would be much more meaningful and relevant to the students. I finally succeeded in getting a very different approach approved.

In this conception, there was no statistics course. Rather, it became a course on the analysis of inequity, a topic that was central to the entire program and that the students were passionate about. In this approach, students would ask questions of a state dataset to understand the nature and degree of inequity, and how their school or district was doing relative to others. They would then learn how to interpret the printouts they were getting, which would have some statistics on them, in order to make judgments about REAL-world inequity. There was no textbook. In other words, the statistics became a needed tool that was learned in the context of making decisions, which is how administrators use data in the real world.

To my limited knowledge, this approach had never previously been used in training school administrators, so I welcomed the challenge to design and teach this course.

Another important piece of information needed to understand the following lesson is that one of the ideals of the program was that a central function of all administrators in a school or district, regardless of their position, was to focus on improving the teaching and learning of underrepresented groups. In addition, all of the students already had administrative experience, and some had been out of school for ten to twenty-five years.

Here is the lesson I designed for the very first class of this course in this brand new program.

The Lesson   I started by handing out the course syllabus. It was a student's worst nightmare. Nothing but technical terms. (I actually compiled terms from three statistics courses.) There was a midterm and a final. Students were expected to memorize a formula for each test and calculate the results by hand.

I expected outright rebellion. When I handed out the syllabus, there was the expected quiet as students read it, then a few murmurs. I did not know what to expect and was surprised when the first comment was, "I like the clean, modern look of the syllabus. What fonts did you use?"

The second comment also surprised me. Another student said, "I am glad we finally have a course where we have a test instead of having to write a paper, and I appreciate that it is an open-book test." She was quickly shushed by the group.

The next question was, "What level of math knowledge do we need?" I assured them that they did not need to know calculus, and that knowing algebra and advanced algebra would be sufficient. When the students asked about support, I told them there would be a help desk they could reach at 415-SOS-MATH.

By now a few students were starting to get pale. A few brave souls wanted to know how this course would help them promote equity and be better administrators. I kept on giving silly answers and pretending that it would help them become better administrators. Finally, a full-scale dissent emerged about the fairness and saneness of this approach. The students were starting to get worried and a bit upset (as well they should have).

I then pretended to be upset by their questioning of my judgment, and then said:

> If you do not like my approach to this course, what ways of doing data analysis would in fact be useful to you as administrators? How do you use data as administrators? What steps do you need to go through to use data in your decision making?

I then went to the board, and we developed a series of steps, starting with the most important one, which is, Ask the right question!

It took ten to fifteen minutes to design a model that everyone agreed with (which is of course what I wanted them to realize). I then said:

> If you really like this model, I happen to have another syllabus here that happens to be built on this model. Maybe we should use this one instead.

I waited a few moments for this announcement to sink in and then handed out the new syllabus. There were stunned looks on the students' faces. When they had looked it over for a few minutes and started to relax, I went on to say:

> The goal of this syllabus is to train you to be *data whisperers*, that is, individuals who can talk to data and listen to what it is trying to tell you. This term is derived from the term *horse whisperers*. These are individuals who can train horses by talking to them and understanding their feelings. We have a state database that you can ask questions of to explore the amount and nature of inequity. Most of the reading we do will be not about statistics but about how researchers define and measure inequity, such as poverty, intergenerational mobility, linguistic isolation, learning gap, and so on. You can then make judgments about these forms of inequity in the state and in your district.

The students began to smile. One student asked if they could get rid of the original syllabus, and when I said yes, they hurled them into a pile. They liked the new syllabus and got excited about the ideas contained in it.

There was then a spirited, excited discussion of the new syllabus. After that was over I asked:

> Why would I give you a phony syllabus?

They could not come up with an idea, although I am sure their collective unspoken thoughts were that their professor was a bit wacko. I continued:

> The first syllabus was a satire of everything that is wrong about how quantitative techniques are taught in virtually every college of education around the United States. The only students who can learn this way are ed-psych students. In addition, the course is generally taught and controlled by ed-psych faculty. However, they are a small

minority in colleges of education. The majority of students have a dismal experience learning this way, quickly forget everything that was learned, and come away hating quantitative analysis.

I then explained to them the struggle I had to go through to be allowed to teach this new version of the course, and that they were in fact the only students in the United States who were going to be taught in this more relevant, interesting way. What was the point? I continued:

I wish you could have seen your faces. You were clearly distraught at the first syllabus. You all knew you would have struggled mightily to get a passing grade, and some would probably have failed. *Remember that feeling!* Right now you have classes in your organizations in which disadvantaged students are struggling, and even where most are failing. They cannot get ahold of the concepts the way they are being taught. This is the closest you will come to truly understanding how they feel. I could have stood by and taught the conventional course, which does not work very well. But I fought to change it, and as a result you will have a unique and successful and valuable learning experience. So, my question to you is, if you with all your successful experience panicked, what is happening to those students who are trying to make sense in key courses who have not had a great deal of success previously? More important, what are you going to do about those courses? Are you going to fight to change them or are you going to let the students continue to flounder? It is your job, regardless of your area of responsibility, to redirect how those courses are taught. The issue is not the title of the course but how the course is being taught.

I then held up the two versions of the syllabus and said:

Both of these syllabi have the same title. However, they are very different, with very different consequences to you as students. The course title does not mean anything. Any course can be conceived in very different ways. What are you going to do about the courses in your schools where the students are struggling to make sense of what is going on? It is not enough to offer services to those who are struggling. What is the nature of those services? Are they state-of-the-art? How can you change the course so that they do not fail in the first place? It is likely that the problems in your school and district with students passing these courses is not unique—but there is always a very creative way to make it better. Your job is to come up with a unique approach, and fight to get it put in place.

There was silence in the room. These highly experienced, highly successful individuals began to murmur to each other. The gist of what they were saying was, "If we as successful leaders, who have previously been successful in school and in the workplace, can become so unsettled and intimidated by a course, what must it be like for struggling students who do not have a history of success when they encounter algebra, or—."

The point was made and I was pleased at their reaction.

I ended the lesson by thanking them for their grace under pressure and for not walking out or throwing things at me.

Comments on the Lesson   Was I nervous as I started the lesson? You bet. I was particularly nervous because the director of the program and several other faculty were watching. I had no idea how the students would react. I simply took a chance. I am confident that five years after they graduate, long after they have forgotten most of what they learned in their classes, they will remember this lesson, and for many or most of them the point of the lesson will become a moral imperative. As far as I am concerned, the lesson about their responsibility to find a way to change the learning environment where students are struggling is the most important lesson that I or any of the other faculty will teach them. However, the only way to bury this lesson deeply in their psyche was to teach it Outrageously.

In the end, everyone complimented me on a brilliant lesson. Whew!

(I am also scheduled to teach several other courses in the program. Of course, the next time I hand out a syllabus, no one will take it seriously.)

Willingness to Pioneer a Lesson

There are presently no compendia of Outrageous lessons other than the examples in this book. Hopefully this will change in the future if large numbers of teachers adopt this approach. However, for now, teaching an Outrageous lesson will probably require that you develop an original one. The result will probably be a lesson that uses an approach that no one has ever thought of before, and you will then become the first person in the history of American education to teach that content objective that way. The pioneering spirit built this country, and it can be a source of improving education and of your professional growth and sense of accomplishment. I know I was a pioneer in how I introduced my students to their quantitative analysis of equity course.

A FORESEEABLE PROBLEM

In the interest of being objective and providing full disclosure, I do predict that one major problem will result from the use of Outrageous lessons. Once a teacher has taught more than one such lesson to the same class, when a substitute teacher comes in and announces that she or he is there because the regular teacher is out sick, I imagine the students will immediately come to attention in the expectation that this is a setup for an Outrageous lesson. Suddenly seeing a sea of expectant faces will be a disconcerting experience for the substitute teacher in and of itself. Of course, once students realize that this really is a substitute teacher, then you can imagine the rest.

SUMMARY

Clearly this book has not invented the concept of role-playing. What it has done is create a specific, systematic, and somewhat unique set of procedures for involving teachers in role-playing to produce content learning in a highly creative and efficient manner. In addition, the power of the Dramatized Content Planning Method is that you can teach the same objectives in only a single lesson, even with the time spent role-playing, with greater degrees of learning for the students and fun for the teacher.

Clearly there are extensive benefits from teaching content Outrageously. These include the following:

- Increased student interest
- Increased student learning, in both quantity and quality
- Reduction or elimination of discipline and classroom management problems
- Increased student respect for the teacher
- Revelations of the capabilities of formerly passive students
- Making teaching fun and awesome

For the education profession to accept and encourage Outrageous lessons, it has to make the same transition of thought that modern physics had to make—the transition to accepting the existence of two very different systems operating simultaneously in the universe. Although Einstein remained skeptical of quantum physics and tried to prove it wrong, over time physicists have come to accept it. The experimental results are simply too compelling, and for now physicists have to work with two different, almost opposite set of laws.

Can the education profession, which is rooted in the one best approach, similarly be able to develop a two-dimensional way to look at instruction? Can it adapt to thinking in terms of two very different sets of rules governing instruction, one for conventional lessons and one for Outrageous lessons—each valid in its own way and circumstances and almost diametrically opposite to the other? Can education come to accept the counterintuitive phenomena that occur during Outrageous Teaching? Will both sets of instructional rules be taught in pre- and postservice education? Will teacher education programs ever teach the dynamics of fascinating students? Will Outrageous lessons ever be routinely accepted and encouraged in practice? Will Creative Authenticity be viewed as a tool as valuable for engaging students as conventional conceptions of authenticity that focus strictly on the real adult world?

If rational scientists can come to believe that a subatomic particle can be in two places at once, educators can at some point come to accept the importance of strategically using Outrageous Teaching. The key, however, is to start the process of demonstrating these benefits on some sort of scale. This will happen only if teachers and administrators make a commitment to Outrageous Teaching (and other uses of drama-based teaching techniques), even if only on an experimental basis initially. Student success will then set us free from our self-imposed chains of sole reliance on conventional instruction to teach content.

Getting Started

Although initially it may take more effort to develop and teach an Outrageous lesson than to develop and teach a conventional one, there are clear benefits to doing so. The time, effort, and innovation needed to incorporate such lessons into practice, however, raise a series of practical, logistical, and political issues, which lead to the following questions:

- How should an individual get started designing an Outrageous lesson?

- How should a school get started encouraging the use of Outrageous lessons?

- How should the profession adapt to the need to incorporate Outrageous Teaching?

In addition, this chapter describes how to extend the Dramatized Content Planning Method to create Outrageous *units* for grades 4–12, and Outrageous lessons for grades K–3.

GETTING STARTED AS AN INDIVIDUAL TEACHER

In the unlikely event that you are a teacher who has a principal who advocates and encourages the use of dramatic technique—great! That makes things easier. If you are not, then you can do what good teachers have always done—they do what they believe to be in the best interest of their students. The primary motivations for you as an individual to start teaching Outrageously are that you want (a) to develop professionally, (b) to experience students hanging on to your every word and emotion, (c) to help your students develop to their full potential, and (d) to have students care as much about the content as you do.

BASIC APPROACH: INCORPORATE OTHER USES OF DRAMA

As you start to plan to incorporate a few Outrageous lessons into your teaching repertoire, you may also want to add to your everyday teaching toolbox some other uses of dramatic technique previously discussed, such as the following:

- Develop an additional, simpler "creating a mood, setting a stage" use of drama once a semester or year (See Chapter 3.).

- Use a game for reviewing content once a semester (at least).

- Add some surprising, dramatic microbursts of exaggerated expression into your teaching.

- Implement a unit once a year that is a more conventional use of dramatic technique, such as a simulation unit.

As discussed in Chapter Six, when you add a different kind of activity or different content that will be of interest to your students, with a bit more thought you can usually link it to existing curricular content objectives. Indeed, one of the most dramatic and effective units I ever saw was the one developed by the Pig Lady. Two reasons it was memorable was the amount of learning it produced and that it lasted a whole year. Here is the unit and the story behind it.

The Pig Lady (Language Arts, High School, Special Education)

In terms of sustainability, the best example of a teacher-initiated Outrageous unit was one that lasted an entire year. I came across this example by chance. I was meeting with another professor when his wife walked in. She was a beautiful, elegantly dressed woman. (You will see the relevance of this description in a moment.) She mentioned that she had just retired from teaching reading to learning-disabled high school students in rural Florida. Her husband mentioned that she had been by far the most successful such teacher in the county. I assumed these were just the words of a supportive husband. I played along, however, and asked her how she did it.

She explained that she wanted to gear her instruction to the students' interest. Having been raised in the city, she had no knowledge of rural life. Her conversations with students indicated that they were very interested in raising animals, so she did research on how to raise pigs. She then developed a manual on how to care for pigs, making sure that all the district-required vocabulary and language development objectives were incorporated. She then spent her own money to buy some baby pigs. The school provided some space to house them.

Over the course of the year the students read her manual and applied the lessons. Their vocabulary and reading comprehension grew by leaps and bounds—as did the pigs.

I never did get to discuss with her whether she used any role-playing. However, there were a variety of roles she could have assumed, such as being a veterinarian who was going to train them to be vet assistants, or being someone who had to become a teacher when she lost her farm and her babies were taken away by the bank (her baby pigs, that is) and she was hoping that the students could replace them, or—

She said that she retired from teaching because the district would not encourage the spread of her techniques, even though her students outperformed every other class in the county by a large margin on the district test. So I think of the Pig Lady often. She is a symbol to me of how great teachers can go against type and instinct to create a powerful and successful learning environment through the use of a dramatic approach (in this case, raising pigs) to produce unusual levels of achievement, and that there are probably many other such examples of similar teacher work out there.

The work of the Pig Lady is also important for how she blended her progressive impulse with a concern for teaching the standard curriculum. She brought a new, discovery-based focus to her teaching and created a new curriculum geared to support it, but in doing so she went the extra step and built in all the content objectives required by the district.

Alas, such work goes unheralded and unsupported in this era of standardized conformity, cookie-cutter staff development, and conventional "successful strategies" that never seem to work. No foundations lined up to support her work, and no government bureaucrat showered her with awards and grants. Instead, they all threw their hundreds of millions of dollars away on the fad of the moment that turned out not to work. Her district was "embarrassed" by her technique. It did not fit the conventional wisdom of practice, so I suspect they were relieved when she retired early, another victim of a profession that often seems embarrassed by unusual levels of success. To me, however, she is an American hero who, although unheralded, represents the best of our profession. We need lots more "pig ladies" and "pig men."

Incorporate Outrageous Lessons

How should you start to develop and teach your own Outrageous lessons? The best advice is to *start judiciously!* Begin by picking one lesson each semester that you will teach using this approach. This will minimize the pressure or anxiety associated with getting started, and maximize the fun and sense of accomplishment you will have. Choose those lessons that you like to teach the least, or that students like the least, or the ones you care most about.

Begin to develop ideas for the initial lesson(s). Brainstorm with peers, friends, and relatives who have a sense of humor to develop and expand the initial ideas.

Once you are ready to teach your first Outrageous lesson, make sure your principal knows what your plan is. Hopefully she or he will not object. Also, if you anticipate a higher noise level during the lesson, make sure that you have the blessing of your peers in the surrounding classrooms.

Then do it!

Then each year, add additional Outrageous lessons and build up your repertoire over time. Continue to embellish each of your prior successful lessons.

At the same time, plan to consciously incorporate other uses of drama into your everyday instruction.

ADVANCED APPROACH: INCORPORATE AN OUTRAGEOUS UNIT

Once you have incorporated a series of Outrageous lessons, you may want to try to develop an Outrageous unit. Up to this point, this book has focused on creating individual lessons. Although creating a series of lessons for different content objectives is the most essential use of Outrageous Teaching, and a major professional accomplishment, for those of you who might also want to explore creating an Outrageous unit, two examples of such units are provided to illustrate some of the key principles. The first example is fairly simple and the second one is more involved.

Stan's Unit on Manipulating Decimals (Grades 4 to 5)

After six and a half years of teaching math in high-poverty New York City schools, I dreamed about one day creating an alternative math curriculum. That opportunity arose when I received a grant from the National Science Foundation. The goal was to design a series of units that would combine the use of software-based "adventures" as the basis for teaching the pre-algebra concepts that were the most difficult to teach and the most challenging for students to learn with any sense of understanding. The goal was to have students engage in real mathematical reasoning and problem solving, and especially to have them derive the mathematical rules whenever possible. In terms of the latter, when students derive the rules on their own by interacting with a Creatively Authentic context, they take ownership of the rules and view them as valuable. So, instead of mathematics being a system of arbitrary, adult-imposed rules, it becomes a system of cool procedures.

The following example is a simple but highly effective unit for enabling students to develop the rules for adding, subtracting, multiplying, and dividing decimals on their own.

On the first day of the unit the teacher puts on the board a series of problems in adding and subtracting decimals. When the usual request for calculators arises immediately from students, the teacher says:

> *You have done such good work recently that I not only am going to let you use calculators to solve these problems, but I also have arranged for you to have special ones that are in your computers. This means you can work on the computers with a partner all period.*

Of course the students approve and eagerly rush to the computers where the on-screen calculator is available. They quickly get to work. However, shortly thereafter a series of complaints echoes around the room: "Teacher, these calculators do not work."

The teacher plays innocent and asks:

> *What do you mean? What's wrong?*

The students respond:

> *"Teacher, there is no decimal point in the answer."*

The teacher asks if they are sure about the problem and quickly determines that this is a problem on all the computers. The teacher then says:

> *I don't know what happened. They worked perfectly before but now they seem to be broken.*

> After acting as though he or she is not sure what to do, the teacher announces:
>
> *I have an idea. The computer is helping by doing the calculation for you. How about helping the computer by using what you know about decimals to estimate where the decimal point should be.*
>
> The students proceed to use common sense to figure out where the decimal points should be. For example, when 25.3 + 13.4 becomes 287, the students realize that 25 and a bit plus 13 and a bit is probably 28 and a bit, so they figure that the computer would have placed the decimal in the answer after the 28, or 28.7.
>
> After the students have placed the decimals in all the answers, the teacher apologizes for the defective calculator but then praises them for helping out the calculator and placing the decimals in the answers on their own. The teacher then asks the students to search all the addition problems and answers for a pattern, then see if they can figure out a rule from the pattern for where the decimal place belongs. They do the same for the multiplication problems.
>
> The next day, when the students arrive they do the same thing with subtraction and division, of course with the teacher making up excuses about how the calculators have not yet been fixed and about why no other calculators are available. The process of students inferring the rules is then repeated.

The use of a slightly broken calculator provided the opportunity for the teacher to role-play, and it was critical for generating an element of surprise that both enhanced the students' interest and provided a highly effective context for them to discover the math rules the same way over a series of objectives and days.

Two benefits of this unit were that thereafter the students were hesitant to request the use of calculators and became confident that they could develop estimation strategies for figuring out how to solve problems.

Zoe (Middle School Social Studies, World History, Beginning of World War I)

Zoe was the only student teacher I had who decided to use the Dramatized Content Planning Method to first design a whole unit instead of just a lesson. Her class was a low-performing middle school social studies class in world history and was one of the most passive I had ever observed. The unit was about events leading up to World War I and how the opposing alliances formed. They were going to get to learn about Prussia. Yawn!

Zoe realized that there was no way the students would be interested in, or understand, these long-ago events using conventional teaching approaches. What to do?

Zoe cast herself as a news reporter who was frustrated because all of the countries wanted to fight each other, and she was afraid that a nondemocratic country would take over the world. She was very worried that the United States was not prepared for war and was underestimating the dangers. Her surprise broadcast framed the world at the precipice of war. She used excerpts from the school's history textbook and some original research from other history books to develop a profile of each country involved in World War I in the years just before the war. After doing her broadcast, she randomly assigned a team of two students to represent each of the countries as ambassadors. The students were then each given the profile of their own country and instructed to form alliances. The alliance with the most overall resources in terms of gross national product, food, and soldiers would win. A number of factors had to be taken into consideration because there was little benefit to having lots of soldiers if you could not feed them.

A map of the world as it existed at that time was also displayed in the room.

Over the course of three days, the students negotiated alliances. The day I was there, one of the teams complained that a team that had formed an alliance with them had gone back on their word and cut them loose in favor of another country. They were understandably upset. Alliances and treaties were formed and broken among a series of groups.

These street-smart students understood and enjoyed the negotiation process. Slowly the number of initial alliances declined, until only two were left. The teacher kept a running color-coded list of the countries in each alliance, which changed daily. Each day the students added up the resources in each group.

The students negotiated with gusto, and the class was filled with constant activity and the sounds of success and frustration. The teams also became more sophisticated in taking into account additional factors in deciding which countries to bargain with. Some ambassadors decided it would not be smart to be surrounded by countries in the other alliance, and some decided they did not want to align with countries that had very different political systems and beliefs.

I was impressed by how much the students knew about each country, and by the facility with which they summarized which countries were banding together and why.

At the end of each day Zoe would list the alliances on the board and do a simulated newscast back to the United States in a somewhat panicky fashion on the status of the world's war preparations. She would also quickly interview some of the diplomats about why they had chosen to align with a particular country.

After three days the students settled into two alliances. In Zoe's last broadcast she was still panicky about the strength of the enemy coalition but voiced optimism that if the United States took seriously the threat of war, it could be part of a winning alliance that would support democracy.

Zoe then assigned students to read the chapter in their text on the period leading up to World War I. The students eagerly read the materials to see how closely their coalition mirrored the coalitions at the start of the war and, most important, which side won. The students were amazed to discover that their two sets of alliances mirrored exactly the opposing coalitions at the start of World War I.

Zoe complimented them on what good bargainers they were and on how well they had predicted history. A discussion of why and how countries form alliances and fight followed. The discussion was sophisticated and passionate. The students began to see that history was a story about how people behaved under difficult circumstances. The discussion was a complete change from what I had observed on my previous visits, in terms of both the students' willingness to participate and share their observations, and the increased sophistication of the discussion.

Zoe's unit exemplified the idea of first teaching the content using a storyline or scenario that was extremely creative and that sustained itself over several lessons. By the time the unit switched to conventional instruction, the students knew all the countries involved and their characteristics, and understood why the coalitions evolved the way they did. They went through the material quickly and with deeper interest and understanding than they would otherwise have done. Even with the student role-playing, this Outrageous unit did not take any more time than a completely conventional approach would have taken to cover the same content, and a lot more learning occurred.

I was curious about whether there would be any carryover in students' interest in history to subsequent units that were taught conventionally. Alas, I did not get the opportunity to find out, because the semester ended shortly thereafter.

Reflection on these Outrageous Units   Note that in both of these units there was a storyline with an element of suspense, and that in both units the teacher role-played at some point. However, as in Outrageous lessons, the role of the students was very different than in traditional units. In Zoe's unit, the students engaged primarily in role-playing while in my unit the students were role-takers. One unit used computers and the other used more traditional materials. In other words, although the details of how the learning occurred differed, both units were highly successful. It is the quality of the storyline and the supporting ideas that matter—not whether technology is used. In addition, although the teachers adopted different roles, the one common element was that they would often act befuddled and surprised as the students figured out the content principles and knowledge. A few well-placed questions by the teacher, such as "Why did you do that?" "What is happening?" "How did you figure that out?" "Do you see a pattern?" and so on, all asked with a quizzical, admiring look, say that you are grateful that they figured this out for you.

The other common elements that makes these examples an Outrageous *unit*, as opposed to a *lesson*, is that the teacher role-play is sustained across a series of lessons, although to varying degrees. The first day is the most dramatic.

The key characteristic of an Outrageous unit that distinguishes it from a conventional role-playing unit is that in both examples the Outrageous unit is the initial, and primary, method of teaching the content. So, for example, when a social studies teacher does a mock election after teaching a unit on government, that is not an Outrageous unit because the content was previously taught conventionally and the teacher directs the activities and only the students role-play. Although the mock election is a valuable learning experience for reinforcing and deepening what the students have already learned conventionally, it is not an Outrageous unit.

At the same time, any simulation, computerized or not, can be the basis of an Outrageous unit if it is used in a discovery mode, that is, if it is used to facilitate students' discovery of the content ideas. So, for example, a mock election can be converted into an Outrageous unit if it is used for the original teaching of concepts. That is, if a teacher sets up a mock election within a role-played scenario prior to the conventional teaching of the formal principles of government and has the students develop a set of principles for conducting the election fairly and in terms of what democracy should embody, these lessons would be well on the way to being an Outrageous unit. The formal textbook content could then be presented for students to consider how well their ideas meshed with the actual governmental rules. Of course the teacher would have to invent a Creatively Authentic reason for the class to hold a mock election. For example, the teacher could role-play at the start of the unit that he or she is thinking of running for office and is looking for a campaign manager.

Finally, it is worth noting that the use of the computer in the Outrageous math unit on decimals was unconventional. The software was not used to present the mathematics. Rather, the software set a dilemma-based context for the storyline and for the subsequent mathematical discussions.

EXPAND YOUR KNOWLEDGE OF DRAMA

As you involve yourself in incorporating drama into your teaching, you may decide that you want to explore the world of drama in more detail. Sarason (1999) has an interesting discussion in the first five chapters of his book *Teaching as a Performing Art* of the view of the playwright and the relationship between artists and audiences; and Kelner and Flynn (2006) provide a glossary of theater and drama terms. Such exploration is optional, however, because the techniques described in this book will be enough to enable you to implement effective Outrageous lessons and units. As previously mentioned, I got so fascinated by how teaching and learning occur in the theater that I spent one sabbatical studying drama at the University of California, Los Angeles. (I adopted some of the approaches to teaching and learning used in the theater in my design of the training workshop for becoming a HOTS teachers.)

If you do decide to increase your knowledge of drama and dramatic techniques, some ideas are as follows:

• *Go to the theater and think of the actors and playwrights as teachers.* As you watch the performance, think about the pedagogical techniques they are using to teach the audience. This can be done with any performing art. What techniques are the actors or dancers or artists or script using? Do you think there is a message, and if so, what are they teaching and how are they teaching it?

- If you need to take additional courses for an advanced degree or to move up the salary schedule and are given flexibility, consider taking a drama class, preferably an acting class. By learning how to put another playwright's words into action, you will increase your ability and confidence to project your own dramatic event.

Indeed, on those days when you present an Outrageous lesson, you are both a playwright and a performer. Unfortunately you are still paid as a teacher, and your name will not be in lights (unless that is part of your drama). Your reward will be the lights in the eyes of your students, in their overall reactions, and particularly in the new things you learn about your students' capabilities.

At the same time, you do not have to follow these suggestions for studying drama to implement a highly effective Outrageous lesson or unit. You can simply rely on using the techniques presented in Chapter Four and on your innate imagination to produce Outrageous lessons and units that are as good as or better than the examples in this book.

Summation of Teacher Practice

Teachers should strive to incorporate the full gamut of dramatic techniques. Consider the examples I provided of my own teaching. In Chapter Three I presented a lesson in which I passed around a banana for students to speak their answers into. That technique was adding a "creating a mood, setting the stage" component to a lesson. Everything else about the lesson was conventional. On the other hand, the lesson I described in Chapter Six in which I passed out the phony statistics course syllabus was an Outrageous lesson. All uses of dramatic technique and humor have value when used in the right place.

GETTING STARTED AS A COLLABORATIVE GROUP

Of course it would be better if a group of teachers at your school was interested in developing Outrageous lessons. You could then build a theatrical learning community around developing such lessons, with an appropriate name, such as the Outrageous Dozen. You could have periodic get-togethers to brainstorm and help each other, and perhaps even go to the theater together and discuss the teaching techniques used by the playwright and the actors. A critical mass of excellent Outrageous lessons would eventually be presented at your school, and the chances would increase that at some point all students in the school would be exposed to an Outrageous lesson or unit—and some to more than one.

If it is difficult to find like-minded teachers at your school, you can try to form a collaborative with teachers from other schools in your area. There are a variety of ways to find collaborators outside your school. Many professional organizations have regional as well as state meetings, and you could post an announcement or even get on the program. You can also post an item in your district newsletter.

Although a multisite or regional cooperative group may not expose more students at your school to Outrageous lessons or units over and above what you teach, it does provide a professional circle in which to bounce around ideas, inspiration, and experience, and it will benefit students at other schools.

With current advances in technology there is another way to construct a collaborative and that is to construct a virtual one over the Internet. I have established a blog for sharing ideas and successful experiences with Outrageous lessons and units nationally: http://www.outrageousteaching.blogspot.com (see Chapter Eight).

GETTING STARTED AS A SCHOOL

The next level of using Outrageous lessons is across an entire school whose principal and staff make a commitment to look for opportunities to incorporate drama into instruction. This is not likely to happen without strong leadership and support on the part of the principal. Such support is most likely if the principal has a background in the theater. I have met few principals with such a background. Indeed, the only report I have seen of an established schoolwide commitment to incorporating drama into instruction was on the Shenton Primary School in England (Dickinson and Neelands, 2006). Another example I got from a recent news clipping was that Laurel Elementary School in Fort Collins, Colorado, just changed its name to Laurel Elementary School of Arts and Technology, with the goal of infusing artistic technique across the curriculum and making instruction more creative.

Viewing Drama as a Key Tool for School Improvement

Regardless of whether the federal No Child Left Behind Act continues in its present form or not, good schools are always seeking ways to improve overall and to reduce learning gaps by raising the performance of students born into poverty, English Language Learners, and special education students. As a result, the use of Outrageous lessons and units will be adopted as a schoolwide priority and encouraged by principals only if it comes to be viewed as an effective tool for improving overall school performance and the performance of the neediest students. A major strength of Outrageous Teaching is that it can in fact be a powerful tool for school improvement.

Strategic Use of Outrageous Teaching for School Improvement

All schools are now getting back highly detailed data on the performance of their students on state tests. Increasingly, principals and staff are looking at these data to establish instructional priorities for improvement. Typically such data are used as the basis for deciding which specific content items require more instruction time or which concepts should be retaught to specific subgroups at specific grade levels. For example, it may turn out that fifth grade English Language Learners are having difficulty finding the main idea in reading passages. That information is used to provide extra instruction in this content objective. Unfortunately, the extra instruction typically involves more of the same type of instruction that was ineffective in the first place. The theory is that if you continue to pound the nail repeatedly into the steel, the more likely it is to penetrate. In reality, this action will only beak the nail. Indeed, historically the remediation approach has indeed produced gains, but they quickly level off after the third grade, and the gap starts to increase.

An alternative approach is to use a different instructional strategy for the key content objectives that are the most problematic. For example, schools could prioritize developing an Outrageous lesson or unit for learning how to identify a main idea. Once the school has identified the key concepts or skills it needs to improve in student performance, the teachers can be challenged and rewarded to develop Outrageous lessons or units as part of a strategy to increase student performance in these skills.

Given the focus of Outrageous Teaching on teaching content in ways that increase learning efficiently, there is clearly the potential for these techniques to increase student performance on key learning needs. Focused use of these techniques will result in near transfer, that is, improving those specific objectives in a given lesson as well as in other objectives that are directly related (see Chapter Two). Chances are, however, that any given school will have a series of high-priority learning objective needs. A series of Outrageous lessons or units targeted at those needs can be developed by teams of teachers. At some point, a critical mass of student experience will be reached and you will achieve not only near transfer but far transfer as well. In other words, once students have experienced a series of Outrageous lessons or units in which they have been captivated and successful, their attitudes toward learning in general, their conceptions of their own abilities, and even their attitudes toward particular content areas begin to change. It is not clear what that critical mass is. In Supermath, after five to seven units students started to change their views of mathematics. They began to see math as interesting and valuable, and to view it correctly, not as a series of arbitrary rules but as a subject that involves solving puzzles and in which they could use their common sense to figure out the rules. In the case of the Pig Lady, she figured out how to incorporate a year's worth of content objectives into a single unit.

The best way to conduct research on what the critical mass is for student exposure to Outrageous lessons or units in order to produce far transfer is to collaborate and share your experience with me and with other teachers. Perhaps we can create a network of schools committed to providing students with multiple Outrageous lessons per semester. This would make it possible to learn more about the conditions under which Outrageous lessons and units produce far transfer, improve test scores, and spark students' interest in school and learning.

Implementing Outrageous Teaching in Grades K to 3   Elementary schools seeking to incorporate Outrageous Teaching into a school improvement plan might want to explore its use at the earliest grade levels. The focus of this book, as well as of my experience, is in grades 4 through 12. The techniques are based on this experience, and they have been validated at these grade levels. Although I have no personal experience yet, or validation, of using the Dramatized Content Planning Method to teach content in grades K to 3, my experience with the HOTS program showed me that it was possible to adapt the thinking-development approach to the youngest students, with some minor modifications. I suspect that this is the case with the Dramatized Content Planning Method as well.

As already noted, however, little has been written on using dramatic technique in the early grades other than for literacy and self-expression. Nor has systematic research been done on the impact of dramatic technique on the academic skill learning of young children. Clearly their natural enthusiasm, curiosity, and naiveté suggest that they are ideal candidates for Outrageous Teaching; as long as their attention span is not exceeded. Sesame Street has mastered using dramatic approaches to teach content to very young children. However, it promotes only a passive form of learning. As a result, little is known about producing learning through classroom use of drama at the earliest grade levels, or about what the best approach is. Can some modification of the Dramatized Content Planning Method work with young children? The only way to find out what is possible is to try and develop some Outrageous lessons and see what happens. Appendix E contains one possible example of a planning process and a resulting Outrageous lesson for the early grades.

APPLYING OUTRAGEOUS TEACHING TO REDUCE THE LEARNING GAP

Reducing the learning gap between advantaged and disadvantaged students is a national priority. The large gap that exists on national measures of achievement is widely considered to be inconsistent with democratic ideals. My large-scale work has shown that the vast majority of underrepresented students can perform at substantially higher levels—regardless of race, ethnicity, language, or whether they are in urban settings or remote areas.

Those of you who have been teaching for a while understand the bewildering array of new reforms that have been advocated, both progressive and traditionalist, liberal and conservative, manual and technological. They appear, the advocates claim success, and then, after everyone has adopted them, it becomes clear they do not work. With all of this back and forth and claims of success, the reality is that despite repeated claims of success for reforms to reduce the gap over the past several decades, Chapter One showed that the gap for fourth grade reading on the National Assessment test was smaller in 1988 than the latest results for 2004. In other words, all of the reforms since 1988 have essentially failed to reduce the gap. We have tried everything, except one possible reform, and that is Outrageous Teaching. (I suspect that most new reforms will merely be recycled from the past using new terminology and buzzwords.)

It is time to accept the reality that we cannot substantially further reduce the learning gap by conventional instruction alone. Despite overwhelming evidence that student boredom is a major problem, virtually no attention is paid to the use of techniques for making learning fascinating to these students. It is also time to recognize that tying content learning to the world of work is not all that exciting to most disadvantaged students prior to high school, and by then many have given up.

The failure of the national reforms of the last two decades stand in stark contrast to what happened in the sample lessons in Chapter Five and in the sample units in this chapter. For example, the Pig Lady reduced the gap for special education students. The Outrageous lessons and units in this book sparked high levels of learning in low-motivated, underperforming students. In those classrooms, and on those days, there was no learning gap.

Roadblocks

So, if the obvious need for and likely benefits from Outrageous Teaching are so compelling, why does it continue to be ignored as a tool for reducing the learning gap? One possible answer is that the profession itself has lost any sense of imagination and wonder. I do not think that is the case, however, because I encounter so many people at all levels of education who are wondering about how to make things better.

Rather, I think the problem is that there is no way that a corporation can make big bucks from the approach, and there is no political constituency. There are no shiny boxes or textbooks to sell at Outrageous prices. In addition, those who are the natural advocates for the specific use of dramatic technique and for creative techniques in general are split in terms of how they want to see such techniques used, and content learning is not currently high on the priority list—even though the initial progressive impulse for the use of dramatic technique in education was in fact to teach content. So, in a sense there is no commercial political base or, as of yet, a professional constituency.

Therefore, a professional constituency and base has to be built, and this can only be done at the grassroots level.

BUILDING A GRASSROOTS MOVEMENT

Change in attitudes about whether and how to incorporate dramatic technique into instruction will probably have to be a grassroots movement for the near future. It will have to be built on the efforts of individual, gutsy teachers and administrators who, one by one, decide they are tired of seeing bored expressions on the faces of their students and come to realize the shortcoming of relying only on conventional and simplistic approaches to teaching and learning. As these individuals produce success, more individuals will join. HOTS started in one school and then spread by word of mouth to 2,600 schools, without an ad budget or salespeople or even an experienced manager, and despite the need for rescheduling students and reallocating budgets. The fact that the program was able to spread despite these barriers is a testimony to the power of grassroots vitality within the profession. Indeed, once teachers started using HOTS on a reasonable scale, Mary Jean Letendre, the national director of Title I, the largest federal program for education, got interested in the program. She then worked to get the Title I law changed to encourage using these funds to provide "advanced skills."

Just as the largest federal program was changed because of grassroots success, I suspect that the same type of grassroots approach, one teacher at a time, will be needed to get the attention of administrators, policymakers, and colleges of education on Outrageous Teaching. Incorporating greater use of Outrageous lessons and units does not involve extra cost or rescheduling students, so there are few barriers to the grassroots spread of such an emphasis. The only real barriers are awareness and prevailing attitudes.

GETTING STARTED AS A PROFESSION

The single most important change that the profession could make to stimulate awareness and change attitudes would be to incorporate the use of dramatic technique into teacher education programs. I am a great believer in the progress made possible by the improved training in learning theory, psychology, and curriculum that has been incorporated into teacher education programs. However, the idea that you can teach effectively without dealing with emotion and fantasy works only for those students who are predisposed to be high performers. The sample Outrageous lessons and units described in Chapters Five and Seven were effective because they were Creatively Authentic.

Teachers, particularly those who work with students born into poverty, need to develop some of the skills of performers and playwrights. We need to shift attention away somewhat from strict reliance on the behaviorist psychological base that underlies most of the efforts to raise test scores, and include the techniques used by artists to learn and to teach.

Most universities with colleges of education also have drama departments. It is time for teacher education programs to develop a joint preservice course to prepare teachers in the use of dramatic techniques and the techniques of performing. This approach would not only better prepare teachers, but it would also reduce the percentage of new teachers who leave the profession in the first few years. The National Commission on Teaching and America's Future estimates that the teacher turnover rate is increasing and that nearly a third of all new teachers leave the profession after just three years, and that after five years almost half are gone—a higher turnover rate than in the past (Dillon, 2007).

Most new teachers are thrown into the toughest classes in a school and need to know how to engage those students creatively. Typically, no such training is provided, and it is hit or miss as to whether they will find a way to engage the students. Many do not, and they get frustrated and disillusioned as a result and leave the profession.

Collaboration between faculty in teacher education programs and those in theater departments, however, will result in more effective training of teachers if both groups come together with a commitment to focus the collaboration on the use of dramatic technique to increase content learning.

Redefine What a Master Teacher Is

As previously discussed, our profession needs to accept and embrace the reality that there are two sets of rules in education: one for how to conduct conventional lessons and one for how to teach Outrageously. In this universe of practice, we need to redefine what it means to be a master teacher. A master teacher is one who can apply the best of both conventional and Outrageous Teaching—that is, teach by direction and teach by creating suspenseful curiosity—and switch between the two modes of teaching as appropriate.

Research the Effects of Intensive Use of Dramatic Technique

Chapter Five provides clear anecdotal evidence of increased learning from even a single Outrageous lesson. Whenever teachers compared how their Outrageously taught students did to how their classes did who were taught the same lesson and unit conventionally, they consistently reported that the Outrageously taught students, even with just one such lesson, did better. So it appears that even a single Outrageous lesson produced benefits that carried over to the remainder of the unit, a form of near transfer. In addition, my observations of these lessons clearly document surprisingly high levels of student participation and learning.

Although these reports constitute only anecdotal evidence, they would seem to be sufficiently compelling to stimulate more formal research and increase use of Outrageous Teaching. One intriguing question that needs to be researched is the following: If one Outrageous lesson can produce near transfer and stimulate learning, what happens when students are exposed to more than one?

Unfortunately, I have found only one assessment of the effects of intensive use of drama techniques in a school, and that is from the Shenton Primary School in England. The evaluation focused only on social and artistic outcomes, and although the desired outcomes are listed by grade level, no evidence of growth is provided. So the effects of intensive use of dramatic technique for learning content in a school remains an open question that needs to be researched.

SUMMARY

We need to train and encourage teachers to go way beyond their comfort zones to reach deeply into the psyches of their students to make learning come alive for them through the use of unconventional dramatic techniques. Until that happens, all the new theories and journal articles, all the additional people in the field with doctorates, and all the additional monies and tutoring programs will have only marginal effects.

Viewing the use of Outrageous lessons and units as a strategic component in any overall school-improvement plan and reform strategy does not diminish thinking about dramatic technique as an important actualization of the human spirit for its own sake or as a part of an individual teacher's quest to improve his or her craft. Indeed, instructional uses of drama should be systematic and self-actualizing, planned and idiosyncratic, strategic and joyful.

So...Let's Do It!

T here is a wellspring of untapped creative potential in both students and teachers that can be harnessed to the more effective teaching of content objectives, whether standards based or not. This is true for even the oldest students and for all content areas. Teachers and administrators alike know that much of the instruction in U.S. classrooms is prosaic and fails to captivate students or get them excited about learning. For self-motivated, highly focused students, this is generally not a problem. For others, it is devastating to their chances of succeeding academically.

To this point schools had to choose between using dramatic technique for enrichment to engage students or the use of conventional instructional techniques to maximize curricular coverage. Outrageous Teaching provides, for the first time, a systematic way to apply humor and dramatic technique to efficiently increase content learning, and strategically contribute to school improvement efforts.

This book has demonstrated that when teachers go outside their comfort zones and exercise their imaginations and courage, their students do the same. When teachers bring emotion into instruction, students bring emotion into learning. This book has also demonstrated the transformative power of Outrageous Teaching as a primary tool for teaching content across the curriculum—regardless of how prosaic or esoteric the content. It not only increases student learning, but also changes how students view learning and the importance of the content ideas to them as individuals.

When teachers exercise their imaginations to teach Outrageously, it engages students and links the content to how they think about life (that is, the instruction becomes Creatively Authentic). The attendant use of social interaction, play, and story increases the likelihood that the content will be encoded in students' memory—and that it will impact how they view the content and subject area, and possibly even other aspects of life.

Teaching an Outrageous lesson or unit was always a transformative experience for my student teachers. Their courage in going forth into the classroom with an untested, divergent idea always changed their conception of what they could achieve as teachers. The process of watching students quickly transition from their initial stage of puzzled surprise to enthusiastic learning was an adrenaline-pumping high, the biggest one our profession offers.

This book has also sought to reestablish a deemphasized, progressive tradition of using dramatic technique for the explicit goal of improving content learning. It is an unabashed and unapologetic melding of the creative with the pragmatic, the imagination with the curriculum mandate, artistic expression with formal technique, with the reality of the bell that starts the ideal of captivating students and ends the period, and the strategic with the joyful. The closest expression to summarize these fusions is Kieran Egan's notion of Imaginative Rationality (Egan, 2007, p. 40).

The effectiveness of Outrageous Teaching also has implications for conceptions of professional practice. Philosophers and scientists now realize that the rational mind and the imagination are interdependent intellectual functions. Physics has now accepted both quantum theory and relativity, although they are almost opposite in their functioning. These examples serve as useful metaphors for what our profession now needs to do. Our profession needs to accept and embrace the reality that there are two critical, almost diametrically opposite instructional processes that must coexist in the classroom in a synergistic fashion if progress is to be made in increasing student interest and learning across the board and in reducing the learning gap and dropout rates. Both conventional instruction and Outrageous Teaching are critical.

It is time for the profession to stop leaning on one technique or the other, and to stop trying to prove that one is better than the other. Rather, we must simultaneously embrace, research, and transmit the best, albeit different, techniques for both conventional instruction and Outrageous Teaching. In most conventional instruction, you teach by directive; in Outrageous lessons and units, you teach by using suspense and curiosity to trigger students' imagination. Maintaining discipline under conventional instruction and over the course of an Outrageous lesson or unit are two very different processes. There are also major differences in planning methods, time allocation during a period, and sequence of events; and the teacher has a very different frame of mind going into each type of lesson. Although both types of teaching require preparation and knowledge, Outrageous Teaching also requires higher levels of imagination and courage. We need to give as much thought to how to develop those creative characteristics in teachers as we do to developing teachers' understanding of the psychological processes that impact learning. We also need to consider teachers as masterful only when they are able to switch back and forth between conventional and Outrageous methodologies as appropriate, and excel at both.

Most important, this book has demonstrated that even the most inexperienced teacher can produce extraordinary instruction and learning, even under the most difficult conditions and with the toughest classes. The book is a testament to the imagination and spirit of my student teachers, both in terms of what they achieved and for putting up with me as a teacher.

Outrageous Teaching makes the following six significant contributions to prior conceptions of the instructional use of dramatic technique:

• It demonstrates that dramatic technique can be used as the primary technique for teaching content in ways that increase learning. Learning is increased when content is taught this way from the beginning rather than relegating dramatic technique to reinforcing content already taught conventionally.

• When the teacher role-plays and the students are active participants, the learning experience is highly efficient as well as highly effective. A lot can be accomplished even within a single lesson rather than requiring a complete unit, so it does not take more time than conventional instruction.

• The fact that Outrageous Teaching is designed to be used in lieu of conventional instruction for teaching selected content objectives makes it as relevant in times of budget cuts and high stakes and accountability as it is in more temperate times when teachers have a say in the curriculum.

• It is possible to have a clear methodology—in this case, the Dramatized Content Planning Method detailed in Chapter Four—and still produce highly diverse and creative lessons and units across the content areas.

• Outrageous Teaching can consistently captivate and increase the learning of even the oldest students, across the content areas.

• It is possible to derive techniques from the performing arts and apply them to a pragmatic end—teaching existing content objectives—and still produce highly creative and thoughtful learning experiences for students, and for their teachers.

Taken together, these contributions of Outrageous Teaching bring the use of dramatic technique into the core missions of schooling and professional practice.

The examples presented in this book also demonstrate that even when an Outrageous lesson is focused on a seemingly prosaic content objective, it does not detract from the creativity and thoughtfulness of both students and teachers. In other words, the content objective does not have to be sophisticated in order for an Outrageous lesson to be creative and inspired, and to stimulate higher-order thinking in students.

OVERCOMING THE BARRIERS—ONE TEACHER AND ONE LESSON AT A TIME

You and I both understand the problems in teaching Outrageous lessons and getting the idea accepted. These problems are summarized in the next section, along with how to overcome them. In the initial draft of this book I placed this discussion of implementation concerns in the first chapter. In the end, I decided to let Dwight's evolution and experience serve as the metaphor for the normal uncertainty and evolution that everyone who develops such lessons and units undergoes—as well as for the rainbow at the end of the journey that we all seek: seeing students excited about learning. Although everyone goes through the stage of wondering "Do I have it in me to teach this way?" "Will it work?" and "Will I look stupid?" hopefully the experience of Dwight and all the other student teachers and teachers in this book will convince you that you do indeed have it in you. If they could do it, so can you.

Ultimately, the only way to overcome the self-imposed doubts and the dilemmas imposed by the existing state of practice is to "Nike" these issues. People have to decide to "just do it" because it makes compelling sense. There is no rationale in this age of ubiquitous entertainment-on-demand and YouTube exhibitionism for education remaining rooted solely in literal and simplistic presentation of content. And even though everyone views taking the plunge into Outrageous Teaching as a bold and daring step—and it is—most teachers I talk to can remember an incident long ago when one of their teachers taught something in Outrageous fashion, and they usually remember it fondly.

The key for teachers is to be bold and creative, yet strategic, in linking their creative vision to the teaching of content. It is not enough to find something that will interest students. You can completely change the learning context into something that students will in fact be interested in while at the same time "backdooring" the content objectives.

Think again of the Pig Lady in Chapter Seven, who took her initial insight for motivating her students and converted it into a yearlong unit on how to raise pigs. She did not just implement this idea for its own sake, however. In preparing the supporting materials on how to raise pigs, she made sure that they encompassed all of the district's formal vocabulary and language arts content objectives.

Linking dramatic context to content learning is a mind-set. Many creative teacher initiatives designed to capture student interest could be extended to cover formal content objectives with just a little more thought and with no loss of student interest or compromising of the teacher's vision.

It is my hope that this book will help inspire the many outstanding teachers in *all* types of schools to engage in teaching content Outrageously. I emphasize the word *all* because too often the most progressive techniques are provided only to the advantaged. Although Outrageous Teaching works for everyone, it is most critical for sparking the learning of children born into poverty, because they tend to be the most resistant to conventional teaching.

So although creating Outrageous lessons is extra work, the results are worth it—for both teachers and students. Learning is increased, deeper connections are established with students, and teachers have the tremendous satisfaction of knowing that they pulled off something masterful and unique in the entire history of U.S. education. In addition, even a little bit of Outrageous Teaching goes a long way in changing everyone's perceptions of one another.

Making the Case: Overcoming Concerns, Fears, and Misunderstandings

I have periodically conducted interviews with teachers to find out how they viewed the use of dramatic technique and why they held these views. This powerful tool is seldom used in the classroom to teach new content. Following are the most commonly expressed concerns and fears about relying on the use of dramatic technique, along with how the principles of Outrageous Teaching address those concerns.

That is not me!   The common perception is that to be dramatic you have to be an extrovert or a jokester. This is simply not true. Indeed, many of the top Hollywood stars are introverts in real life. They use acting as a way to break out of that shell. In other words, one's professional personality need not be the same as one's real-life personality. The true personality key for incorporating drama into teaching is that the individual believes that he or she will do anything to help his or her students learn.

I do not have time due to accountability pressures!   Incorporating dramatic techniques into instruction is largely viewed as taking time away from "real" teaching time. In Outrageous Teaching, however, you are teaching the same content objectives you would otherwise, and chances are that you will produce more learning in less time and with greater retention. This is evidenced by the sample lessons and units presented in this book. Outrageous Teaching is thus consistent with accountability requirements.

No one else is doing it!   Unfortunately, this is probably true, particularly in high-poverty schools. The sad irony is that the students who can most benefit from incorporating drama into teaching and learning are less likely to experience it in school. My experience working with student teachers in high-poverty schools was that the mentor teachers often resented my encouraging their student teacher to conduct a drama lesson. The mentor teachers would often argue that I was being unreasonable because "no one in the school teaches that way." But that is the problem! And it is all the more reason for you to embrace the challenge, exert leadership, and demonstrate the benefit of Outrageous Teaching to your peers.

I will be reprimanded!   Unfortunately, this could be true, because administrators have not been trained to recognize the value and encourage the use of dramatic approaches to teaching and learning. But it is not likely. All a teacher is doing in an Outrageous lesson is teaching the same lesson differently and not deviating from the established curriculum.

In addition, there are lots of good administrators out there, many of whom are trying to figure out how to establish the types of instruction that will better captivate their students. So there is opportunity to convince open-minded administrators to value the use of dramatic techniques.

In general, communication is the best way to avoid problems. First talk to your peers about your interest in trying out an Outrageous lesson. Perhaps others will be interested in exploring the use of the technique or in assisting you. Then have a dialogue with the administrators at your school. Once the administrators realize that you are still teaching the expected content, and once they see the reactions of students to an agreed upon pilot lesson, few will question the value of Outrageous lessons, and they may even encourage other teachers in the school to get on board.

I will lose control of my class!   It is natural to fear that giving up routine discipline and lesson structure will result in chaos in your classroom and total loss of control. Although these are all possibilities, I have never seen a teacher lose control of a class while doing an Outrageous lesson. Quite the contrary! I have seen usually rambunctious classrooms in absolute silence and awe, wondering what would happen next. Many such examples are scattered throughout this book. Not only is drama the most underused instructional teaching technique, but it is also the most underused technique for maintaining classroom control. Indeed, the best form of classroom control is to surprise and fascinate students.

It may work for younger students, but I teach high school!   Outrageous Teaching works equally well at the high school level, as demonstrated by the sample lessons and units in this book.

I do not have the time to plan lots of Outrageous lessons!   Outrageous lessons are so powerful that a little bit goes a long way toward stimulating student interest and learning and increasing student respect for the teacher. Students typically react to teachers who occasionally incorporate dramatic contexts into their teaching by saying, "Our teacher really cares about us because he or she works hard to make the lessons interesting." You do not need to teach many Outrageous lessons. Even a few, judiciously used, have a lot of impact on students. What is really important is to take some of the elements of an Outrageous lesson and incorporate them into your everyday teaching.

What if it does not work and I end up looking stupid?   It is true that anytime you do an Outrageous lesson for the first time you are not sure what the reaction of the class, is going to be. Yet, I have never seen an Outrageous lesson not work in the classroom. All you need to do is take a deep breath and go forward. Outrageous lessons always work because the students appreciate any divergence from the typical lesson, and because they appreciate the opportunity to be introduced to ideas in ways that make those ideas more meaningful and accessible to them—which is the primary purpose of Outrageous Teaching.

I have not been trained in the use of dramatic techniques! That is probably true. Few teacher education programs train teachers how to use dramatic techniques. The typical graduate of a teacher education program knows the latest class management techniques, knows a lot about learning theory, knows a lot about content, knows how to organize a lesson, and so on, but he or she does not know how to fascinate and not bore kids.

It is my hope that this book fills that void, and that teachers will use it to train themselves and one another in how to construct fascinating lessons and units.

Web Sharing Your Creative Genius

As mentioned in Chapter Seven, to facilitate the sharing of Outrageous ideas, experiences, lessons, and units, I have established a blog to provide a forum in which to discuss your experiences with Outrageous Teaching. Please send your lesson ideas, questions, suggestions, and experiences to me at http://www.outrageousteaching.blogspot.com. It is my hope that this blog will serve as an ongoing discussion community of teachers interested in Outrageous Teaching. (Should the name of the blog change in the future, you can locate the site via Google by searching on keywords such as my name, *Outrageous Teaching*, and *student engagement*.)

I may also create a compendium of the best examples of Outrageous lessons in a follow-up book.

IN CONCLUSION

Let the show begin!

Lights, Camera, Action!

—applause—applause—applause—applause—

TEACHER: Wow! They liked it—they learned it—they cared about it!

—take a bow—

STUDENTS: Why can't we learn this way all the time?

Encore!

APPENDIX A: THE ORIGINS OF DRAMA

EARLY FORMS OF DRAMA

It is believed that drama emerged from the myths and rituals of ancient times. Some believe that drama originated with the Egyptians in the form of reenacting the death and resurrection of the god Osiris. Brockett and Hildy (1999) concluded, however, that the first records of drama we have are Greek. Greek drama evolved from dithyrambic rituals consisting of a hymn sung and danced in honor of Dionysus, the Greek god of wine and fertility, at religious festivals. The worship of Dionysus was designed to "keep a balance between the civic values of patriarchal Athenian society, law and order, intellect, culture (all under the aegis of Apollo and Athena herself) and everything the city walls excluded—untamed nature, the passions, the female" (Sagar, 2004). The dithyrambic ritual consisted of an improvised story sung by a choral leader, and a traditional refrain sung by a chorus (Brockett and Hildy, 1999).

The dithyrambic ritual further evolved when the Athenian government accorded official sanction and financial support in 534 B.C. Athens sponsored a contest for the best tragedy presented at the City Dionysia, a major religious festival. It was at the City Dionysia that a tragedy was first presented. The name *tragedy* derived from *tragoidia*, which means "goat song." It was probably derived from the tradition of awarding a goat to the best singing and dancing performance at the Dionysia (Brockett and Hildy, 1999). According to Aristotle, tragedy emerged out of improvisations by the leaders of dithyrambs (Brockett and Hildy, 1999). Thespis is considered to have initiated the evolution of dithyrambic song and dance improvisations into the tragic dramatic play in 534 B.C. (This, of course, is the origin of the modern term of *thespian* for actor.) Thespis won the first tragedy contest. He is credited with introducing an actor who wore masks and costumes and engaged in dialogue with the leader of the chorus (Cheney, 1935).

In addition to sparking the evolution of the City Dithyrambic ritual into drama, the link of state and theater also led to the writing down of major plays of the times. The main structural features of the surviving Greek tragedies are:

1. A prologue
2. A parados (entrance of chorus, which begins the play)
3. A series of episodes (three to six separated by choral dance songs) that develop the main action
4. An exodus: a concluding scene that includes the departure of all the characters and the chorus (Brockett and Hildy, 1999, pp. 17–18).

Even as the dramatic form was evolving, the events that made up Athens' Dionysia were altered to meet changing social conditions. Around 508 B.C., Athenian democracy was created. To facilitate democracy, the family structure of Attica society that had fomented extensive rivalries was replaced and the population was divided into ten tribes. It may have been out of the desire to stimulate loyalty to the recently created tribes that a new contest—for dithyrambic performance—was inaugurated at the City Dionysia. Each tribe, in competition with the other nine, presented two dithyrambs each year, one for men and one for boys. The dramatic events went on for three days, with five plays a day. The three-day event was judged and the winners were given a laurel wreath and a goat, which was then sacrificed (Conway, 1934).

Over time, the heightened dithyrambic competition became more involved, which led to new forms of expression. Around 501 B.C., reorganization of the City Dionysia added a contest for satyr plays. This type of play was a burlesque treatment of mythology that generally ridiculed gods or heroes and their adventures. The satyr form contained boisterous action and included vigorous dancing as well as indecent language and gestures. The play was divided into series of episodes separated by choral odes, with a chorus of satyrs who sang and danced as they carried large phallic symbols aloft on poles (Brockett and Hildy, 1999). The satyrs were as unheroic and grossly physical as it was possible to get. They represented natural and amoral man, as opposed to civilized man, and extolled everything that man shares with beasts: acquisitiveness, lust, drunkenness, lying, boasting, and cowardice.

In time, dramatists emerged—a small group of individuals who were recognized as having special talent to produce dramas. To enter the City Dionysia competition, each dramatist was required not only to write a tragedy, but also to supply a satyr play as an afterpiece. The satyr plays provided comic relief from the serious plays that had gone before (Brockett and Hildy, 1999).

The City Dionysia continued to become more sophisticated. By 500 B.C., in order to enter the competition, each dramatist was required to present three tragedies and a satyr play. In 487–486 B.C. a new dramatic form was added to the City Dionysia: comedy (Brockett and Hildy, 1999). Aristotle credited comedy with growing out of the improvisations of the leaders of phallic songs in the satyr. Another influence on Athenian comedy was mime, which supposedly first appeared in Megara, a city some twenty-five miles from Athens, shortly after 581 B.C. No records of the mimes from this early period survive, but later mimes are short satirical treatments of everyday domestic situations or burlesqued versions of the myths that formed the basis of the satyrs (Brockett and Hildy, 1999).

Whereas satyr plays focused on parodying myths, comedies often focused on contemporary events. In addition, while satyr plays were written by the same dramatists who wrote the tragedies, new dramatists emerged who specialized in comedies.

THE EARLY DRAMATISTS

The dramatists built on the innovation of spoken dialogue by an actor begun by Thespis. In addition, they began to link the multiple sequences of tragedies they were required to develop for each contest into a plot (Cheney, 1935).

Although Arion (625–585 B.C.) may have been the first to write down dithyrambs and give them titles, knowledge of Greek tragedy is derived almost entirely from the works of Aeschylus, Sophocles, and Euripides (Brockett and Hildy, 1999). Aeschylus (525–456 B.C.) wrote ninety plays and added a second actor to his works. He has been called the father of tragedy, and he brought his sensibilities as a poet to his works. Sophocles (496–406 B.C.) wrote at least one hundred plays and added a third actor. He was the first to have the actor-spoken dialogue supersede the role of the chorus (Cheney, 1935). In addition, he was the first dramatist not to act in his own plays (Johnson, 1969). Euripides (486–406 B.C.) wrote ninety-two plays (Conway, 1934). His plays humanized drama by probing more deeply into the emotional and psychological nature of characters while also portraying gods as malignant (Cheney, 1929). Although satyr plays constituted a quarter of the entire output of these early dramatists, only one and a half have come down to us.

Aristotle credited Epicharmus, who wrote plays from 485–467 B.C., with inventing comedy (Brockett and Hildy, 1999). Some of the early comic dramatists were Chionides, Magnes, Ecphantides, and Eupolis. However, the only surviving comedies of the fifth century are by Aristophanes (448–380 B.C.). He is thought to have written about forty plays. Probably the most noteworthy characteristic of Aristophanic comedy is its "commentary on contemporary society, politics, theater, and above all the Peloponnesian War" (Brockett and Hildy, 1999, p. 21).

It is these works that form the basis of the evolution of drama from ancient to modern times. These dramatists developed all the bases of modern theater. Their works led to the growing sophistication of dramatic forms as festival and religious ritual branched out into formal drama.

APPENDIX B: GAMES AND QUIZZES—SELECTED RESOURCES

I f you choose to use software to organize review games and puzzles, make sure it has the following characteristics:

• *It is simple to learn and inexpensive.* The more bells and whistles it has, the more expensive it will be and the longer it will take to learn to operate. Simple is better.

• *It requires, or at least allows, teachers and students to input the contents of the puzzle or quiz.* Much of the lower-priced software comes with the questions and answers already provided and have no provision for creating your own, which is the reason for getting the software.

• *It does not put time pressure on responses or reward speed.* Unless you are using the software with high-performing students, no pressure should be placed on students to answer questions quickly, nor should the player or players who are first to respond be rewarded. The focus should be on accuracy of response.

• *It provides a free trial period.* This period gives you a chance to learn whether you feel comfortable using the software, and whether it works well on your computer system.

Table B.1
Crossword Puzzle Software

Name	Platform	Comment/URL	Site License Cost
Crossword Compiler	Windows	Can place puzzles on Web page http://www.crossword-compiler.com	School $499 District $1,900
Crossword Construction Kit	Windows	http://www .crosswordkit.com	Thirty users $340
Crossword Express	Mac, Windows	Lite version. http://www .crauswords.com	$35 per single user No site license price listed
Crossword Studio	Mac, Windows	Can add pictures and sounds http://www .nordicsoftware.com/ web/product_index/ crossword_studio	$29.95 for single user Site license available
Crossword Weaver	Windows	Use the freeform style version (not the professional style version) http://www .crosswordweaver.com	School site license $99–$159, depending on grade levels
Puzzle Maker	Mac, Windows	Includes nine other word puzzles in addition to Criss-Cross http://puzzlemaker .discoveryeducation.com	CD-ROM version $300

Note: List does not include shareware or freeware, or software that costs more than $500 for a site license.

A wide variety of crossword puzzle creators are available. Table B.1 lists the most widely used versions along with their prices either for a site license or for all the computers in a thirty-computer lab. Please note that inclusion in the list is not an endorsement; I have not tested them.

Table B.2
Quiz Show Software

Name	Link	Cost
TGI Quiz Game Show XF	http://www.training-games .com/classroom_quiz_show.html	Ten users $599
FRS Classroom Game Show	http://fastrabbitsoftware.com/ gameshow.htm	Site license $249.95
The Ultimate Quiz Show	http://www.decsoftware.com/ quizshow.htm	Five users $170
Learning Ware	http://www.learningwarek20 .com	

Note: Given the high cost of software, the HOTS project developed its own crossword puzzle and quiz show software. For information about obtaining this relatively low-cost software, contact me by e-mail at stanpogrow@att.net

Quiz show software is available both for specific games, such as Jeopardy (see http://www.nextag.com/jeopardy-game/search-html for a comparative listing of both board and computerized versions of Jeopardy), and in a general quiz show format that allows for a great deal of customization. Such software tends to be more expensive than crossword games because it is often used by industry for training programs, which encourages the developers, who seek the greatest possible market, to add lots of features, most of which are not needed for classroom use. Table B.2 lists a variety of quiz show software options.

APPENDIX C: SIMULATION UNITS—SELECTED RESOURCES

Part One of this Appendix presents sources for social studies simulation units. Part Two lists sources of computer simulations for use across the curriculum. Part Three discusses general concerns about using existing computer simulations to teach content objectives and develop thinking skills.

PART ONE: SOURCES OF LOCAL AND NATIONAL SOCIAL STUDIES MOCK PROCEEDINGS UNITS

Some states have developed their own trial, election, or government proceedings simulations based on state courtroom, election, and government practices. To find these simulations, Google, for instance, "mock trial" or "mock election" and the name of your state. Googling "mock trial" and "Maryland," for example, will lead you to such sources as http://www.courts.state.md.us/mocktrial/index.html, and Googling "mock elections" and Utah will lead you to such sources as http://www.mockelection.utah.gov.

Table C.1 lists national sources for obtaining social studies simulation units.

Table C.1
National Sources for Mock Social Studies Units

Social Studies School Service	http://catalog.socialstudies.com	Mock trial
Constitutional Rights Foundation	http://www.crf-usa.org/marketing/catindex.html	Mock trial
American Bar Association	http://www.abanet.org/publiced/mocktrials.html	Mock trial
National Student/Parent Mock Election	http://www.nationalmockelection.org	Mock presidential election, every four years
Youth Leadership Initiative	http://www.youthleadership.net/index.jsp	Mock elections, congressional proceedings, election campaigns
Center for Civic Education	http://civiced-store.stores.yahoo.net/wepeciandco.html	Mock congressional hearing

PART TWO: SOURCES OF COMPUTER-BASED SIMULATIONS

Professional journals provide sources for and reviews of computer-based simulations. For example, the National Science Teachers Association's Web site (http://www.nsta.org) offers links to online sources. A wide variety of such simulations are also available from http://www.sunburst.com and http://www.tomsnyder.com. Sunburst specializes in simulations that are installed on computers in a lab, and Tom Snyder Productions offers simulations that are installed on a teacher's computer station that is connected to a projector for classroom screening. Lots of additional websites, some of them content specific, offer both electronic and text-based simulation materials. For example, http://www.pbs.org and http://www.nationalgeographic.org both offer a wide variety of games and simulations in a range of content areas, and http://nsdl.org focuses on science materials, both print and computerized.

PART THREE: GENERAL CONCERNS ABOUT USING COMPUTER-BASED SIMULATIONS

Although both Supermath and HOTS revolved around the use of computers, I use computer software not to present content but rather to provide a context in which to discuss content. Alas, I have found it increasingly difficult to use commercial simulations as a basis for enhancing content learning and have turned to developing my own software. Indeed, it is ironic that as technology has advanced I have found it increasingly difficult and inefficient to use commercially available computer simulations.

The problem is that commercial software is becoming more automated and complicated, with tons of whiz-bang features. Consequently, the learning process must include spending more time mastering the technology and the bells and whistles, which means that less time is available for learning and integrating the content. In addition, there are so many visual and audio distractions that it is hard to remain focused on the pragmatic learning objectives. "Edutainment" software is becoming more entertaining and less educational.

For example, I always wanted to develop an extended, integrated math and science unit that had students use a flight simulator. I thought this would be a great way to integrate math and physics content. Students would play the role of pilot or pilot trainee. A variety of flight-simulator computer programs provide extensive documentation, and the approach lends itself to developing many math concepts such as angles and coordinates.

Although the process of learning to use a flight simulator is in itself an interesting experience, the point was to figure out how to apply it to teaching math and science content. Whenever I looked into the possibility of developing such a unit, I was deterred by three problems. First, it would take so long for the students to learn how to use the software that little time would be left over to tie in the math and science content from the curriculum. Second, an extraordinary amount of work would be required to link the specific math and science concepts to the use of the software. Third, students could master the software without the math and science knowledge I was trying to teach, so in the end it could be an artificial exercise. Therefore, even though I knew the students would enjoy learning to fly an airplane, I judged this simulation to be an inefficient way to teach the math and science concepts.

I also had to reconsider my use of the venerable program Oregon Trail. I used it to teach metacognition skills. (Metacognition is the ability to reflect explicitly on why a chosen strategy for solving a problem did or did not work.) In the original, simple, black-and-white version of Oregon Trail, students would find out in ten to fifteen minutes whether they would reach Oregon alive. The teacher could then quickly engage them in a brief discussion about why their strategy did or did not work, and what strategy they would try next. The students could then try a different approach. In two to three periods, the teacher could provide the students with four to six such debriefing experiences, thus enabling them to refine their explicit strategies and improve their ability to reflect on those strategies verbally. It is the student-teacher conversation about the strategies, about why they did or did not work, and about what they were going to change that enhanced the students' metacognition skills, which underlie all learning. In the new versions of Oregon Trail, it takes two to four periods for students to find out whether they have reached Oregon, so metacognition development opportunities are almost nil. So, when the vendor refused to continue to sell the original version to me, even though I was willing to pay the same price as for the new version, I had to develop my own version of the original program.

Another problem with using recent versions of simulation software is that it is often "dumbed down" from earlier, more primitive versions. For example, I used to use *Where in the World Is Carmen Sandiego?* to teach note-taking skills. In the early versions of the program, to figure out who the criminal was, the students would have to take notes to keep track of the clues acquired as they played the game. In later versions, the note taking was automated. At first this feature could be turned off; later on it could not be. Finally the software was automated to the point that the computer would indicate who the criminal was. In each new version, the note taking and the thinking-development activities, which were the critical features for teaching specific content and problem solving, were rendered increasingly obsolete by automation. Isn't progress great? Once again I had to develop a note-taking program of my own to teach the content objective in a dramatic context. The software that my team developed was always bare-boned so that the students could learn to operate it quickly and most of their time was spent discussing the content rather than learning how to use the software. Consequently, technology coordinators often thought our software, and hence our program, was backward. Alas, often the sophistication of the technology and the sophistication of the learning that can be produced are often inversely related.

RECOMMENDATIONS

Teachers need to be careful when adopting computer-based simulations as instructional tools. The greatest value of computers at this time seems to be their use as tools for writing down ideas, keeping score, constructing geometric proofs, and so on, rather than their use in simulations.

Above all, it is critical to remember that *the best and most important teaching technology is conversation, and the best graphics are the images in the mind. As a result, the development of powerful Outrageous lessons and units requires not computers or software but nothing more than knowledge, imagination, and guts.*

DWIGHT'S LESSON PLAN

Content objective: For students to learn the definition of persuasive writing and to write several paragraphs of a persuasive essay

Props and media	Content materials
Large tree stump and a sack full of common everyday items such as a large comb. Disguise.	Definition of persuasive writing

Who are you? Visitors/conspirators?	Disguise elements
I am a visitor who is a supersalesman.	Old fashioned stovepipe hat, large and long bushy white cotton beard, coveralls, and change of voice.

Opening surprise and setting

Supervising teacher tells the class that there is a special visitor and I walk in wearing a disguise and emphatically place a large tree stump on the floor.

Storyline or scenario and method (such as role-playing or anthropomorphizing and so on)

I role-play a salesman trying to convince students to buy a tree stump, and who is conducting tryouts for hiring another salesperson.

Transition to student activity phase (the *what* and *why* for the assigned work)

Have students try out for a great job as a TV infomercial salesperson.

Ending discussion (debriefing and completing content objective)

Explain that the writing they did was persuasive writing, define what it is, and congratulate the class on doing a great job of persuasive speaking and writing.

TAMARRA'S LESSON PLAN

Content objective: To learn the history of early efforts to unionize the coal mines

Props and media	Content materials
Sad blues music, lighting, single lamp to focus light just on her	Social studies textbooks

Who are you? Visitors and conspirators?	Disguise elements
Sad, weary, sick, exploited coal mine worker who has appeared from the past to ask for help because no one in her present time will help her.	Black smudges on face, head down on the desk, tattered blouse, and unkempt hair

Opening surprise and setting

Room is dark when students walk in. Supervising teacher announces that Tamarra is sick and that a visitor has taken her place.

Storyline or scenario and method (such as role-playing or anthropomorphizing, and so on)

Visitor is sick, dying, starving, desperate. Through fits of coughing and soft blues music, the visitor tells her tale of woe to convey to the students what it was like to work in the mines before unionization.

Transition to student activity phase (the *what* and *why* for the assigned work)

Visitor needs their help and advice to figure out a way to improve her life and that of her coworkers. The students are her only help.

Ending discussion (debriefing and completing content objective)

Origins of the union movement, reaction of employers to unionization efforts, how and why the struggles to unionize were finally successful

SHIRLEY'S LESSON PLAN

Content objective: To learn how an author creates a mood in a story, and why setting an appropriate mood is important for engaging the reader

Props and media	Content materials
Disguise	Literature text, students read the short story "The Sniper" by Liam O'Flaherty

Who are you? Visitors and conspirators?	Disguise elements
I am me, as someone who is being stalked.	Long coat (raincoat) with hood, sunglasses to hide my face

Opening surprise and setting

Rush into class, hide under a table, and ask students whether there is someone they do not recognize outside of the class.

Storyline or scenario and method (such as role-playing and anthropomorphizing, and so on)

Act worried that the person stalking me may spot me teaching so I have to hide while teaching and talk softly so that no one passing by will see me

Transition to student activity phase (the *what* and *why* for the assigned work)

Just have students continue to read the story out loud, taking turns, from early in the period until its dramatic ending.

Ending discussion (debriefing and completing content objective)

Discuss the mood of the story, how the author created a mood, how what I did was like what the author did. I hope they will realize that both the author and I created a mood of foreboding. End by thanking the students for their cooperation.

VIERA'S LESSON PLAN

Content objective: To get students interested in reading a classic story, Edgar Allen Poe's "The Tell-Tale Heart," and thinking about its meaning.

Props and media	Content materials
Disguise	Literature textbook
Who are you? Visitors and conspirators?	**Disguise elements**
I am me, but I come in late in my disguise.	Hospital cap and blouse, with straitjacket. Wild look with hair askew

Opening surprise and setting

The supervising teacher tells the class that I have had a nervous breakdown and have been sent to the mental hospital. Then I burst into the room looking indeed like I have just escaped from a mental institution.

Storyline or scenario and method (such as role-playing or anthropomorphizing, and so on)

I have been sent to a mental hospital because I hear sounds that no one else does. I escape, come to the classroom, start wandering around the classroom pretending to hear sounds in the floor and in the walls, constantly asking either the class as a whole or individual students whether they hear the sounds, whether they think I am crazy. I then ask them to read the story on the appropriate page in their reader, and go into a corner of the room so that no one will find me until the students figure out a way to help me.

Transition to student activity phase (the *what* and *why* for the assigned work)

Students need to read the story to find information that can be used to help me prove that I am not crazy and to figure out why I acted the way I did.

Ending discussion (debriefing and completing content objective)

They will have only started the story, so all I will do at the end of the period is tell them that I am really okay but when they continue to read the story tomorrow I want them to see if they can figure out why I pretended to be hearing all those sounds.

JOSE'S LESSON PLAN

Content objective: To teach students thirty-four new Spanish words related to ordering food in a restaurant

Props and media	**Content materials**
Small towel on the arm	Copies for each student of a handout of the new words along with an overhead projector
Who are you? Visitors and conspirators?	**Disguise elements**
I am a bumbling waiter who does not speak any English.	I am not trying to hide my identity, but rather to assume the persona of a moonlighting waiter, so I put on a white shirt, black jacket, and bow tie.

Opening surprise and setting

Teacher announces that I will be late because I have to moonlight at night as a waiter because I am not being paid for teaching, then I breathlessly run in dressed in my waiter outfit and apologize for being late. I tell them that they must have gotten very hungry waiting for me to come and take their order.

Storyline or scenario and method (such as role-playing or anthropomorphizing, and so on)

I am a waiter who does not speak English and who goes to each table and gets each group's order. I pantomime the meaning of the new words, and constantly repeat them from group to group.

Transition to student activity phase (the *what* and *why* for the assigned work)

There is no real transition. For most of the period I will be stumbling around the room taking orders, repeating and pantomiming key words until they start to understand them.

Ending discussion (debriefing and completing content objective)

Go through about half of the list of new words and have students provide definition generated inductively from the context of the ordering experience. Compliment them on how many new words they were able to learn so quickly, and ask whether they prefer learning new words by this approach or the traditional one.

SERENA'S LESSON PLAN

Content objective: To read poetry expressively and to appreciate the expressiveness of poetry.

Props and media	Content materials
Coffee essence, candles, quiet mood music, swaths of cloth, signs with the name of the coffee shop and slogan, dark juice to simulate coffee, cups	Text of about twenty poems previously discussed, and list of the available poems on the blackboard or poster

Who are you? Visitors and conspirators?	Disguise elements
The beat poet Allen Ginsberg, or perhaps more appropriately, Alena Ginsberg	Beret, sunglasses, and a painted goatee. A Nehru-like jacket.

Opening surprise or setting

The opening surprise is when the supervising teacher announces that I am absent that day and that she does not have any lesson to teach them, and it is announced that they are going to hang out in the new coffee shop on campus. The second surprise is when they enter the dimly lit coffee shop and see the figure sitting on the desk and wonder who that is, and why the lights are out, and gradually come to realize that it is me.

Storyline or scenario and method (such as role-playing or anthropomorphizing, and so on)

A beat poet is running a coffee shop in the school and the students are invited to the grand opening. The supervising teacher brings them to Nick's coffee shop. Nick turns out to be Allen Ginsberg, the beat poet.

Transition to student activity phase (the *what* and *why* for the assigned work)

After welcoming fellow beat poets to his coffee shop, Allen Ginsberg explains that the audience is expected to do a poetry reading and that if the audience approves, they signal that approval by clicking their fingers.

Ending discussion (debriefing and completing content objective)

Praise the students' poetry readings and how they captured the expressiveness of the ideas and words. Review some of the different types of emotion they portrayed in their reading. Finally, explain about the period of beat poetry and its influence on American poetry.

JOHN'S LESSON PLAN

Content objective: To learn about how the Wright brothers came to design the first successful flying machine and to develop understanding of the basic principles of flight

Props and media	Content materials
Several pieces of metal to clang together to make sounds outside the classroom door, something to make a boom or crash sound with, a long piece of cloth or paper attached to a balsa wood frame to simulate a wing frame that can be lifted above my head	Science books

Who are you? Visitors or conspirators?	Disguise elements
I am Orville Wright, who for some reason was transported to the future when he crashed his plane.	Goggles covering face, old pilot's hat, smudges all over face

Opening surprise or setting

Class is told that we do not know where the teacher is. There is a boom or crash sound, and in staggers a strange visitor dressed in goggles and old flyer hat and with smudges of black on his face.

Storyline or scenario and method (such as role-playing or anthropomorphizing, and so on)

Strange visitor is a failed inventor who is always crashing. In his last crash he is transported to the classroom of the future, where there is secret, magical science information. The visitor then notices the strange electronic devices that the students have, and their strange mode of dress, and decides that they are magical people. Then he notices their science book and sees all kinds of magical information that he asks the class to share with him.

Transition to student activity phase (the *what* and *why* for the assigned work)

The strange visitor needs the magic information in their books to figure out how to design a better plane, and he asks for their help while he recovers from his crash.

Ending discussion (debriefing and completing content objective)

Discuss what the key breakthroughs were that led to the first successful flight, and the importance of combining perseverance and knowledge. Then use the experience of transforming as a metaphor for the students and how it is critical not to give up on your dreams, and that they too can use science knowledge to become inventors and enrich their own lives and the lives of others.

STAN'S LESSON 1 PLAN

Content objective: For students to infer the rules for multiplying signed numbers, starting with $- \times - = +$

Props and media	Content materials
Two CDs or other music source, one with old-fashioned boring music and one with contemporary music, large + and −signs to tape to the walls, and possibly a number-line banner	None
Sign with the signed number choreography for the first four moves	
Who are you? Visitors or conspirators?	**Disguise elements**
I am myself, but as a choreographer with an irrepressible urge to dance and to teach new dances.	None

Opening surprise or setting

The opening surprise is when I start to dance around the room and talk about how I am a choreographer and would rather dance than do math that day.

Storyline or scenario and method (such as role-playing or anthropomorphizing, and so on)

I decide not to teach math today and let the students dance, that is, learn a new dance.

Transition to student activity phase (the *what* and *why* for the assigned work)

The students apply the signed number choreography to infer the other rules for multiplying signed numbers.

Ending discussion (debriefing and completing content objective)

Quickly review the rules for signed numbers, and why using numbers made it easier to learn the dance moves than using words, and what that tells you about numbers.

STAN'S LESSON 2 PLAN

Content objective: For students to understand the importance and structure of fractions

Props and media	Content materials
Several posters of a jungle and another of a mastodon	None
Jungle music. Sand box with a stick, or black paper and chalk.	

Who are you? Visitors or conspirators?	Disguise elements
The teacher is a visitor from the future.	Lots of unkempt hair, long nails, feathers in the hair, primitive-looking clothes.

Opening surprise or setting

When students arrive in a darkened room, they hear jungle music and see the teacher sitting or lying on the floor, looking very strange.

Storyline or scenario and method (such as role-playing or anthropomorphizing, and so on)

The chief of the prehistoric tribe has to divide up the mastodon steak fairly.

Transition to student activity phase (the *what* and *why* for the assigned work)

Students figure out how to describe the process of sharing fairly without numbers or words.

Ending discussion (debriefing and completing content objective)

Quickly review the significance of fractions.

APPENDIX E: TEACHING OUTRAGEOUSLY IN THE EARLY GRADES

There are a variety of books that focus on the use of dramatic techniques in the earliest grades (Kelner, 1993; Cresci, 1989; Kelner and Flynn, 2006; Greenberg, 1996; Dickinson and Neelands, 2006; and Jossart and Courtney, 1997). A way for teachers of younger children to start developing Outrageous lessons with a high probability of success is to look through children's drama books for ideas and inspirations, and then try to extend those ideas according to the principles of how to create Outrageous lessons.

For example, Kelner (1993, pp. 53–54) presents a wonderful idea for a game to *reinforce* basic punctuation for second graders. It is inspired by one of the great comedy routines of all times; Victor Borge's routine on phonetic punctuation. In this routine, Borge would read a passage using sounds and gestures to indicate the punctuation. Of course he would select a passage with lots and lots of punctuation and that would involve lots of spitting.

Kelner's idea of extending this comedy routine to the classroom is brilliant. Any second grade teacher who is a Victor Borge fan will be enticed to try the game. In her suggested lesson, the teacher tells the students what sounds and gestures to make for each punctuation mark. The lesson ends up being a cute way to review and reinforce the use of punctuation marks and embed them in the students' memory. Although this is a valuable lesson, I believe her creative idea can be extended further to use the approach for original teaching of the punctuation marks. I therefore decided to develop an alternate version of this lesson built on the same wonderful idea, and that retained some of her suggestions such as using only a few punctuation marks at a time.

KELNER'S MODIFIED LESSON—EXTENDED (PUNCTUATION, SECOND GRADE)

The following is my extension of Kelner's idea into an Outrageous lesson for *teaching* (as opposed to *reinforcing*) punctuation to second graders.

The Lesson

The teacher can introduce a special guest, John, who pretends to be blind (or someone who is actually blind). The teacher indicates the following:

> My friend John is blind and therefore likes to have people read to him. I told him how you are a very good group of readers, and he wanted to listen to you read stories out loud. It would make him feel so good if you would do that. Is that OK?

The students will of course say yes. Then the teacher asks the students to turn to a story that has periods and commas. The teacher asks one of the students to please start reading. As soon as the student finishes the first sentence and starts the second, John asks the student:

> Why did you slow down after [whatever the last word in the sentence was]? How did you know to pause there?

The student will probably respond that there was a dot or period there. If the student says "period," John says:

> What does a period look like?

If the student says it looks like a dot, John asks:

> What does a dot look like? Remember, I can only feel and hear things.

At that point, the teacher asks the class:

> If John can only feel or hear things, how can we explain to him what that mark is at the end of the sentence?

Students will probably realize that they can make him feel it if they draw it for him on his hand. They may or may not come up with the idea of making a sound that gives the feeling of the shape. If they do not, the teacher can suggest using a sound that describes the shape. The teacher can then say:

> There are marks on the page to help you read the story better. This is called a sentence and this is called a comma. Let's read the story for John and help him feel and hear the marks also.

The teacher then divides the class into teams of three. One student is the group reader; the second is the marker, who will draw the mark on John's hand; the third is the sound maker, who makes the sounds for the marks. Each team is assigned two sentences to read and given a few minutes to practice the sentences and develop their own sounds for the comma and period. (Ideally, the marker and sound person do their things at the same time.)

After some noisy planning, the teacher says:

> I want each team to come up and read their two sentences to John. As the reader in your team reads the words, pause for each comma and period, and the marker will draw it on his hand while the sound-effects person makes the sound your team agreed on.

After all the teams have read the two sentences with sounds and marks, John says:

> Thank you for sharing your story with me and helping me understand what a comma and period look like and sound like. You read very beautifully.

John then leaves.

The teacher compliments the students on the wonderful sounds they invented for periods and commas. The teacher then asks the students how commas and periods help them read and understand what they read.

COMMENTS ON THE PROPOSED LESSON

In this approach, the students get to explore creative ideas for communicating while also learning about punctuation. The Outrageous lesson also provides the basis for ongoing learning about punctuation. In this adaptation of a terrific drama idea, the drama is used to teach the content objective, that is, the elements of punctuation, while at the same time enhancing the creative and discovery elements of how the idea is implemented.

The lesson also provides a shared experience that is then useful for teaching additional punctuation marks. In subsequent lessons on punctuation, the teacher can have the students quickly go through the same process of making up sounds and gestures for the new marks. Each team can keep its own sounds.

Will you be able to hold the students' attention through this more involved lesson? What additional modifications would be needed to make it work smoothly? Not having direct experience with second grade classrooms and students, I cannot say for sure, but I am confident that teachers can figure it out. I am also confident that teachers in the early grades can figure out ways to incorporate the principles of Outrageous Teaching into their lessons with the students for the original teaching of content.

IMPLICATIONS FOR DEVELOPING OUTRAGEOUS LESSONS FOR GRADES K TO 3

There are lots of other wonderful ideas in these children's drama books that can be similarly extended. Most teachers of young children also have lots of their own resource ideas for games and role-playing that they have developed over the years. These too can be similarly extended into Outrageous lessons, and their role can be expanded from something that will interest students to something that can also be used to teach content.

REFERENCES

Black, A., & Stave, A. M. (2007). A comprehensive guide to reader's theater: Enhancing fluency and comprehension in middle school and beyond. Newark, DE: International Reading Association.

Bolton, G. (2001). Changes in thinking about drama in education. *Theory into Practice*, *24*(3), 151–157.

Bower, G. H., & Forgas, J. P. (2000). Affect, memory, and social cognition. In E. Eich, J. F. Kihlstron, G. H. Bower, J. P. Forgas, and P. M. Niedenthal (Eds.), *Cognition and emotion* (pp. 87–168). New York: Oxford University Press.

Bresler, L. (2005). Music and the intellect: Perspectives, interpretations, and implications for education. *Phi Delta Kappan*, *87*(1), 24–31.

Bridgeland, J. M., Dilulio, J. J., & Morison, K. B. (2006). *The Silent Epidemic: Perspectives of High School Dropouts*. Washington, DC: Civic Enterprises.

Brockett, O., & Hildy, F. (1999). History of the theatre (8th ed.). Boston: Allyn and Bacon.

Catterall, J., Chapleau, R., & Iwanaga, J. (1999). Involvement in the arts and human development: General involvement and intensive involvement in music and theater arts." In E. Fiske (Ed.), *Champions of change: The impact of the arts on learning* (pp. 1–18). Washington, DC: Arts Education Partnership, President's Committee on the Arts and the Humanities.

Catterall, J. S. (2007). Enhancing peer conflict resolution skills through drama: An experimental study. *Research in Drama Education*, *12*(2), 163.

Cheney, S. (1935). The theatre: Three thousand years of drama, acting and stagecraft. New York: Tudor.

Conway, J. (1934). A history of the theatre syllabus. Seattle, WA: University of Washington Bookstore.

Cresci, M. M. (1989). Creative dramatics for children. Glenview IL: Scott, Foresman.

Darmer, M. (1995) Developing transfer and metacognition in educationally disadvantaged students: Effects of the Higher Order Thinking Skills (HOTS) program. Unpublished dissertation, University of Arizona.

Dewey, J. (1931). *Art as experience.* New York: Capricorn Books.

Dickinson, R., and Neelands, J. (2006). Improve your primary school through drama. London: David Fulton.

Dillon, S.(2007, August 27). With turnover high, schools fight for teachers. *New York Times.* Available at http://www.nytimes.com/2007/08/27/education/27teacher .html?scp=1&sq=with%20turnover%20high,%20schools%20fight%20for %20teachers&st=cse

Egan, K. (1992). Imagination in teaching and learning: The middle school years. Chicago: University of Chicago Press.

Egan, K. (2007). Imagination past and present. In K. Egan, M. Stout, and K. Takaya (Eds.), Teaching and learning outside the box (pp. 3–20). New York: Teachers College Press.

Flynn, R. M. (2007). Dramatizing the content with curriculum-based reader's theater, grades 6–12. Newark, DE: International Reading Association.

Gardner, H. (1993). *Frames of mind: The theory of multiple intelligences.* New York: Basic Books.

Goodman, N. (1968). *Languages of art: An approach to a theory of symbols.* Kansas City, MO: Bobbs-Merrill.

Goodwin, J. (2006). Using drama to support literacy: Activities for children aged 7 to 14. London: Paul Chapman.

Greenberg, C. R. (1996). Little plays for little people. Portsmouth, NH: Teacher Ideas Press.

Greene, B. (2008, June 1). Put a little science in your life. *New York Times*, OP-ED, http://www.nytimes.com/2008/06/01/opinion/01greene.html?_r=1&scp=3& sq=greene&st=nyt&oref=slogin

Harris, P. (2000). *The Work of the Imagination Boxford*, UK: Blackwell.

Hart, B., & Risley, T. (1995). Meaningful differences in the everyday experience of young American children. Baltimore: Paul H. Brookes.

Heath, S., & Roach, A. (1999). Imaginative actuality: Learning in the arts during the nonschool hours. In E. Fiske (Ed.), *Champions of change: The impact of the arts on learning (19–34).* Washington, DC: Arts Education Partnership, President's Committee on the Arts and the Humanities.

Heathcote, D. (1984). *Dorothy Heathcote: Collected writings on education and drama.* London: Hutchinson.

Heathcote, D., and Bolton, G. (1995). Drama for learning. Portsmouth, NH: Heinemann.

Heller, P. G. (1996). Drama as a way of knowing. Portland, ME: Stenhouse.

Hiatt, K. (2006). Drama play: Bringing books to life through drama in the early years. London: David Fulton.

Jensen, E. P. (2008). A fresh look at brain-based education. *Phi Delta Kappan*, *89*, 408–417.

Johnson, A., & Johnson, B. (1969). Drama for classroom and stage. New York: A. S. Barnes.

Jossart, S., & Courtney, G. (1997). Story dramas K–3. Tucson, AZ: Good Year Books.

Jossart, S., & Courtney, G. (1998). Story dramas for grades 4 to 6. Tucson, AZ: Good Year Books.

Kelner, L. B. (1993). The creative classroom. Portsmouth, NH: Heinemann.

Kelner, L. B., and Flynn, R. M. (2006). Dramatic approach to reading comprehension: Strategies and activities for classroom teachers. Portsmouth, NH: Heinemann.

McCaslin, N. (1990). Creative drama in the classroom (5th ed.). New York: Longman.

Papert, S. (1980). *Mindstorms: Children, computers, and powerful ideas.* New York: Basic Books.

Pogrow, S. (2005, September). HOTS Revisited: A thinking development approach to reducing the learning gap after grade 3. *Phi Delta Kappan*, 64–75.

Ramani, G. B., & Siegler, R. S. (2007). Promoting broad and stable improvements in low-income children's numerical knowledge through playing number board games. Unpublished paper, Carnegie Mellon University.

Read, H. (1945). *Education Through Art.* New York: Pantheon.

Reisberg, D., and Heuer, F. (2004). Memory for emotional events. In D. Reisberg and P. Hertel, Eds., *Memory and emotion* (pp. 31–41). New York: Oxford University Press.

Rooyackers, P. (1998). 101 drama games for children: Fun and learning with acting and make-believe. Alameda, CA: SmartFun Activity Books.

Sagar, K. (2004, February). [Online]. Interview with Rutter. Programme Notes: Keith Sagar Essay. Retrieved from http://www.northern-broadsides.co.uk/Pages/prev_alcestis_sagar.htm

Sarason, S. B. (1999). Teaching as a performing art. New York: Teachers College Press.

Schank, R. E. (1999). Dynamic memory revisited. Cambridge, UK: Cambridge University Press.

Shuman, R. (Ed.). (1978). *Educational drama for today's schools.* Metuchen, NJ: Scarecrow Press.

Silberman, C. E. (1971). *Crisis in the classroom: The remaking of American education.* New York: Knopf.

Tauber, R. T., and Mester, C. S. (2007). Using performance skills in the classroom (2nd ed.). Westport, CT: Praeger.

Taylor, P. (2000). *The drama classroom: Action, reflection, transformation.* London: RoutledgeFalmer.

Vygotsky, L. S. (1978). Mind in society: Development of higher psychological processes (M. Cole, V. J. Steiner, S. Scribner, & E. Souberman, Eds.). Cambridge, MA: Harvard University Press.

Wagner, B. J. and Heathcote, D. (1976). Drama as a learning medium. Washington, DC: National Education Association.

Wilhelm, J. D. (2002). Action strategies for deepening comprehension. New York: Scholastic.

Wilhelm, J. D. (2008). *You gotta be the book*. New York: Teachers College Press.

INDEX

A

Accountability pressures, 190
Adolescents, connecting with, 12–13
Aeschylus, 195
Age of Enlightenment, 33
Analogy dramas, 52
Arion, 195
Aristophanes, 196
Aristotle, 4, 5, 33, 193, 196
Assessment and Outrageous Lessons, 85
Authentic learning experiences, 12

B

Barriers to Outrageous lessons, overcoming, 188–192
Black, A., 53
Blog for sharing ideas, 176, 192
Bolton, G., 4, 18, 19, 22, 54, 146
Boredom, student, 1–2
Borge, V., 217
Bower, G. H., 32
Bresler, L., 27
Bridgeland, J. M., 10
Brockett, O., 193, 194, 195, 196
Bruner, 21

C

Catterall, J. S., 21, 24, 27
Chapleau, R., 21, 24, 27
Character or persona, developing a, 72–73
Characters used in sample lessons, 139–140
Chase, Chevy, 73
Cheney, S., 194, 195, 196
Chionides, 196
Classroom games: enriching learning experience with, 48–49; resources for, 197–199; student-created, 49–52
Classroom use of dramatic techniques: instructional management, 42–48; introducing new content, 57–59; maintaining discipline, 40–42; overview of, 39–40; reviewing content learning, 48–57
Cognitive psychology, 31–32
Cognitive transfer: defined, 20–22; evidence of, 27–31
Computerized simulations, 55, 201–205
Confessional element in the debriefing, 80
Confucius, 4

Content debriefing, 71, 79–81

Content learning: introducing new content, 57–59; reviewing, 48–57

Controversy over dramatic technique, 22–24

Conway, J., 194, 195

Costume, voice, and mannerisms, 73–74, 139–140

Courage and Outrageous Lessons, 156–157

Courtney, G., 52, 217

Creatively authentic learning, 12

Cresci, M. M., 53, 217

Crisis in the Classroom, 2

Crossword puzzles, 49–50, 198

Culture and reality, tapping into students', 10–12

D

Dancing, for discovering math rules, 121–131

Darmer, M. A., 29

Decimals, manipulating, 168–170

Designing Outrageous Lessons: character or persona, 72–73; components of lesson plan, 70–71; content debriefing, 79–81; content materials, 79; disguise, 73–74; Dramatized Content Planning Method for, 69–70; Dwight's problem in, 81–82; emotional reaction, 78; key steps in, 82–84; props, 77–78; setting, 74; state of mind for, 155–162; storyline, 75–77; summary on, 87; surprise, 71–72; transition to students' learning activity, 78–79; trepidation over, 86–87. *See also* Examples of Outrageous Lessons; Getting started

Dewey, J., 21

Dickinson, R., 176, 217

Dillon, S., 182

Dilulio, J. J., 10

Discipline, maintaining, 40–42, 144–145, 191

Disguises, 70, 73–74, 138, 139–140

Drama: early forms of, 193–195; expanding your knowledge of, 174–175; as instructional tool, 4–5

Dramatic techniques: controversy in using, 22–24; defined, 3–4; integrative perspective on, 24–26; learning improvement from, 26–31; recent evolution of, 18–22

Dramatists, early, 195–196

Dramatized Content Planning Method: defined, 69–70; role-playing in, 152–155; storyline, suspense, and fantasy in, 151; uniqueness of, 150–151

Dwight's Outrageous Lesson: complete lesson, 59–62; introduction to, 7–8; lesson continued, 35–37; lesson plan for, 207–208; what can be learned from, 62–67

Dwight's problem in planning his lesson, 81–82

E

Early grades, Outrageous Teaching for, 178, 217–220

Ecphantides, 196

Egan, K., 33, 34, 186

Einstein, A., 34

Emotional reaction, eliciting of an, 70, 78

Epicharmus, 196

Eupolis, 196

Euripides, 195–196

Evolution of dramatic technique as instructional tool: cognitive transfer, 20–22; progressive origins, 18–20

Examples of Outrageous Lessons: comparison of, 136–141; Jose's lesson (Spanish), 109–113, Julie's lesson (language arts), 90–95; lesson plans for, 207–216; math and science lessons,

113–136; overview of, 89–90; Serena's lesson (poetry), 106–109; Shirley's lesson (literature), 99–102; social studies lessons, 95–99, 170–172; summary of, 141; Tamarra's lesson (social studies), 96–99; Viera's lesson (literature), 103–106

Expressive microbursts, 42–43

F

Far transfer, 22
Fast Food Nation, 54
Finlay-Johnson, H., 18, 19, 20, 37
Flynn, R. M., 52, 53, 56, 65, 174, 217
Forgas, J. P., 32

G

Games: classroom, 48–49; resources for, 197–199; student-created, 49–52
Gardner, H., 34
Getting started: as a collaborative group, 175–176; as an individual teacher, 165–175; as a profession, 181–183; as a school, 176–178; summary on, 183
Ginsberg, A., 107, 212, 213
Goodman, N., 21
Goodwin, J., 52
Grassroots movement, building a, 180–181
Greek drama, 193–195
Green, B., 114, 115
Greenberg, C. R., 217

H

Harris, P., 33
Hart, B., 11
Heath, S., 28
Heathcote, D., 19, 20, 23, 37, 53, 54, 56, 77, 146, 152
Heller, P. G., 52
Heuer, F., 32

Hiatt, K., 52
Higher Order Thinking Skills (HOTS) program: computer use in, 147; ideas from, 25; poetry contest, 108; student achievement and, 149, 150; training for, 174; transfer of skills and, 28–30, 37–38; word of mouth and, 180–181
Hildy, F., 193, 194, 195, 196
History lessons, developing, 95–99, 170–172
History of dramatic technique as instructional tool: cognitive transfer and, 20–22; progressive origins, 18–20; summary on, 37
Humor and strangeness, changing persona with, 6, 43–44

I

Ideas, blog for sharing, 176, 192
Imagination and learning, 6, 33–34
Instructional management: advanced techniques, 44–48; basic techniques, 42–44
Iwanaga, J., 21, 24, 27

J

Jensen, E. P., 32
Johnson, A., 195
Johnson, B., 195
Jossart, S., 52, 217

K

Kelner, L. B., 52, 56, 65, 174, 217, 218

L

Languages of Art: An Approach to a Theory of Symbols, 21
Learners, reluctant, 8–9
Learning: imagination and, 33–34; increasing efficiency of, 145–147

Learning gap, reducing the, 9–10, 179–180

Learning objectives for sample lessons, 137–138

Lesson plans for sample lessons, 207–216

Letendre, M. J., 181

Lighting, 74

Lombardo, G., 123

Loungers, 14

M

Magnes, 196

Master teachers, redefining, 182

Math and science lessons, 113–136, 168–170, 213–216

McCaslin, N., 53

Memories, vivid, 32

Mental models, 31–32

Mester, C. S., 43, 55

Miller, G., 21

Misunderstandings over Outrageous lessons, 189–192

Morison, K. B., 10

N

National Assessment of Educational Progress (NAEP), 10, 179

Near transfer, 22

Neelands, J., 176, 217

Neuroscience, perspectives from, 32–33

No Child Left Behind Act, 176

Noises Off, 119

Northwestern University's School of Speech, 19

O

Objectives, learning, 6, 137–138

Outrageous Lessons, designing: character or persona, 72–73; components of lesson plan, 70–71; content debriefing, 79–81; content materials, 79; disguise, 73–74; Dramatized Content Planning Method for, 69–70; Dwight's problem in, 81–82; emotional reaction, 78; key steps in, 82–84; props, 77–78; setting, 74; storyline, 75–77; summary on, 87; surprise, 71–72; transition to students' learning activity, 78–79; trepidation over, 86–87. See also Getting started

Outrageous Lessons, examples of: comparison of, 136–141; Jose's lesson (Spanish), 109–113, Julie's lesson (language arts), 90–95; math and science lessons, 113–136, 168–170; overview of, 89–90; Serena's lesson (poetry), 106–109; Shirley's lesson (literature), 99–102; social studies lessons, 95–99, 170–172; summary of, 141; Viera's lesson (literature), 103–106

Outrageous Teaching: barriers to, 188–192; building blocks of, 58–59; defined, 5–7; as powerful tool, 3, 6–7; reasons for, 8–13; six significant contributions of, 187; theoretical bases for, 31–35

Outrageous unit, incorporating an, 168–174

P

Papert, S., 136

Passive classroom, handling the, 47–48

Pedagogy, cutting-edge, 34–35

Perspectives on dramatizing instruction: historical perspective, 18–24; integrative perspective, 24–26

Pig Lady (Language Arts), 166–167, 178, 179, 189

Plato, 33, 34

Poe, E. A., 105, 137, 146, 210

Poetry contest, annual, 108

Poetry lesson, 106–109, 212–213

Pogrow, S., 21

Props, 70, 77–78, 138, 139–140
Punctuation, lesson reinforcing basic, 217–220

Q
Quiz show software, 199

R
Ramani, G. B., 49
Rapport with students, 147–148
Read, H., 21
Reader's Theater, 53
Reading gains for low socioeconomic status students, 27–28
Reisberg, D., 32
Reluctant or resistant learners, 8–9
Repeating students' answers, 45
Repertoires, expanding teachers', 148
Reprimands for teaching Outrageous lessons, 190–191
Risley, T., 11
Roach, A., 28
Role-playing: description of, 52–54; Dramatized Content Method and, 152–155; limitations of, 55–57
Role-taking, 53–54, 152–153
Rooyackers, P., 53
Russell Simmons Def Poetry Jam series, 108

S
Sagar, K., 193
Sample Outrageous Lessons: comparison of, 136–141; Jose's lesson (Spanish), 109–113, Julie's lesson (language arts), 90–95; learning objectives for, 137–138; lesson plans for, 207–216; math and science lessons, 113–136, 168–170, 213–216; overview of, 89–90; Serena's lesson (poetry), 106–109; Shirley's lesson (literature), 99–102; social studies lessons, 95–99, 170–172; summary of, 141; Tamarra's lesson (social studies), 96–99; Viera's lesson (literature), 103–106
Sarason, S. B., 174
Schank, R. E., 34
School improvement, drama as tool for, 176–178
Science and math lessons, 113–136, 168–170, 213–216
Self-expression perspective, criticism of, 22–23
Self-fulfillment, achieving, 85–87
Shuman, R., 19, 20
Siegler, R. S., 49
Silberman, C., 2
Silent classroom, handling the, 44–46
Simon, H., 21
Simulated experiences, 54–55
Slade, P., 19, 22
Snapshot and tableaux drama, 52
Social studies lessons, developing, 95–99, 170–172
Social studies simulation units, 201, 202
Software for puzzles and quiz shows, 197–199
Sophocles, 195
Sound effects, 74, 139, 140
Spanish lessons, 109–113, 211–212
State of mind for developing Outrageous Lessons, 155–162
Stave, A. M., 53
Storylines: developing, 70, 75–77; inventive, 6; of sample lessons, 137–138
Student achievement, creating a new physics of, 149–150
Student role-playing, 52–57, 152–155
Student teachers, Outrageous lessons taught by, 14–16

Student-created games, 49–52
Students: culture and reality of, 10–12; engaging, 146–147; passive, 47–48; rapport with, 147–148; silent, 44–46
Substitute teachers, 162
Supermath program, 30, 120
Surprise, planning the, 70, 71–72
Surprises, giving away the, 81
Suspense and fantasy, 151

T

Tauber, R. T., 43, 55
Taylor, P., 23, 56, 65
Teacher education programs, 181–182, 192
Teacher turnover rate, 181–182
Teachers' repertoires, expanding, 148
Teacher-student interaction, 144
Teaching, Outrageous: barriers to, 188–192; building blocks of, 58–59; defined, 5–7; as powerful tool, 3, 6–7; reasons for, 8–13; six significant contributions of, 187; theoretical bases for, 31–35
Teaching as a Performing Art, 174
Television, 11
Theater, interest in, 23
Theoretical bases for teaching content outrageously, 31–35
Theories of learning and Dwight's lesson, 66
Thespis, 193–194
Thinking development, inhibiting, 23–24
Thought experiments, 33–34
Time for lesson planning, 191
Title I program for education, 181

To Tell The Truth Game, 53
Transfer: defined, 20; evidence of, 27–31; as new rationale, 20–22
Transition to the students' learning activity, 71, 78–79
Tucson Poetry Festival, 108
Turnover rate, teacher, 181–182

U

Units, Outrageous, 168–174

V

Voice, costume, and mannerisms, 73–74, 139–140
Vygotsky, L., 21, 31, 47, 149

W

Wagner, B. J., 20
Ward, W., 19
Way, B., 19
Weirdness, embracing, 155
Welk, L., 123
Wilhelm, J. D., 34, 52, 53, 54, 114
Williams, R., 112
World history lesson, 170–172
Wright, O., 116–118
Wright brothers, 117, 118

Y

Yelling teachers, 41
You Gotta Be the Book, 34
Young children, Outrageous Teaching for, 178, 217–220

Z

Zone of proximal development, 149